TEACHING READING
IN
CONTENT
AREAS

HAROLD L. HERBER
Syracuse University

PRENTICE-HALL, INC.
Englewood Cliffs, New Jersey

To Janice and "The Friends"

13–894105–X

Library of Congress Catalog Card Number 71–94427

Printed in the United States of America

Current printing (last digit) :

10 9 8 7 6 5 4 3

PRENTICE-HALL INTERNATIONAL, INC., *London*
PRENTICE-HALL OF AUSTRALIA, PTY. LTD., *Sydney*
PRENTICE-HALL OF CANADA, LTD., *Toronto*
PRENTICE-HALL OF INDIA PRIVATE LTD., *New Delhi*
PRENTICE-HALL OF JAPAN, INC., *Tokyo*

CONTENTS

ACKNOWLEDGMENTS

Many people have contributed to this text, and they have done so in a variety of ways.

Two gentlemen shared generously their experience and knowledge as I needed it while taking on new responsibilities: Mr. Peter Coffin, my principal when I began teaching in Hamilton (Mass.) High School; and Mr. Harry Spencer, Director of Curriculum and Instruction when I began serving as reading coordinator in Sewanhaka High School District (Franklin Square, New York). Ideas of both of these men are embodied in the text.

Dr. Donald D. Durrell and Dr. Mabel (Noall) Clayton made clear to me the value of balancing theory with practice—and they showed me ways to do so.

Numerous teachers in many schools contributed significantly by their willingness to try, analyze, and revise many ideas presented in this text. Over the past ten years classroom teachers have helped me crystallize my own thinking by their cooperation in attempting different teaching procedures.

Graduate students in my classes and seminars aided considerably in the refinement and translation of the ideas presented in this text. Their challenging questions and the analyses of their own experiences with these procedures, have been extremely useful.

Professional friends and associates from many fields, colleagues in business, law, medicine, theology, education, have shared ideas generously in long discussions concerning education. Ideas in this text cannot be claimed as completely original; most are adaptations of ideas discussed with these people. Though I cannot single out each contributor, I do recognize, and appreciate, what they have done.

Although I am aware of many contributions to my experience and thinking concerning *Teaching Reading in Content Areas,* I alone take responsibility for the manner in which ideas and suggestions have been assimilated into the writing of this text. I am hopeful that both personal and professional pleasure will come to all who shared in its development.

H.L.H.

PREFACE

One of the basic purposes of formal education is to develop independent learners. Formal education cannot provide an individual with sufficient knowledge to last a lifetime. The continuing explosion of knowledge dramatizes this fact. Formal education should acquaint students with the structure of various disciplines and equip them with skills with which to explore these disciplines independently. Niles says it another way: "school exists, not to cram facts into the students' heads, but rather to help them acquire power in learning for themselves." [1] At best, formal education can expose students only to broad areas of knowledge and guide their exploration of basic concepts within those areas. If we fail to help students develop skills for independent learning, their "education" will cease when they leave school.

This understanding sets the *teaching of reading in content areas* in its proper perspective. Its purpose is to help students acquire the skills they need for adequate study of all the materials required in their subjects. Using subject-related material, regularly assigned, as the vehicle for this instruction, content teachers can provide for the simultaneous teaching of reading skills and course content. Neither has to be sacrificed to the other.

To teach well we must show the learner how to do what is required of him and do it in such a way that he develops an understanding of the process. The content teacher applying this principle as he gives reading assignments in his course is, without doubt, "Teaching Reading in Content Areas."

The purpose of this text is to present methods and materials which make "Teaching Reading in Content Areas" more than a cliché. The basic questions, for which answers are presented, are: (1) How can a content teacher help his students understand his subject as fully as their capabilities will allow, and (2) how can he concurrently help his students develop skills needed for this understanding?

[1] Olive S. Niles, "Developing Essential Reading Skills in the English Program," in *Reading and Inquiry* (Newark, Del.: International Reading Association, 1965), p. 35.

RELATED PURPOSES

This text is addressed to content teachers, elementary and secondary, whose primary interest is the content of the courses they teach. Many are "unaware that a dichotomy need not exist" [2] between content and process. Consequently they provide a distillation of the content for their students and frequently neglect the skills by which students can obtain the knowledge independently.

Assistance offered to content teachers interested in bringing about a balance between content and process generally has been a series of admonitions and objectives. Only infrequently are they told *how* to develop content and process simultaneously. Admonitions only produce animosity and rejection. Prescriptions, as simple and intellectually unattractive as they may be in some circles, are welcomed if they produce results.

Prescriptive approach

This text is not a theoretical treatise. It is a practical handbook that suggests ways to teach students how to read their content materials and increase their understanding of the content at the same time. In other words, it is quite prescriptive. This is very presumptuous because educational research indicates that there are many educational means to accomplish the same educational ends. Therefore, within the prescriptions, latitude is given by suggesting ways to modify the procedures.

Being prescriptive is the alternative to merely exhorting, and if we err, it is better to do so on the side of prescription than admonition.

Assumptive teaching

A prescriptive text implies the conviction that much teaching is governed by chance rather than by design, that many teachers are searching for ideas to develop a strategy for teaching and to give structure to their lessons so that their students will learn what they are supposed to learn. There seems to be automatic reliance on the *recitation method,* "characterized by assignment, study, and report . . . [It is] considered to be the one with which other methods are compared . . . [but] . . . there is little experimental support for [it]" [3] This method is filled with assumptions: that students have

[2] Mary Austin and Coleman Morrison, *The First R* (Cambridge: Harvard University Press, 1963), p. 50.

[3] Norman E. Wallen and Robert M. W. Travers, "Analysis and Investigation of Teaching Methods," in *Handbook of Research on Teaching* (Chicago: Rand McNally, American Educational Research Association, 1963), p. 483.

sufficient maturity and skill to handle the assignments; that they have sufficient command of skills to ferret out the significant points on which to
report; that they have sufficient organizational skills to marshall all of the
information and present it in coherent form. Frequently structure is lacking
in lessons and assignments; students occasionally are uncertain *what* they
are to do; they often are uncertain *how* to do what has been assigned. They
receive inadequate preparation for the tasks they are to do; they are not
assisted in performing the task; they are not aided in making use of the
information and ideas they are expected to acquire through the task. This
is *assumptive teaching.* That is, the teacher assumes students already have
the skills and already know the concepts he is supposed to teach them. If
he were not making such assumptions, he would show them *how* to study;
how to develop and use concepts. The "recitation method" and assumptive
teaching are nearly synonymous. The fact that so many content teachers
engage in the recitation method suggests that assumptive teaching is prevalent in most content areas.

To engage in assumptive teaching is to abdicate the major responsibility
of a teacher. If the students know before a course begins what they take
the course to learn, why take the courses? Preston states the problem in
the context of social studies, but it could well relate to any other subject:

Some social studies teachers assume their students should know how to master
the textbook assignments without instruction. This is an unsound assumption.
The acquisition of reading-for-mastery should not be left to chance.[4]

The alternative, obviously, is to have teachers present carefully structured lessons which develop both the concepts and the skills essential to
the course. The question is, however, "Can teachers enhance or accelerate
growth by trying to direct it? They undoubtedly can, and the most effective
means is by purposeful guidance of reading activities." [5] This text is written
in an effort to eliminate assumptive teaching. It suggests procedures by
which students are guided as they develop subject related *concepts* and *skills*
simultaneously.

This text is organized so that readers experience many of the procedures
they are urged to provide for their students. Purposes are set for reading;
technical vocabulary is presented before chapters are read; study guide
materials accompany each chapter and are of the type recommended for
use in content areas. Ample illustrative lesson materials accompany ex-

[4] Ralph C. Preston, J. Wesley Schneyer, and Franc J. Thyng, *Building Social Studies
Reading of High School Students,* Bulletin No. 34, National Council for the Social
Studies (1963), p. 136.
[5] James M. McCallister, "Promoting Growth in Interpreting in Grades One through
Fourteen," in *Reading: Seventy-Five Years of Progress* (Chicago: University of Chi-
cago Press, 1966), p. 93.

planations. The Appendix of the text contains additional reading guides designed by classroom teachers.

The design of the text has merit because there is assumptive *teaching of teachers* too, an assumption "that all one has to do is to tell a teacher what pattern to exhibit and that the teacher can then act out this pattern. Such an assumption is, of course, contrary to what is known about the modification of behavior." [6] Whether the learner is a student or his teacher, the learner must be shown how to perform the behavior requested of him; admonitions will not bring about the desired change.

This text does prescribe a structure—one for teaching reading skills simultaneously with course content; one that has been used successfully for many students by many teachers. Its significance lies in the fact that it shifts the responsibility for learning to the student where it belongs and, importantly, that it shows the teacher how to help the student handle this responsibility. This "how" has sufficient latitude so that many "methods" can be employed.

[6] Wallen and Travers, "Analysis and Investigation of Teaching Methods," p. 457.

1

INSTRUCTIONAL
PROBLEMS

VOCABULARY

Several terms used in this chapter are defined in context. You should give
particular attention to:
- recitation
- reading through content
- reading
- vocabulary load
- concept load
- functional teaching

IDEA DIRECTION

This chapter reviews several problems teachers face. You should determine
if your particular teaching problems are represented in the discussion. If not,
you might list other problems at the end of the chapter and, through sources
listed in the bibliographies as well as throughout this book, search out the
answers.

READING DIRECTION

An exploration of problems generally contrasts the way conditions are with
the way they should be. Look for these contrasting relationships as you read.

This text presents methods and materials which can make *Teaching Reading in Content Areas* more than a cliché. Two significant questions underlie the presentation: How can a content teacher help his students understand his subject as fully as their capabilities will allow? How can skills needed for this understanding be developed at the same time?

There is a story, perhaps apocryphal, of the university professor who informed his students that questions on the final examination for his course were the same each year; only the answers changed. Similarly, problems in education remain the same, but the alternatives for solution change.

For many years research has focused on basic problems in learning through reading, yet problems still remain. We are closer to the knowledge of how to solve the problems than we once were; our curricula have improved; the achievement of our students has increased in comparison with previous generations. Yet there is much dissatisfaction with our educational product.

One reason for the dissatisfaction is that we still apply old methods to new materials, perhaps with more intensity but in the same pattern. The explanation, of course, is simple: teachers tend to teach the way they were taught rather than the way they were taught to teach.

Principals commonly voice the opinion that most teachers do not teach in accordance with the pattern prescribed by teacher-training institutions, but rather teach in accordance with the pattern they observed when they were pupils and which they believe is expected of them. This is hardly surprising. Imitation is a well-established phenomenon. The long period of exposure to teachers during the growing years provides a body of experiences and a pattern to imitate which may well serve the new teacher as a guide to action. This rich background of direct experience with teaching probably provides a much more vivid guide to action in the classroom than does the period of teacher-training which consists so largely of verbal experiences.[1]

The method thus perpetuated is the "recitation" method, the teacher-talk/student-listen procedure that dominates the vast majority of content classrooms.

The traditional recitation method used in content areas allows almost no time for teaching students how to read their texts. Unfortunately, ". . . with a need to cover much more material in many different sources, the study skills have rather abruptly increased in value to the learner while

[1] Norman E. Wallen and Robert M. W. Travers, "Analysis and Investigation of Teaching Methods," in *Handbook of Research on Teaching* (Chicago: Rand McNally & Co., American Educational Research Association, 1963), p. 453.

the school's respect for these skills and its ability to effectively teach them has lagged." [2]

However,

The contemporary explosion of knowledge . . . has effectively put an end to the notion that the teacher's primary role is to be a single source of facts and knowledge. It has also made clear, on the other hand, that the teacher's knowledge is a more critical element than ever. In a bewildering, fast-changing world, knowledge about how to inquire, knowledge of critical ideas, and knowledge about how to acquire and handle facts and theories are the important kinds of knowledge to possess. [3]

"The goal of education is disciplined understanding; that is the process as well." [4] If a teacher accepts this position, then he will be more than an "information dispenser." Rather, he will emphasize the means for acquiring, interpreting, and using knowledge independently.

Though the "teaching of reading and evaluation of proficiency in the content areas are at present not very satisfactory," [5] there are those that believe "we are moving gradually toward a time when reading will be taught mainly in the subject fields with regular content materials and regular daily lessons of the course. It never should have been otherwise." [6]

The point not to be lost is the general agreement that some systematic, structured approach to teaching does matter and that "it is the teacher . . . who makes the difference between effective and ineffective learning." [7] Flanders found that teachers demonstrated different patterns in teaching. Different patterns do affect learning of children. [8] Teachers need a repertory of methods to use so that they can better meet the needs of all children, adjusting the patterns until one or a combination is found to meet the needs of children in a given class. But this demands flexibility, an awareness of a variety of patterns of instruction, a structure with sufficient latitude to adjust to students' needs. It means that one cannot hold on to

[2] Arthur W. Heilman, *Principles and Practices of Teaching Reading* (Columbus, Ohio: Charles E. Merrill Books, Inc., 1967), p. 374.

[3] Bruce R. Joyce and Berj Harootunian, *The Structure of Teaching* (Chicago: Science Research Associates, 1967), p. 13.

[4] Jerome S. Bruner, "After John Dewey, What?" in *On Knowing* (New York: Atheneum Publishers, 1965), p. 122.

[5] Miles A. Tinker, *Bases for Effective Reading* (Minneapolis: University of Minnesota Press, 1965), p. 286.

[6] Olive S. Niles, "Developing Essential Reading Skills in the English Program," in *Reading and Inquiry* (Newark, Del.: International Reading Association, 1965), p. 36.

[7] A. Sterl Artley, "Influence of Specific Factors on Growth in Interpretation," in *Reading: Seventy-Five Years of Progress* (Chicago: University of Chicago Press, 1966), p. 78.

[8] Ned Flanders, *Teacher Influence: An Interaction Analysis,* U. S. Office of Education Cooperative Research Project No. 397 (Minneapolis: University of Minnesota, 1960).

the traditional merely because it is traditional and comfortable. "What is needed is the daring and freshness of hypotheses that do not take for granted as true what has merely become habitual." [9]

At present, then, there is great disparity between knowledge and practice, between what we know to be good procedure and what we actually practice in the classroom.

. . . there is an enormous time lag before the best of innovations finally make their way to our schools, a resistance of education to the product of research that is unmatched in other fields. . . . In education, the process often takes 30 years or more.[10]

Consider some of the problems which plague classroom teachers at all grade levels and in all subject areas. Many have been researched, but they persist, reflecting the knowledge-practice time lag.

PROBLEMS

The descriptions vary but generally one can categorize the problems under four headings: (1) students' competence; (2) curriculum pressures; (3) content materials; (4) teacher education.

Students' Competence

Teachers become frustrated when their students are unable to achieve success while reading content materials. Teachers at the secondary level believe that the reading skills taught in elementary school should be adequate for successful reading in various content areas. Even though this assumption is tempered with the understanding that achievement relates to ability, many teachers hold "grade-level standards" without considering their students' capabilities for attaining them.

Certainly content teachers are aware that ability and achievement are closely related and that not all students can attain the same level of competence. Nevertheless, many feel that had students been exposed to better reading instruction in the earlier grades, they would perform much better and meet adequately the demands of the various subject areas.

It does seem logical to think that instruction at the elementary level should prepare students for the reading required in secondary schools. However, certain factors qualify this position. At the primary level students are taught basic reading skills—decoding and simple interpretation—prin-

[9] Jerome S. Bruner, *Toward a Theory of Instruction* (Cambridge: Harvard University Press, 1967), p. 171.
[10] Francis Keppel, "Research: Education's Neglected Hope," *Journal of Reading,* May 1964, p. 5.

cipally through narrative material; and this extends through elementary grades. Even though students are required to read expository material in subjects other than *reading,* they are not taught how to handle it as well as they are taught to handle narrative. Yet students at the secondary level are required to read increasingly complex and abstract exposition, and teachers assume they are equipped to do so.

Somewhere during their years of formal education students should experience the transition from simple narrative material to abstract exposition. Even where the elementary reading programs are of high quality and provide this transition, students need continued instruction to learn to adapt skills to the more demanding content materials. Not only the level of abstraction in content materials but also the technical language is more complex at each successive grade level. Successful achievement at one grade level within a subject does not guarantee the same at another. Students must be shown *how* to read the material at each successive level.

Content teachers are particularly troubled by the wide range of competence among their students. Neither organizational structures (tracking, grouping, isolating) nor content materials (multitexts, multilevel texts, companion texts) eliminate the obvious necessity *to teach* students and *to provide learning experiences* for each member of each class. When the teachers feel pressured to "cover the curriculum," any suggestion that related reading skills should also be taught as part of the curriculum is met with incredulity.

Curriculum Pressures

The knowledge explosion is such that for each grade level and in each subject area, information is increasing at a tremendous rate. For example, one source states that "67,000 words of scientific research are being written every minute, the equivalent of enough scientific matter to fill eleven sets of a 30-volume encyclopedia every 24 hours." [11] Information in the social sciences and the creative production of literature is also increasing. The impact of this new knowledge is felt by classroom teachers as it is incorporated into curricula. Content teachers generally have "so much to cover" that they feel forced to teach more superficially than they know they should. Emphasizing concept development rather than accumulation of information is recommended for handling the growing curricula; but for many this requires considerable adjustment in teaching procedures. The thought of adding the teaching of reading to their responsibilities causes teachers to throw up their hands in absolute despair.

[11] *Concepts in Science,* advertising brochure (New York: Harcourt, Brace & World, Inc., 1967).

An emphasis on reading instruction, they believe, would jeopardize students' understanding of the subject because the time available for learning content would be diminished. This concern is prevalent among elementary as well as secondary school teachers. As long as teachers feel pressed by administration to "cover" a subject, they will continue to view related reading instruction as an intrusion and will resist devoting curriculum time to reading skills instruction. Administrators who deny exerting this pressure need to convey to teachers—in concrete terms and plain English—the fact that this pressure does not exist.

The error that underlies these problems is, of course, the assumption that teaching the content of a subject and teaching the skills that are related to the subject are somehow separate entities. Austin and Morrison state the problem well. Teachers "reportedly do not have sufficient time to 'teach everything' and, unaware that a dichotomy need not exist, feel it more important to cover the content than to teach the reading skills in the content areas." [12] Research evidence shows that reading and study skills related to a course need not be taught in isolation, as an appendage to the curriculum.[13] Skills can be taught simultaneously with the course content; content and process need not be separated. Subject-area teachers have been urged to do this for many years; however, surveys rarely reveal this kind of instruction being practiced.[14] The gap between what is known and what is practiced is most unfortunate.

Content Materials

Teachers frequently believe that texts required for their courses are too difficult for most students in their classes. If these materials cannot be used as sources of information, how can they be used as vehicles for skill development? Distribution of texts is often an empty gesture used to placate the administration and parents; the students rarely open the books. Teachers

[12] Mary Austin and Coleman Morrison, *The First R* (Cambridge: Harvard University Press, 1963), p. 50.

[13] Guy L. Bond and Miles A. Tinker, *Reading Difficulties: Their Diagnosis and Correction* (New York: Appleton-Century-Crofts, 1957), pp. 349–72; Harold L. Herber, "Concept Association in PSSC Physics," *The Reporter* (Spring 1964), pp. 9–12. Harold L. Herber, "Teaching Reading Through Seventh Grade Science Content" (unpublished research sponsored by the Division of Research, New York State Department of Education, Central High School District No. 2, Franklin Square, New York, 1962); Ralph C. Preston, J. Wesley Schneyer, and Franc J. Thyng, "Building Social Studies Reading of High School Students," Bulletin No. 34 (Washington, D.C.: National Council for the Social Studies, 1963); Ruth Strang, "Developing Reading Skills in the Content Areas," *The High School Journal,* April 1966, pp. 301–6.

[14] Austin and Morrison, *The First R,* p. 50; Leonard S. Braam and Marilyn A. Roehm, "Subject-Area Teachers' Familiarity With Reading Skills," *The Journal of Developmental Reading,* Spring 1964, pp. 188–96.

provide the information by means of extensive lectures, and many students do not learn how to read the special materials in various subjects.

The adequacy of texts raises several problems. One is the vocabulary load. Particularly in science, the content is highly saturated with complicated and abstract terminology. Students find it difficult to read the material because they are unfamiliar with the language of the subject, so teachers generally rely on lectures to convey the information.

A related problem is the concept load. Authors develop abstract concepts with complicated language. Concepts are presented rapidly—faster than many students can absorb—and are not carefully paced. Moreover, the concepts are not developed sequentially; that is, sophistication needed to handle certain concepts is assumed by the authors rather than ensured. If students are not prepared to handle abstractions, they cannot be expected to develop concepts through their reading. Again, sensitive to students' inadequacies, teachers resort to the lecture to convey concepts.

Teachers lecture to compensate for other problems: texts that do not "follow the curriculum" and therefore are considered useless; texts that are of questionable validity because they treat topics superficially; "primary sources" that are inaccessible. These real problems confront teachers every day, and unless realistic solutions are proposed and practiced, students will have little opportunity to learn—under guided instruction—*how* to read a variety of subject-related materials.

In a program for teaching reading in content areas, the adequacy and appropriateness of texts obviously is a major concern. A solution to the problem is proposed in chapter 2 and explored further throughout the text.

Teacher Education

Earlier we noted that teachers tend to teach the way they were taught rather than the way they were taught to teach. To the degree that this is true, problems that have plagued teachers for several generations will continue. New generations of teachers attack new problems with old solutions, and many drop out of teaching because of frustration. Their inability to help students comprehend material in their texts causes many to seek other careers. Teachers believe their education courses "did little or nothing" to help them meet this problem. It is true that very few content teachers ever take a course in reading. We cannot be certain, however, that methods courses related to subject specialties completely ignore the teaching of study skills.

Beyond the content of the courses teachers take during their preparation, there is the question of how to change understandings and methods of teaching.

. . . there appears to be a growing conviction that teacher education does little to generate appropriate patterns of teacher behavior in students of education. Indeed, there are serious doubts in some quarters whether teacher education can even be considered to generate any teaching pattern. . . .[15]

However, "patterns of teacher behavior and the teaching methods they represent are mainly the products of forces which have little to do with scientific knowledge of learning." [16] Teachers are comfortable with familiar procedures and are reluctant to change. Even beginning teachers are reluctant to change, that is, to teach differently from the way in which they themselves were taught. When a new teacher stands before his first class, much of what he was taught *about* teaching fades, and he falls back on what is natural to him, the way he was taught. Thus, the old solutions are perpetuated. A teacher will utilize a new, unfamiliar procedure only under duress.

One can hardly expect a teacher to put full effort into the utilization of a teaching method which he does not consider sound or personally congenial. The latter factor may become a much more important determinant of what happens than differences in the prescribed patterns.[17]

The precise content of teacher education courses is not the subject of this chapter. However, it is important to note that omissions in this education (including failure to help teachers make new practices "their own"), contribute to the current difficulty teachers have in helping students become successful readers of content materials.

Specialization by content teachers presents another kind of problem. Teachers spend many years studying, and become very knowledgeable in, their specialties. Gradually their tolerance for people who are ignorant of their field diminishes. As they intensify their specialty and, in many cases, contribute to the literature, their acceptance of the "uninitiated" rapidly lessens. Unless teachers make a consistent effort to overcome this attitude, they can develop a moderate, or even strong, hostility toward students new to their subject area.

In a related syndrome, a teacher often attributes to students much more knowledge than they actually possess. Subconsciously he says, "Surely the students must know _____! It's absolutely impossible for a student to be at this level in the curriculum and not know it." His superior knowledge of the content plays tricks on him. He "fills in" those gaps in the students' understanding, not by presenting information but by assuming the students already possess it. Bright students play the game and wait for clues in subsequent lectures that will help to identify the missing information. Others sense inconsistencies or unknowns but cannot handle them. The teacher

---

[15] Wallen and Travers, *Analysis and Investigation of Teaching Methods,* p. 456.
[16] *Ibid.,* p. 464.
[17] *Ibid.,* p. 458.

needs to adjust the instruction to suit students' actual weaknesses rather than to stress his own strengths. But then we are back to methodology in the classroom—the subject of this text.

DEFINITIONS

"Reading Through Content"

There is much confusion about the responsibility of content teachers for teaching reading. Pervading the literature is the feeling that content teachers just do not understand—they are ignorant of—what they can and should do for their students. Bruner makes a significant point about "understanding":

Let us recognize that the opposite of understanding is not ignorance or simply "not knowing." To understand something is, first, to give up some other way of conceiving it. Confusion all too often lies between one way of conceiving and another better way.[18]

The "better way" of conceiving reading in content areas has not been made clear. There is a definite difference between teaching reading in a reading class and in a content class. When this distinction is made clear, confusion fades, and content teachers are more inclined to engage in "reading instruction," to the benefit of students and of their own peace of mind.

The most satisfactory way to define teaching reading through content is to compare the responsibilities of the reading teacher with those of the content teacher. Each has a specific set; each has a curriculum to teach.

The reading teacher's curriculum is a set of reading skills. Certainly he hopes to develop students' interests in the use of these skills to enlarge their interests, appreciations, and understandings of life around them, but his primary responsibility is to teach the skills. He arranges the skills in logical sequence, following a pattern prescribed by a manual or one he has established through study and experience. He analyzes the needs of students in his classes, and this analysis determines where he enters the sequence for a given student, as well as the level of sophistication at which he teaches the skill (or skills).

He selects reading material through which he can teach the skill and through which the students can practice the skill after they have received the initial instruction. He is not primarily concerned about the content of this material, as long as it is interesting and informative. The content can be related to any curriculum area in the school or it can be general material that has no bearing on a specific content area. He is not teaching the *con-*

[18] Bruner, "After John Dewey, What?" *loc. cit.*

tent of the material. He wishes to develop understandings of the *processes* being applied to these materials.

The content teacher has a set of ideas as his curriculum. These ideas have order; definite relationships exist among them. He establishes a sequence for these ideas based on logic, study, and experience. Either the basic text for the course or the curriculum guide may determine the sequence.

He analyzes the needs of his students, decides where in the sequence of his curriculum they require instruction, and plans a teaching program accordingly. They are weak in specific concepts; they need more exposure to specific ideas; they need to see relationships among various principles; they need to enlarge the base on which they have established their own points of view. The content teacher finds materials (or selects parts from his textbook, if that is all he has available) which contain the information and ideas he wants his students to encounter, understand, and use. He is not primarily concerned with the skills students must use in reading materials. When he teaches the students *how* to acquire the information and ideas from an assigned selection, he has to be aware of the skills inherent in the selection. But those skills are *not* the reason for using that material. He teaches students only the skills needed to understand the ideas his curriculum calls for them to understand. He does not teach a reading skill for its own sake, as does the reading teacher. He concerns himself not with the sequential development of reading skills, but with the sequential development of ideas. Skills are developed functionally, not directly. The skills to be taught are determined by the content of the material assigned for a given lesson, never the reverse.

Again, to state the difference in a somewhat different way, the reading teacher says: *I have to teach these skills. What materials can I use to give instruction and provide practice on these skills? I don't care what the subject matter is just as long as the students have to use these skills in order to understand what they read.*

And so the reading teacher finds the material, teaches the skills, and has the students engage in reinforcing practice. He hopes, of course, that the students will transfer these skills to their subjects and that the instruction they receive in reading class will help with assigned readings in each of their courses.

Meanwhile, the content teacher says: *I have these ideas to get across to my students and this text—or these texts—develop the ideas quite well. I'll assign this material for homework so students, through their reading, will develop some understanding of these ideas. Now, in order for them to develop and use those ideas, there is a specific skill that the students have to use. It isn't "main idea," because the mere apprehension of the central thought is not the key to understanding this concept; nor is it "inference," because the author is rather straightforward in his statements; nor is it "recognition of assumption," because the author has identified his premises and has not relied on assumptions. No, in this particular selection the students have to read to "evaluate argument," and so that's the skill I will discuss with them for a moment before they begin reading the selection. Some of them will need more assistance than others so I'll have to provide a bit more guidance for them, but all of the students will have to employ this skill.*

This is the difference between the reading teacher and the content teacher with respect to the teaching of reading. The cliché "Every teacher a teacher of reading" has been interpreted by content teachers in light of the reading teacher's role and responsibility for teaching reading. Content teachers have rejected that role, and rightly so. Moreover, there has been a concerted effort to force on all content teachers the direct reading instruction properly engaged in by the reading teacher. This is unfortunate. There is no place for reading instruction, as reading teachers generally employ it, in content areas. There is a need for a whole new strategy in teaching reading through content areas, a strategy that uses what we know about the direct teaching of reading but adapts that knowledge to fit the structure of and responsibilities for the total curriculum in each content area.

Regular curriculum materials—basic and supplementary texts—can be used as vehicles for reading instruction in each content area with teachers showing students how to become successful readers of the required materials. There is no wasted time, no separate emphasis, no risk to the curriculum. The strategy *does* require modification in teaching behavior, changes in the role of both teacher and learner; but the modifications and changes are realistic and practical.

"Reading"

The view that reading instruction should be part of the curriculum in each content area necessarily implies a broad definition of the term "reading." Though there are many definitions, there is general agreement that reading is not a unitary act, that reading comprises several functions. For example, ". . . the complete act of reading has four dimensions—word perception, comprehension of stated and implied meanings, critical and emotional reaction, and application of perceived ideas to behavior." [19] Dechant also views "reading" as a four-step process: recognition, understanding, reaction, and integration.[20] Russell summarizes his survey of the literature on reading instruction, saying:

[19] Artley, "Influence of Specific Factors," p. 79.
[20] Emerald V. Dechant, *Improving the Teaching of Reading* (Englewood Cliffs, N. J.: Prentice-Hall, Inc., 1964), p. 375.

. . . it is apparent that there are at least three broad aspects of interpretation and reading; namely, word knowledge, apprehending the meaning of passages, and thoughtful reaction and the use or application of the ideas read. The speed at which the reader interprets what he reads also merits emphasis.[21]

In this book, "reading" is defined as a thinking process which includes decoding of symbols, interpreting the meanings of the symbols, and applying the ideas derived from the symbols.

DECODING   There are those who hold a very restricted view of "reading," defining it only as a decoding process.[22] From this point of view, reading is simply a matter of associating symbols with sounds. A student viewing a symbol—whether a letter or a word—internally compares that symbol to all other symbols with which he is familiar. His perception of that symbol and the experience he associates with it determine whether he can handle the symbol successfully. As Bruner says,

Perception involves an act of categorization. Put in terms of the antecedent and subsequent conditions from which we make our inferences, we stimulate an organism with some appropriate input and he responds by referring the input to some class of things or events.[23]

Stimulated by a symbol, the student searches through his experiences with sound and symbol relationships to associate a sound with that symbol. If he cannot, he must learn the sound; or if he applies an incorrect sound to the symbol (incorrect perception), he must learn the correct variation or the new sound.

Meanings associated with the decoding of symbols are rather restricted in that they relate generally to what the symbol "says" and not to what the symbol "means." Thus it is possible for a person to decode a word and associate sounds with that symbol so as to "pronounce" it, yet have little or no understanding of the concept represented by that word. Decoding obviously is important, but, standing alone, it has limited usefulness. One can see that:

Word recognition is a pre-requisite to reading, but does not guarantee understanding. Comprehension requires knowledge, not only of the meaning of words but other relationships in sentences, paragraphs, and longer passages. It involves understanding of the intent of the author, and may go beyond literal recorded facts to hidden meanings or implications.[24]

[21] David H. Russell, "Reading," in *Encyclopedia of Educational Research* (New York: The Macmillan Co., 1960), pp. 1100–1101.

[22] Charles Walcutt, *Tomorrow's Illiterates* (Boston: Little, Brown and Company, 1961); Leonard Bloomfield and Clarence L. Barnhart, *Let's Read* (Detroit: Wayne State University Press, 1961).

[23] Jerome S. Bruner, "On Perceptual Readiness," *Psychological Review,* LXIV (1957), 123–52.

[24] David H. Russell and Henry R. Fea, "Research on Teaching," in *Handbook of Research on Teaching* (Chicago: Rand McNally & Co., American Educational Research Association, 1963).

Nevertheless, Artley reports, "As I travel about and meet and talk with teachers and supervisors, it seems to me that their primary preoccupations are still word perception and factual recall . . . this is not the point where the reading process should stop." [25]

INTERPRETATION   The second aspect of "reading" is interpreting the meanings of the symbols. The reader should not only associate sound with the symbol but also associate meaning with the symbol, drawing on ideas he has developed in relationship to the symbol. If the symbol is a word, he associates it with an experience he has had—real or vicarious—in connection with it. That is his meaning for the symbol. If the symbol is other than a word, perhaps a formula, an equation, a sentence, or a paragraph, the process is the same, differing only in degree of complexity.

Many students successfully decode words but fail to find meaning in what they read; their failure reflects lack of experience associated with the words or longer units. This kind of reading is a rather futile exercise, particularly when viewed in light of the reading demands placed on students in content areas. "Any instructional program which overemphasizes the mechanical aspects of reading tends to lead to verbalism, a poor substitute for true reading." [26] Students are expected to derive meanings from what they read. Failing to do so frequently means failing the course.

But associating meaning with successfully decoded symbols does not complete the total act of "reading." There is yet a third factor.

APPLICATION   It is important to use the ideas which are developed through the decoding and interpretive processes. "For learnings to become the full property of the learner, he must *use* them. So long as his knowledge is a passive thing, it is immature and impermanent. Its maturation depends on its active use in new situations." [27]

In what manner are these ideas used? They are applied to previous knowledge and experience to determine if there is corroboration or contradiction. If the former, then specific ideas are strengthened; if the latter, specific ideas are modified. Ideas acquired through decoding and interpretation may not be immediately applicable and therefore may be "stored" and used later when they have particular bearing on an activity or other idea that is considered. The principal problem to be considered then "is not storage, but retrieval. . . . The key to retrieval is organization." [28] Teachers can show students how to organize ideas and keep them readily accessible for appropriate use.

"Reading" cannot be narrowly defined when associated with instruction

---

[25] Artley, "Influence of Specific Factors," p. 79.

[26] Tinker, *Bases for Effective Reading,* p. 39.

[27] Henry P. Smith and Emerald V. Dechant, *Psychology in Teaching Reading* (Englewood Cliffs, N. J.: Prentice-Hall, Inc., 1961), p. 77.

[28] Bruner, *On Knowing,* p. 124.

in the content areas. Proper reading of resource materials requires that students interpret what they decode and effectively use the ideas they acquired.

REACTION GUIDE

Directions: Several ideas were contrasted directly or by implication. The two columns below contain many of these ideas. By matching items in Column B to those in A, show how you perceive the contrasts explored or implied in the chapter. Items in Column B may be used more than once.

Column A	Column B
_____ 1. curriculum saturation	a. functional teaching of skills
_____ 2. teacher's interests	b. selective instruction
_____ 3. knowledge about teaching	c. decoding-interpretation-usage
_____ 4. direct teaching of skills	d. experience in teaching
_____ 5. separating content and process	e. students' potential
	f. students' needs
_____ 6. decoding	g. guiding by structure
_____ 7. changing instructional materials	h. developing skills and concepts simultaneously
_____ 8. grade-level standards	i. teaching practices
_____ 9. inertia	j. changing instructional procedures
_____10. assumptive teaching	k. flexibility

2

INSTRUCTIONAL
PROVISIONS

VOCABULARY

Several terms used in this chapter are defined in context. You should give particular attention to:

— reading grade-level score
— transformation
— grouping
— student interaction
— multilevel texts
— single texts
— continuum of independence

IDEA DIRECTION

This chapter suggests ways to meet problems expressed in chapter 1. Most of these means will be explored in detail in subsequent chapters. Note whether provisions and problems really match.

READING DIRECTION

Since this chapter is somewhat anticipatory, it should be read so that specific details can be recalled—or referred to—during the reading of subsequent chapters.

Certain instructional provisions need to be made in order to instruct students in content-related reading skills. They represent factors apparent to any experienced teacher, yet they also represent rather illusive objectives.

Range of Ability and Achievement

A teacher needs to be with a class only a short time before he discovers a considerable range of ability and achievement, regardless of the criteria used for grouping students into classes. If a reading grade-level score is the criterion for homogeneous grouping, he will find a range of ability represented among the students. There is not a sufficiently high correlation between IQ scores and reading scores to be certain of homogeneity of the latter when the former is used as the criterion for homogeneous grouping. Moreover, students' reading performance will vary considerably even though their scores are identical. This is because *reading* is too complex a process to be expressed in a single score. The procedures for deriving single scores which designate reading achievement reflect this fact. Reading scores are generally derived from several subscores; therefore, different combinations of strength and weakness can produce the same reading grade-level score. It is quite possible for two students to have the same reading grade score with the areas of strength for one being the areas of weakness for the other. For example, the advanced form of the *Iowa Silent Reading Test* has nine subtests and the total test score is computed by using the median score from among the nine subtests. It is possible that Student A will be relatively strong in subtests one through four and relatively weak in subtests six through nine, his median being subtest five. Student B, then, might be relatively weak in subtests one through four, relatively strong in subtests six through nine, his median being subtest five with a score identical to Student A. Both would have identical total scores, but they would have opposite strengths and weaknesses.

When *ability* is used as the sole criterion for grouping, one will find a range of *achievement* in reading. The relatively low correlation between IQ and reading again is evident. Moreover, because ability scores are also composites, as they are in reading, comparability is similarly limited. Composite scores mask differing strengths and weaknesses in intelligence even as they mask differences in specific reading skills.

Frequently students are grouped by two criteria: reading achievement and intelligence. Even so, there is a range of actual ability and achievement among students within the class.

The need is not only to admit to the existence of differences in ability and achievement, but also to discover how to accommodate the range that is present in most classes. Service to individual differences can be realistic, within the framework of the curriculum as it now exists and the present organizational structure of schools, and can have sufficient flexibility to meet the demands of new educational developments. Each student can understand the content and experience success in reading the required material at his level of competence.

Differences in Learning Rate

Though students may have the same relative achievement and ability, they may differ in the rate at which they work and learn. Each paces himself and absorbs information at a different rate from any other student; he assimilates and applies generalizations differently. Teachers cannot expect students to function at the same pace even though they are grouped homogeneously.

Experiments on the factor of repetition in instructional media have reflected a prevalent educational philosophy which tends to grade students on how much they learn in a given time rather than . . . to the length of training (e.g., 'number of trials') necessary . . . to achieve some predetermined criterion of mastery.[1]

Allowance for differences in learning rate, coupled with provisions for a range of ability and achievement, eliminates much learner frustration.

Transfer and Transformation of Skills

"Transfer is the application of our previous learnings to our current problems." [2] The great hope in education is that what students learn in one situation can be transferred and applied to comparable situations. "When one utilizes his past experience in reacting to a situation that has in it some element of newness, we conclude that there has been transfer of learning." [3]

On development of this ability we predicate much of our teaching. Were it not possible for students to transfer knowledge from one subject area to another and one grade level to another, we would have to reteach continually everything that students need to know. This is impossible, impractical, and unnecessary.

[1] A. A. Lumsdaine, "Instruments and Media of Instruction," in *Handbook of Research on Teaching* (Chicago: Rand McNally & Co., American Educational Research Association, 1963), p. 643.

[2] Henry P. Smith and Emerald V. Dechant, *Psychology in Teaching Reading* (Englewood Cliffs: Prentice-Hall, Inc., 1961), p. 68.

[3] *Ibid.*, p. 69.

However, transfer does not occur automatically; "it cannot be taken for granted." [4]

Much cognitive learning does not reflect itself in general behavior; this is a problem of transfer . . . persons who have acquired given responses frequently do not use them in the problem situation. The major point seems to be that cognitive learnings may not become part of the individual's general response repertoire but remain as isolated responses elicited only by 'academic' stimuli.[5]

We must teach concepts and skills in such a way that students can use them not only in situations comparable to those in which they were learned but also in many other situations. "An understanding of fundamental principles and ideas . . . appears to be the main road to adequate 'transfer of training'." [6]

The need to develop the ability to transfer has been a basic consideration in reading instruction. Skills are taught in elementary grades with the hope that children will transfer them to the reading of content materials in these and succeeding grades. Particularly, the assumption has been widely held that skills taught in the elementary grades are sufficient for the needs of students entering junior and senior high schools. We need only witness teachers "passing the buck" from secondary to elementary levels to realize that the *assumption* of transfer is true even though the *fact* often is not.

Teachers can provide instruction in how to read the content materials used in their subjects so that students are not dependent on this assumed transfer.

The amount of transfer induced can be increased by the method of teaching used. Although no set principles can be expected to apply to all conditions, there are a few very general rules that cover a fairly wide range of situations: bring out the feature to be transferred, develop meaningful generalizations, provide a variety of experiences, practice the application to other fields. . . .[7]

Each subject-area teacher can assure a degree of transfer by attending to these features and devising methods for their application.

It is helpful to content teachers to think of a factor *beyond* transfer when they consider ways to help their students read the materials in their courses. This important factor is *transformation* or the adaptation of skills. Skills taught in reading classes are applicable to content materials but students

[4] Olive Niles, "Developing Essential Reading Skills in the English Program," in *Reading and Inquiry* (Newark, Del.: International Reading Association, 1965), p. 35.

[5] Norman E. Wallen and Robert M. W. Travers, *Analysis and Investigation of Teaching Methods: Handbook of Research on Teaching* (Chicago: Rand McNally, American Educational Research Association, 1963).

[6] Jerome S. Bruner, *The Process of Education* (New York: Random House, Inc., 1960), p. 25.

[7] J. M. Stephens, "Transfer of Learning," in *Encyclopedia of Educational Research* (New York: Macmillan Co., 1960), p. 1542.

must adapt the skills to meet the peculiarities of each subject they study. There is "horizontal transformation" as students adapt reading skills to various subjects within a grade level. There is also "vertical transformation," as students progress from grade to grade within a subject and adapt skills to meet the increased sophistication of content materials at successive levels. The concept of *transformation* is directly related to the earlier discussion of the differences between teaching reading in reading classes and in content classes. *Transformation* is discussed in detail in chapter 6.

Concept Formation and Application

The definition of *reading* established earlier includes the need for development of ideas from reading and, subsequently, the application of those ideas. The formation of concepts (ideas) and their use is of critical importance to the student who wishes to be successful in his studies, but students frequently lack facility in handling concepts.

A concept is defined as "a generalization drawn from particulars." [8] As a student reads he gathers specific information (particulars) which he attempts to organize in some fashion so as to identify relationships among them. A relationship that he identifies, and subsequently uses, is a generalization. "The learner originally makes specific responses to specific stimuli. When he learns to apply these responses in other situations, he has generalized his behavior. This generalization of behavior is a most important kind of transfer." [9] "Studies on transfer have stressed the value of generalization. Generalization provides for applications to new learning situations. . . ." [10]

A physics teacher observed: "It seems apparent we are training good memorizers rather than good thinkers." The factor that gave rise to his comment was the inability of his students to make use of information acquired from their texts. They could recite details and interpret the significance of some information, but when asked to analyze interrelationships or to generalize from the information, their achievement was far from satisfactory. They had not learned how to make good use of the information they had acquired. When given instruction on the development and use of concepts, they improved significantly in their achievement in the subject. [11]

But this problem is not unique to above average students in physics

[8] *Webster's Seventh New Collegiate Dictionary* (Springfield: G. and C. Merriam Company, 1963).
[9] Smith and Dechant, *Psychology in Teaching Reading,* p. 69.
[10] *Ibid.,* p. 72.
[11] Harold L. Herber, "Teaching Reading and Physics Simultaneously," in *Improvement of Reading Through Classroom Practice* (Newark, Del.: International Reading Association, 1964), p. 84.

classes. Even less able students, poorer readers, rely extensively on identification and memorization. They have as much need to develop and use
concepts as more able students do, and they need to be shown how.

There appears to be more retention and better learning when attention
is focused on development of concepts rather than on identification and
memorization of detail.[12] However, teacher-made examinations and standardized tests have fostered the latter procedure. Being test wise, students
reject concept-centered instruction because "it won't be on the test." [13] Education perpetuates generations of students conditioned to view learning as
the storing of information rather than the development, evaluation, and
use of ideas. Gardner comments on this kind of instruction:

All too often we are giving our young people cut flowers when we should be
teaching them to grow their own plants. We are stuffing their heads with the
products of earlier innovation rather than teaching them to innovate. We think
of the mind as a storehouse to be filled when we should be thinking of it as an
instrument to be used.[14]

Active Student Participation in Learning

Durrell refers to students who engage in "lonely learning." [15] This expression aptly describes what happens to students in many classrooms. "The
teacher-centered style [of teaching] is typically defined as one in which
the teacher does most, by far, of the talking, directing, explaining, goal
setting, assignment making, and evaluation." [16] Analysis of classroom practices reveals that much classroom time is thus dominated by teachers.[17]
Teachers are active; students are passive. Teachers lecture; students attempt
to absorb what is said. Recitation on assignments is nearly always directed
to the teacher rather than to fellow students. Teacher-oriented discussion
limits student involvement.

This is unfortunate. Studies show that good learning is promoted when
the orientation of discussions is among students with the teacher a participant, rather than between students and teachers with the teacher playing
the dominant role. Teachers can create a new role for themselves by be-

[12] *Ibid.*

[13] Estes, Thomas, "Teaching Reading in Social Studies." Unpublished study, Syracuse University, 1969.

[14] John W. Gardner, *Self Renewal* (New York: Harper & Row, Publishers, 1964),
pp. 21–22.

[15] Donald D. Durrell, *Improving Reading Instruction* (New York: Harcourt, Brace,
& World, Inc., 1956).

[16] Lumsdaine, *Handbook of Research on Teaching*, p. 705.

[17] Ned Flanders, "Teacher Influence, Pupil Attitudes, and Achievement," in *Studying Teaching,* eds. J. Rath, J. Pancella, J. Van Ness (Englewood Cliffs: Prentice-
Hall, 1967), pp. 42–68.

coming guides to learning rather than dispensers of information; and they will observe the positive effects of students' achievement and feelings of success.

Active participation means interaction among students. Consider a classroom activity in which students are grouped in various combinations: threes, fours, fives. Given a structure to which he can react in this group activity, each student has opportunities for participation in group discussion and individual recitation much more frequently than in traditional classroom activity. The needs of individuals can be more easily met. The hesitant student feels freer to express his views in a group of four or five than in competition with thirty students in his class. Durrell refers to this experience as "multiple recitation." [18] The principle is obvious: students become active participants in the learning process rather than casual or passive onlookers. Consequently Bruner, among others, urges "that reading be rescued from its passivity and turned into a more active enterprise." [19]

Group activity must have purpose. Teachers should not group just for the sake of grouping. Each group can be guided so that students learn how to react to ideas, how to develop concepts, how to employ skills, how to express ideas, how to use ideas that have been developed, how to react to one another—expressing, defending, accepting ideas. Learning becomes more intense; students confront ideas of importance; involvement in learning is total. Group activity bridges the gap between memorization of detail and application of concepts. Students learn how to manipulate detail, how to sense relationships, and then how to express those relationships.

INSTRUCTIONAL MATERIALS

As previously discussed, reading instruction in content areas should be provided through reading materials required in the courses. If reading is taught through separate materials, reading instruction becomes a separate activity, indirectly related to the subject. Teachers become dependent on transfer, hoping students can apply to their texts the skills that they learned and practiced in the separate materials. Skills are taught more or less in a vacuum.

Using regular subject-area texts as vehicles for learning and practicing skills, as well as for sources of information, seems logical and practical. This view is rather widely accepted in principle, but there is some rather emotional disparity as to what form the instructional materials should take,

[18] Durrell, *Improving Reading Instruction.*
[19] Jerome S. Bruner, *Toward a Theory of Instruction* (Cambridge: Harvard University Press, 1967), p. 105.

and various solutions have been proposed: use of single texts; use of multiple texts; use of multilevel texts.

Single Texts

Given the fact that the ability and achievement of students in a given class range across several levels, the use of a single text seems, according to some, quite unrealistic.[20] Though adequate for the needs of some students in a class, the single text is too difficult for some and too simple for others.

Strong opinions are expressed on the question of exposure to points of view in history, science, math, or literature. Marksheffel asks, for example, "Would you, as a social studies teacher, feel that you were meeting your professional obligations to your country, school, and students if you deliberately limited students to the point of view of a single textbook?" [21]

The epithet "textbook teacher" is leveled at those who use a single text. Teachers who begin with page one and "grind through" the text, using it, in reality, as their curriculum guide, are "textbook teachers." They use the text not as one resource among many or as an instrument for developing skills, but as the course itself. Much emotion is generated by such teaching and use of curriculum materials.

Two alternatives to a single text are suggested in the literature: multilevel texts and multiple texts. They are often confused and referred to interchangeably.

Multilevel Texts

To meet the range of ability and achievement represented in a given content course, a teacher can gather resource materials written at a wide range of difficulty, representing various points of view, treating topics outlined in the curriculum guide. Each student is given material appropriate to his reading achievement level. During general class discussions he represents the point of view of his author but is exposed to other points of view from materials read by other students. The teacher pursues the curriculum as outlined in the course of study, not as dictated by a specific textbook.

Multiple Texts

To expose students to various points of view, teachers gather a number of titles for each topic and assign readings in each; or teachers may select one text for each topic within the course of study. Each text provides more

[20] Ned Marksheffel, *Better Reading in the Secondary School* (New York: The Ronald Press, 1966).
[21] *Ibid.*, p. 178.

specialization on its topic than possible in one generalized text. Though not necessarily allowing for exposure to many points of view on each topic, the latter variation does allow for greater depth of study on each topic. In neither case are materials selected on a basis of readability level.

The multiple text and multilevel text approaches are easily confused. Both emphasize exposure to multiple points of view but only one provides for students' achievement levels. Many teachers believe they are using the multilevel approach when they gather a variety of materials for their students. Because of the scarcity of materials treating the same topic on several levels of difficulty, teachers settle for multiple sets which treat the same topic though not necessarily on different levels of difficulty. Consequently, they may feel they are using the multilevel approach, providing for differences among students in their courses, while in reality they are only providing a variety of points of view.

Analysis of These Approaches

The views expressed concerning the use of a single text versus multilevel texts in a content area seem logical, theoretically sound, and practicable. However, there are several basic flaws in the arguments. First, there is the faulty assumption that a teacher will not be a "textbook teacher" if he uses more than one text. If a teacher is inclined to teach through a text, he will still assign readings beginning on page one and continuing through to the end of the book, whether he uses one or six books! A teacher can abuse several texts just as easily as one.

Another fallacy is the assumption that if a student has material written at his reading achievement level he will read it successfully, with relatively little instruction in how to read the material. The argument seem to be that if the teacher provides a text written at the student's reading achievement level, the student's reading problems will disappear. Unfortunately, overcoming a student's reading problems is not that simple. If it were, we would not have so many poor readers in content areas as we now do. Such assumptions are dangerous and lead teachers to use this approach, only to be discouraged when it does not work. Students do not read well merely because they have a book "written at their level." They have to be taught *how to use* the material.

Durrell makes a very important observation on this point.

Although there has been a constant concern about materials being written on "different levels" for children with different reading abilities, materials of the same reading level can be used for an entire class if the teacher provides the right amount and type of study help. It is possible that the differences among pupils in their need for study guides of different levels is greater than the differences in vocabulary load required to adjust to them.[22]

[22] Durrell, *Improving Reading Instruction,* p. 288.

The crucial factor is how one guides his students in the use of materials required in the course.

It certainly makes sense to have material written at a level approximating the achievement level of the students, as long as the students are shown how to handle it successfully. Students can read at various levels of comprehension from the same text (discussed further in chapter 5). Durrell is suggesting that if we guide each student's reading at levels appropriate to his needs, a basic text can be used for the initial instruction in concept and skill development followed by independent reading in multilevel materials. Experience has shown that such guidance does result in the improvement of students' reading comprehension and understanding of course content.[23]

Using a single text in a class doesn't make a poor teacher any more than using multilevel texts makes a good teacher. The kind of use made of the text or texts is what counts; needs of individual students can be met in either case.

Suggested Use of These Categories

There seems to be a logical sequence in the use of these sources. First, we must grant that all students need guidance in the proper use of their texts and that the level of comprehension at which students are led to respond to the text is as important to successful reading achievement as the vocabulary level at which the material is written. This being accepted, the content teacher has a sensible plan to follow. He uses his basic text for initial exposure to the ideas of the unit being studied. By guiding students in their reading of the text so that individual students are responding at different levels of comprehension, the teacher is able to provide for individual differences as he shows students how to cope with the reading difficulties posed by the text. Having experienced success in this guided reading experience and having had an initial exposure to the ideas of the unit, the students are ready to do some "independent" reading in materials written close to their various levels of achievement. This is when the teacher makes use of the multilevel materials available. With much less guidance, due to the successful experiences they have had with the basic text, the students continue their exploration and study of the unit. As they grow in achievement, some may continue on to the use of multiple texts, engaging in in depth study of selected topics, preparing reports for the class or just enriching their understanding.

If we accept the thesis that the essence of good teaching is showing students how to do what they are required to do, then whether a single or multilevel text approach is used, students must be guided as they read. Until

[23] Ruth Strang, "Developing Reading Skills in the Content Areas," *The High School Journal,* April, 1966, pp. 362–69.

a teacher knows how to do this with one text, he is not in a good position to attempt it with several. If he learns how to do it with one, then the close guidance of students as they read multilevel texts is not as essential; students will draw upon their successes in reading the single text.

One other point should be made. Nearly every class has a basic text identified for the curriculum. Very few classes have multilevel materials available even though more money is now available to purchase such materials. The problem is finding texts which are appropriate to the units to be studied in a given curriculum and also written at several levels of difficulty. In relation to the total number of units to be studied in all of the curriculum areas in school, there are relatively few suitable materials to be found. Consequently, it is important for content teachers to know how to make the best possible use of the material available: basic texts. It is not helpful to discredit these as inadequate. In themselves they are nothing, neither good nor bad; in the hands of a skillful teacher, they can be potent instruments for improved reading achievement and for an initial exposure to and understanding of the basic ideas in the curriculum.

This is the approach advocated in this text: proper use of the basic text and then proper use of multilevel texts. What a teacher does with the single text, in terms of guiding students as they respond at several levels of comprehension, can be applied to multiple texts as well; but the student must learn to walk before he runs. The important point to remember is that individualization of instruction is accomplished by what is done with the material, whether single or multiple sources. Individualization does not lie in the material itself.

OBJECTIVES

Independence

Producing independent learners is the goal for which content teachers should strive, but *independence* is a relative term. There seems to be a "continuum of independence," running from complete dependence on the teacher to complete independence from the teacher. In any course a teacher will find his students scattered all along this continuum. The teacher's task is to move them along the continuum as rapidly as possible, toward independence. Obviously some will never make the optimum; others will; but the teacher moves everyone as far as he has the capability to go.

Interestingly, a class will show one pattern of distribution of students along the continuum of independence in math, another pattern for that same class in science, another in history, another in English. The demands change; students' interests and talents come into play; curriculum expectations vary. Consequently the level of independence attainable for any one student will vary considerably as he moves from subject to subject. The same will occur as students move up through the grades. Following a given class through school and plotting levels of independence along the continuum for each of their subjects, we find a redistribution of students along the continuum *within the same subject* as the class moves through the grades.

The achievement level which a very able student can attain is higher than the level possible for a student of lesser ability. Both achieve independence in the use of skills if our expectatoin is appropriate to the ability of each. The bright student handles sophisticated levels of abstraction and independently applies concepts at this level. On the other hand, a student of limited ability may do well to achieve success in the accurate identification of detail. He can develop independence at this level of achievement.

Success

This is the factor which encourages the development of independence. But even as independence is a relative condition, as stated above, so is success. Because of differences in ability and previous achievement, "success" for one student might be considered "failure" for another. Both independence and success must be qualified in light of the individual to whom these conditions are attributed.

In any case, the challenge to the teacher is clear. He must find methods and materials that will show his students how to be successful in the study of his subject and how to attain independence in that study! This is the essence of good teaching: *to show students how to be successful in doing what is required of them.* With this as the teacher's purpose, students cannot help but be successful. And when students are successful, they are highly motivated and will learn.

REACTION GUIDE

Directions: Listed below is a series of statements. Place a check on the line before those items that are supported in this chapter. Circle the number before those statements you support. Examine the results to determine what the differences are. Compare your responses with your colleagues' and discuss possible reasons for differences you encounter.

_____ 1. Passivity in learning is nonlearning.
_____ 2. The lecture method prevents learning.
_____ 3. Students can learn from one another as well as from the teacher.

_____ 4. Assumptive teaching diminishes students learning opportunities.

_____ 5. Students should derive more than facts from their reading.

_____ 6. If a student cannot read his text the teacher should substitute the lecture for reading.

_____ 7. When given opportunity to be active participants in the teaching/learning act, students are more receptive learners.

_____ 8. Students must develop reasoning skills as well as reading skills.

_____ 9. Individualization of instruction is a theoretical principle that rarely works out in practice.

_____10. Achievement of success is dependent on ability.

_____11. Good teaching methods instruct in "how" to perform the required task and "how" to develop the required concepts.

_____12. Students should be held to grade-level standards to insure a quality education for all.

_____13. Multilevel texts answer the problems of students' reading achievement range.

_____14. All students in a given class might be "marching in the same academic parade" but ". . . to different drummers."

_____15. A teacher making good use of a basic text need not be considered a poor teacher.

_____16. "Independence" is a relative condition.

_____17. "Success" is a relative experience.

_____18. There is more commonality of skills than uniqueness among subject areas.

3

INSTRUCTIONAL FRAMEWORK

Several terms used in this chapter are defined in context:
- — structure *of* lessons
- — structure *within* lessons
- — directed reading activity

Other terms are touched on briefly, to be discussed in detail in later chapters:
- — reading guides
- — reasoning guides
- — functional analysis

Some critical terms are not clearly defined in context; therefore, a brief definition of each is given:
- — structure: as a noun form, the organizational scheme which simulates or ensures awareness of certain learning experiences
- — framework: the context into which structures are placed to give them meaning
- — guide: as a noun form, used synonymously with "structure"

IDEA DIRECTION

An old procedure is given more than a new name. Wherein lies the difference? Must change relate only to the procedure or also to the mind-set of the teacher?

READING DIRECTION

The use of the Instructional Framework assumes certain preparatory steps by a teacher. As you read, speculate about and identify (where expressed or implied) what these steps should be.

A third grade teacher expressed concern about the experiences her students would confront when they entered fourth grade. Because of departmentalization of sorts and because of stronger emphasis on the content areas of the curriculum, fourth graders were expected to function quite independently. They would receive relatively little instruction of a highly structured nature. The teacher's concern was how to prepare her students for this level of independent study. Her solution: "I put them on their own here in grade three!" Suggestions that students need to be guided in the development of independence in the use of skills were met with the rejoinder, "That's just spoon feeding." The assumptive teaching continued.

Of course, when these third grade students reach the fourth grade, the fourth grade teacher will prepare them for the independence required at the fifth grade. And what will be the preparation? Placing students on their own in grade four. Again, the response to suggestions for guiding students toward independence at their current grade level is: "Spoonfeeding!"

Teachers from grade three through twelve have expressed the same sentiment with almost identical wording. To prepare students for the independence they will be expected to demonstrate at the "next" grade level, teachers withhold guidance in learning activities, avoid "spoonfeeding," and require independence at the current level. Teachers prepare fourth graders for grade five, fifth graders for six, sixth for seven . . . eleventh for twelve. Then, of course, teachers of high school seniors know that colleges require the capacity for independent study. What better preparation is there than to require students to function independently in the twelfth grade?

One wonders, not unreasonably, who shows students *how* to become independent readers! Obviously a great responsibility is placed on the shoulders of first and second grade teachers who, presumably, prepare students for a life of independent study. At each level the students' independence is assumed as they are "prepared" for independence required at the succeeding level. Clearly the students are shortchanged, never being shown how to apply those skills which teachers at each level assume they can handle independently.

What is the role of the teacher in this unfortunate sequence? If he assumes students' independence, then his role is testing rather than teaching—testing to see how well students are performing with the skills they are assumed to possess; testing to see what knowledge they have acquired while exercising the skills in which, it is assumed, they have independent power. Teaching consists mainly of daily assignments on which students recite the following day in a teacher-led discussion. The teacher and the text become mere information dispensers, a role for which machines are better suited. However

When teaching no longer consists chiefly of assigning tasks and hearing recitations, guiding students' study becomes a recognized responsibility of the teacher. It should become an intrinsic part of the teaching process. Learning how to learn is surely as important an outcome of education as the facts learned.[1]

Independence should be looked upon, not as the means, but as the end product of skills and content instruction.

As discussed in chapter 2, independence is a relative term. Teachers need to move students along the continuum with forethought and calculation. "One way to describe the process of instruction is to say that the teacher strives to change the response pattern of a student from mere compliance to independent action. . . ." [2] The critical consideration, of course, is what constitutes the "striving." There needs to be a design, a structure, within which students are led to potential independence. If independent activity is expected and students have not been *shown how* to perform that activity, this is assumptive teaching. It neglects the critical factor in good instructions, that is, that students must be *shown how* to do whatever it is they are *expected* to do independently. With respect to any skill, independence is an ultimate state, not an immediate one.

Teachers can help students experience immediate success and ultimate independence if they provide a structure, or framework, within which students are guided through the process being taught, developing an understanding of both the process and the concepts to which the process is applied. "Teachers may feel that there is too much 'hand-holding' in this . . . approach. In a sense good teaching IS hand-holding; it is literally leading the pupils through a process until such time as they can walk alone. Rarely does that time come abruptly." [3]

This chapter presents a structure that teachers can provide for their students. The structure is a lesson framework designed in reference to the act of reading. It incorporates what is to be accomplished prior to, during, and after the reading of a given assignment. Although there are many non-reading activities related to any subject area and although it is possible to learn in ways other than reading, the purpose here is to focus attention on

[1] Ruth Strang, *Guided Study and Homework* (Washington: National Education Association, 1955), p. 8.
[2] Ned Flanders, "Teacher Influence, Pupil Attitudes, and Achievement," in *Studying Teaching,* eds. J. Raths, J. Pancella, J. Van Ness (Englewood Cliffs: Prentice-Hall, Inc., 1967), p. 49.
[3] Olive S. Niles, "Developing Basic Comprehension," in *Speaking of Reading* (Syracuse: Syracuse University, 1964), p. 70.

the reading phase of learning and on those elements of instruction which support this activity.

Structure of Lessons

Bruner believes that "Instruction consists of leading the learner through a sequence of statements and restatements of a problem or body of knowledge to increase the learner's ability to grasp, transform, and transfer what he is learning." [4]

INSTRUCTIONAL FRAMEWORK

The structure through which such instruction is provided consists of three major parts: preparation; guidance; independence.

Preparation

An activity designed to promote learning—whether of concept or process —is more effective if the participants are prepared to engage in that activity. Preparation has several components.

MOTIVATION   People seem to learn best those things in which they are interested. As interest is aroused, attention is more acute and minds are more receptive. As part of the structure for ensuring success in learning reading skills and subject content, motivation makes an important contribution. Each teacher has his own techniques by which to arouse his students' interest in a particular topic. He has learned that "It is often the case that novelty must be introduced in order that the enterprise be continued," [5] or even that it be begun in the first place!

Any discussion of motivation raises the interesting question of what happened to the students' natural curiosity that makes it necessary for teachers to find ways to generate some interest in the curriculum they are studying. Getzels raises this issue, saying

. . . the change in the basic question from how we can instill interests in children to why this child is not interested leads us to look at the individual child rather than the children in the mass, to focus on causes rather than on symptoms, and to think of ways to prevent the loss of interest rather than to deal with the lack of interest as if lack of interest were the child's natural state. This is a signal gain not only theoretically but practically, for in the long run

[4] Jerome S. Bruner, *Toward a Theory of Instruction* (Cambridge: Harvard University Press, 1966), p. 29.
[5] *Ibid.,* p. 59.

it may be easier to head off the loss of capacity to be interested than to try to instill interests after the capacity for interests has been damaged.[6]

This is an important issue, practical and worthy of close study. Until we find ways to prevent loss of interest, teachers will have to cope with the task of arousing, or restoring, as the case may be, students' interests in specific units of study in content areas.

Techniques for motivation are as varied as the teachers who employ them. It is unrealistic and unnecessary to be prescriptive in this area. But consideration of motivation raises another issue: motivation involves not only arousing interest but also establishing purposes for learning.

Education being what it is, a person must study some things in which he has no particular interest. If the purpose for the study is evident, the time and energy expended will bring a reasonable return in knowledge gained and used. Assuming that students are not equally interested in all areas of intellectual endeavor, and acknowledging the reality of Getzel's point, a content teacher must devise interest-arousing activities to capture the attention of students.

BACKGROUND INFORMATION AND REVIEW   When a student begins a a new unit of study and reads material related to that unit, he needs a frame of reference for new ideas he will acquire. Otherwise his idea intake will be erratic and lack organization. He will recall isolated bits of information, which may or may not have bearing on what he has studied previously. He will find it difficult to draw generalizations from that information.

Background information refers to those major and minor concepts which identify, qualify, and support the specific unit to be studied. As part of his motivational procedure, the teacher may draw upon students' experiences, asking them for information that will enlighten the class on specific points and prepare it for an in depth study of the topic. The teacher may also draw on his own knowledge of the topic to provide information that arouses interest and sets the problem in bold relief.

Whether the teacher draws from his own fund of knowledge or from students' experiences, his purpose is to provide a context into which new information can be fitted, subsequently enlarged into a major concept, and possibly explored in depth. Regardless of the individual teacher's style, his intention is to prepare students to read an assignment successfully. Background information also aids the motivation factor. When a student has little experience with or knowledge of a topic, his interest is minimal. "The cumulative effect of outdistancing his experience will generally inhibit his interest and progress."[7] Through his teacher and fellow students, he can

[6] J. W. Getzels, "The Problem of Interests: A Reconsideration," in *Reading: Seventy-Five Years of Progress* (Chicago: University of Chicago Press, 1966).

[7] James M. McCallister, "Promoting Growth in Interpreting in Grades Nine through Fourteen," in *Reading: Seventy-Five Years of Progress* (Chicago: University of Chicago Press, 1966), p. 90.

gain sufficient vicarious and actual experience to maintain his interest.

Review provides the true frame of reference into which students fit new ideas acquired through their reading and study. Review provides intellectual hooks on which new ideas can be hung. Review has a narrower focus than "background information." The latter is assumed not to be part of the students' immediate understanding or direct experience; it is provided by the teacher to enrich the context for the new unit.

Review assumes a previous experience, common to all students, which has bearing on the new unit. This common experience is recalled and related to the new unit, enlarging and strengthening the context for the topics within the unit.

A student will experience learning difficulties if he does not have the benefit of review. If he does not go over previously learned information to speculate on its relative value and bearing on the new topic, his only recourse is to memorize isolated bits of information with little purpose or focus.

ANTICIPATION AND PURPOSE   ". . . Students should cultivate the habit of questioning and surmising the coming ideas." [8] The combination of *background information* and *review* creates this sense of anticipation in students, an "I'm-looking-for-something" attitude. This is how purposes for reading are established. They are not dictated by the teacher; they are evolved by the students through the structure provided by the teacher. "The capable teacher is the one who helps children recognize various purposes for reading and then gives them opportunities to improve their abilities to read for these somewhat distinct and different purposes." [9]

Develop a purpose and it will be realized. Read without anticipation and you are reduced to word calling. A student who looks for ideas as he reads will find them; but if he looks for nothing he finds that too! "If the pupil is to understand what he is reading, he must know why he is reading." [10]

Two broad areas of purpose need to be established: 1) the ideas to be discovered; 2) the skills to be applied. The structure provided by the teacher should reflect his own preparation for the lesson: he has determined the ideas he believes are important enough for the students to acquire. He encourages students to be receptive to those ideas as they read. He also determines how the students must read the material in order to develop those ideas, and he gives students direction in the application of those skills. Consequently, students read for the purpose of developing specific ideas, and they do so with a conscious application of specific, appropriate

[8] Ruth Strang, Constance M. McCullough, and Arthur E. Traxler, *The Improvement of Reading* (New York: McGraw-Hill Book Company, 1967), p. 355.

[9] David H. Russell and Henry R. Fea, "Research on Teaching Reading," in *Handbook of Research on Teaching* (Chicago: American Educational Research Association, 1963).

[10] Emerald V. Dechant, *Improving the Teaching of Reading* (Englewood Cliffs: Prentice-Hall, Inc., 1964), pp. 354–55.

skills. Obviously *purpose* is closely allied to another aspect of preparation: *direction.*

DIRECTION   The teacher determines major ideas his students are to acquire and the skills needed to discover them in reading a given assignment. Based on this analysis, he can give students specific directions in how to apply the necessary skills. Chapter 4 discusses this analysis in detail; chapters 5, 6, 7, and 8 explore the specific processes the teacher would look for during this analysis.

For example, when he is about to read an assignment in his text,

> . . . it is never appropriate to tell a student merely to read a certain chapter. We must help him set his purpose for reading. If we want him to draw general conclusions from the material, then we must indicate this purpose before he reads it. . . . If we want him to read the material for certain kinds of specific details, once again we should point out this purpose and direct him toward those details.[11]

Students can achieve greater success with this direction than they would if the teacher assumed they already knew the skills to be used and knew how to adapt them to the assignment.

This direction can take many forms. A teacher can "pull out" one skill and emphasize it through oral descriptions. A teacher might lead students in a survey of the text to identify the specific skills that they need to use, speculating on their adaptation to the content. However, teachers should always make certain that skills for which direction is given are associated with the content of the material, so that skill development supports an understanding of the subject and is not isolated from it.

Teachers may feel uncomfortable about giving all of this direction because they think they are helping students too much. Some may be afraid students will never achieve independence (and this has already been discussed), or believe they will be looked on as soft touches (apparently the "tough teacher" image is to be preferred by many and that is, seemingly, equated with having students fumble along on their own, uncertain as to what to do). Hopefully we will come to the point in education where instruction is conceived of as showing students how to perform required tasks and where not providing such instruction is viewed as professional negligence.

LANGUAGE DEVELOPMENT   Each subject has its own language, its own technical vocabulary. To study the subject, students must know the language which serves as the basis for communicating ideas within that subject. They do not develop an understanding of this vocabulary by chance, but only by design. The design should include calculated exposure

[11] William K. Durr, "Improving Secondary Reading Through the Content Subjects," in *Reading as an Intellectual Activity* (Newark, Del.: International Reading Association, 1963), p. 68.

to the technical vocabulary of the subject and opportunity to use that vocabulary sufficiently often to insure familiarity and facility with it. Through the design, meanings of words are reinforced and understandings of concepts extended.

When students discuss the technical vocabulary before reading a selection, their understanding of the content is much greater than when the vocabulary is ignored or handled only superficially. Moreover, reinforcement of word meanings by frequent exposure to and manipulation of the vocabulary makes learning more permanent.

Vocabulary development is discussed in detail in chapter 8. Many questions about selecting, teaching, and reinforcing vocabulary in content areas are explored.

Guidance

After the preparatory steps in the structure of lessons have been completed, students are ready to read. What does the teacher do at this point? He makes certain that students apply the skills for which they have been given direction and that they pursue the ideas embodied in the assigned materials. The teacher guides the students in this experience, *not* assuming they already know what he is attempting to teach them. This guidance has sufficient flexibility and latitude, however, to permit students to use their own systems for pursuing ideas and applying skills, because

The learning process is highly individual. Each student may be at a somewhat different stage in effective study methods; each may have worked out methods that make sense to him. These methods may be more helpful to him at the time than methods suggested by the classroom teacher.[12]

The need is for latitude in the guidance of students' skill and concept development ". . . learning that starts in response to the rewards of parental or teacher approval or the avoidance of failure can too readily develop a pattern in which the child is seeking cues as to how to conform to what is expected of him." [13] Obviously this is not the result the teacher should seek. "Since the role of the teacher is to guide and direct learning activities, we should seek to examine every approach or technique that will further that purpose." [14] The purpose is not conformity but ultimate independence.

Consequently, guidance must be sufficiently structured to give purpose and direction but sufficiently "loose" to allow personal strengths, prefer-

[12] Strang, *Guided Study and Homework,* p. 7.
[13] Jerome S. Bruner, "The Act of Discovery," in *On Knowing* (New York: Atheneum Publishers, 1965, pp. 87–88.
[14] Arthur W. Heilman, *Principles and Practices of Teaching Reading* (Columbus: Charles E. Merrill Books, Inc., 1967), p. 384.

ences, discoveries, to emerge. The more induction is used in the guidance procedure and the more "discovery" one puts into his structure, the more enthusiastic the response from students and the greater the chance for ultimate independence on the students' part. As Bruner states,

The hypothesis that I would propose here is that to the degree that one is able to approach learning as a task of discovering something rather than "learning about" it, to that degree will there be a tendency for the child to carry out his learning activities with the autonomy of self-reward or, more properly, by reward that is discovery itself.[15]

The reason for incorporating careful guidance in one's instruction is obvious. "When a pupil fails to develop adequate study skills, the educational process may become dull and unpleasant. Therefore, guidance and specific instruction must be provided to help children develop these skills." [16]

This chapter and, more particularly, chapters 5, 6, and 7 give specific suggestions and examples for guiding the development of skills and concepts.

DEVELOPMENT OF SKILLS   Reading guides are designed to show students how to apply skills as they read. Merely telling students what skills they should use is not sufficient, though it is essential. Suggestions such as the following are only a partial solution: "If we want (the student) to draw general conclusions from the material, then we must indicate this purpose before he reads it, preferably by giving him or helping devise questions which require general conclusions." [17]

Asking questions that "require" the use of a skill does not necessarily teach the skill. Such procedures, based on the notion that to require the use of a skill is to teach its use, are assumptive. The two are quite different. *After* the skill has been taught and the student has had opportunity under some direction to develop familiarity with it, it is useful reinforcement to ask questions requiring use of the skill. But while it is being *taught,* some procedure, other than merely asking questions requiring use of the skill, should be used.

This should be a structure that will give students a conscious experience in the application of the skill and, simultaneously, an understanding of the course content; provide for individual differences in ability and achievement among students in classes; ensure success in the assigned reading. Reading *guides* can be designed for these purposes.

A thorough discussion of the construction and use of guides appears in chapters 5, 6, and 7. There is some evidence [18] that students of average

[15] Bruner, "The Act of Discovery," *loc cit.*

[16] Heilman, *Principles and Practices of Teaching Reading,* p. 373.

[17] Durr, "Improving Secondary Reading," p. 68.

[18] Harold L. Herber, "Teaching Reading and Physics Simultaneously," in *Improvement of Reading Through Classroom Practice* (Newark, Del.: International Reading Association, 1964), pp. 84–85.

and above average ability need and respond to assistance offered by guides as much as students of below average ability. Bruner does suggest, however, that "Good teaching that emphasizes the structure of a subject is probably even more valuable for the less able student than for the gifted one, for it is the former rather than the latter who is more easily thrown off the track by poor teaching." [19] The same can be said about teaching reading, though there is not sufficient research evidence to say so with certainty. Valuable research studies can be conducted in this area.

Another profitable research area concerns the nature of instruction, and related materials, provided for students at various levels of ability and achievement. Again, Bruner suggests that "intellectual activity anywhere is the same, whether at the frontier of knowledge or the third grade classroom. . . . The difference is in degree, not in kind." [20] It is not clearly known what adjustments are needed to accommodate the degrees of difference nor is it clear what duration of guidance is required at each of the levels. Hopefully, research studies will yield the needed information.

DEVELOPMENT OF CONCEPTS   Students have the innate capacity for accurate assimilation of material they read, but to assume that this skill, in well-developed form, is a natural condition is not valid. To teach a subject by requiring memorization of detail is to give incorrect emphasis. Concept development is the more profitable emphasis, collection of facts much less valuable. Bruner suggests,

One cannot "cover" any subject in full, not even in a lifetime, if coverage means visiting all the facts and events and morsels. Subject matter presented so as to emphasize its structure will perforce be of that generative kind that permits reconstruction of the details or, at very least, prepares a place into which the details, when encountered, can be put.[21]

Students must acquire skills for deriving information from reading— reading skills. Likewise, it is essential that they acquire skills by which to assimilate and react to ideas acquired through reading—reasoning skills. Guides can be designed to insure profitable experiences with reading skills; models also can be created to serve as patterns of behavior for students as they learn how to reason critically and creatively about concepts. Subsequently, they learn how to apply those concepts to their own lives, to their environment, and to ideas they have developed previously on the same topic.

The construction and use of reasoning guides is discussed in chapter 7. When students are exposed to such experiences within a subject area, there is growth in their understanding of the course content because their ability to reason about the content is improved.

[19] Jerome S. Bruner, *The Process of Education* (New York: Vintage Books, 1960), p. 9.
[20] *Ibid.*, p. 14.
[21] Jerome S. Bruner, "After John Dewey What?", *On Knowing* (New York: Atheneum Publishers, 1965), p. 121.

The need exists for research studies such as the following on reasoning guides as well as reading guides: making comparisons among various kinds of guides and within specific guides with respect to their relative effectiveness in promoting learning; studying the duration over grade levels and the intensity within grade levels with respect to the usefulness of guides in promoting learning. The knowledge gained from such studies could make a significant difference in instruction in content area classes.

Independence

APPLICATION OF SKILLS   As has been mentioned previously in this chapter, there is the widespread concern that students need to develop and demonstrate independence in the use of reading skills in all of their subjects. This is an important concern, but independence is not produced merely by expecting or demanding it. It is produced only by structuring lessons with sufficient care so that the students are clearly shown how to apply the skills and are guided for a sufficient duration so they develop a "feel" for the skills.

The structure of lessons presented in this chapter does develop independence. It prepares students for a task and then carefully guides them as they perform it. Having developed a pattern of behavior, students will repeat it with fewer and fewer external controls until they are able to adapt and modify it to suit their personal idiosyncracies. True independence has then been reached.

The road to independence is long. It is damaging to students for teachers to assume that independence is required at the beginning of the instructional journey rather than found at the end.

APPLICATION OF CONCEPTS   A chemistry teacher was disturbed because his students could not "handle concepts" in his course. The statewide final examination required independent application of concepts developed throughout the course. The suggestion was made that he prepare study guide material showing the students how to develop and apply concepts, as expected of them in the examination. He replied that to do so would take the time he needed to cover the course, and would, therefore, jeopardize the students' performance on the examination. It was pointed out to him that his students already were doing poorly because of their inability to "handle concepts"; it would be to the students' advantage if he were to teach them how to develop the concepts they were expected to handle. He persisted that he could not afford the time; if the students could not handle concepts when they came to his class "they didn't belong there." He was then asked, "What is it that you have responsibility to teach? If they *must* know when they come to your class what they *should* know when they take the end-of-the-year examination, you really have nothing to teach them!" The conversation ended in stony silence.

Independent use of concepts is, indeed, a proper goal for teachers to hold for students. Reasoning guides walk students through simulated experiences in the development and use of concepts. These successful experiences under close guidance develop a behavior pattern that students can repeat when required to function independently. As students become more proficient, they begin to modify the pattern to suit their own special needs. True independence, then, is achieved. As has been said, independence is not the starting point but, rather, the end product of good teaching.

STRUCTURE WITHIN LESSONS

The critical part of the structure *of* lessons is the structure provided *within* lessons: the reading and reasoning guides. These guides provide a model, a simulation, of the desired behavior. They assume the preparatory part of the Instructional Framework and point toward the ultimate independence which the Instructional Framework fosters. The structure within lessons is the part frequently omitted for reasons already discussed.

The structure within lessons has three elements, each applied according to the students' sophistication in the use of the procedure being learned.

Reaction to Pattern

Both skills and concepts have specific components. If students are to acquire a feeling for the skill or an understanding of the concept, it is necessary for them to manipulate the components of the skill or concept. Through such manipulation they see how the concept is formed or how the skill operates. The teacher can develop a guide (structure) which incorporates the components of the skill or concept and includes distractors, which students must sort out. This sorting and arranging of the components of the process or concept develops a sensitivity to the relationships essential to the development of concepts; a sensitivity to the process by which the relationships are formed and applied. The guide, then, becomes a simulator of the experience and understanding which is being taught. When the guide follows the "direction" of the instructional framework, the simulation is a powerful learning experience. "There is a relationship between the development of content and the nature of the control exercised by structure. When the structure permits no exploration on the part of children it serves to delimit and restrict." [22] The alternatives, which incorporate the components needed for the desired learning, provide this exploration. Students explore, through discussion, the differences they find in comparing their selections from among the alternatives, and the learning is reinforced. A pattern of

[22] Marie M. Hughes, "What is Teaching? One Viewpoint," *Educational Leadership,* January, 1962, pp. 251–59.

behavior is started which will lead to independence. Such a structure is in direct contrast to that frequently observed in classrooms: "The questions teachers used for structure were usually closed; that is, asked for one *right* answer. It was suggested that one right answer evoked the use of recall as a mental process instead of stimulating a large range of mental activity." [23] Subjected to closed questioning, students' mental activity is reduced to guessing what is in the teacher's mind; he is rewarded if the guess is correct, punished if other possibilities, even though valid, are presented.

ILLUSTRATION   The essential elements of this phase of the structure within lessons, *reaction to a pattern,* is illustrated in the following material provided for fifth graders. Teachers wanted to observe ways to teach the use of "inference" as a reading skill. They wished to see development of the early stages of the skill, and then receive suggestions for follow-up and sequential development of the skill.

Reading pictures inferentially was selected as the first step in the sequence. The problem was to provide a structure within the lesson which would simulate the experience of reading for inference. The first phase of the structure within lessons was applied: providing for *reaction to patterns.* The following picture was selected from their text.

From Marjorie W. Hamilton, *Pirates and Pathfinders* (Canada: Clarke, Irwin, and Company, 1954), p. 149. Reproduced by permission of the publisher.

[23] *Ibid.*

In reading pictures inferentially, students first identify objects actually within the picture. Second, they speculate on possible objects or ideas related to what they see in the picture but not actually appearing in the picture. (Objects, suggested in this manner, would be of a concrete nature and ideas more abstract.) Third, students frame statements to represent the inferences that can be drawn by relating the given with the possible.

Part One lists objects one possibly can observe in the picture. These are the components necessary to the first step in inference. Asking students to list the objects they observe would be assuming competence in the skill one is attempting to teach. Providing a list of alternatives which students can manipulate gives them guidance within which they can exercise some judgment and, thereby, develop a feeling for this aspect of the skill.

Students were asked to check the names of the objects they observed in the picture and to add the names of those objects not listed, which they could identify. Students worked together discussing the alternatives, determining which were appropriate to select and, finally, listing items which should be added.

Part One

Directions: Place a check before all words that name something you see in the picture. Add any others you can support.

_____ 1. Wrecks	_____10. Bread
_____ 2. Animals	_____11. Fire
_____ 3. Men	_____12. Sky
_____ 4. Smoke	_____13. Sails
_____ 5. Ship	_____14. Clouds
_____ 6. Sand	_____15. Trees
_____ 7. Birds	_____16. Guns
_____ 8. Sea	_____17. Knives
_____ 9. Meat	

The same procedure was followed in Part Two. It lists objects or ideas that can be related to the picture, but are not actually shown in the picture. Again alternatives were given. Each alternative had to be compared with the picture and discussed in light of its relevance. Students were required to draw on their past experience in order to perceive the relevance.

Part Two

Directions: Place a check before all words that name an object or idea that the picture makes you think of. Add any others you can support.

_____ 1. Transportation	_____ 2. Pirating
_____ 3. Exploration	_____ 4. Whaling

_____ 5. Tropics   _____11. Work
_____ 6. Army   _____12. Long journeys
_____ 7. Resourcefulness   _____13. Carpentry
_____ 8. Caution   _____14. Plunder
_____ 9. Danger   _____15. Preparation
_____10. Farming

If students had been asked to produce this list independently, it would have been a test to determine whether or not they could draw inferences from pictures. By providing alternatives, and allowing discussion among students, they were being shown how to draw inferences from pictures.

Part Three presents a list of alternative statements, each of which might possibly be an inference one might draw from the picture. The presentation and manipulation of alternatives, again, allowed a reaction to the pattern of behavior which was being taught. Selection and discussion of the alternatives reinforced the use of the pattern.

Part Three

Directions: Place a check before all statements that you believe tell about the picture. You may add other statements you can support.

_____ 1. The men are seamen.
_____ 2. The men are going on a long voyage.
_____ 3. The men are strangers to this country.
_____ 4. The men are explorers.
_____ 5. The men are used to danger.
_____ 6. The men are in the Queen's Navy.
_____ 7. The men enjoy their work.
_____ 8. The men are pirates.

When coupled with the preparation phase of the Instructional Framework which, in part, gives specific direction on the use of the skill, this material develops an awareness of how the skill "feels" and of the information and ideas the student can acquire by using the skill. Of special interest is the fact that this material was used with both a below average class and a fast class. There was a similar response from both classes, the difference being "in degree, not in kind." The experience supported, again, Bruner's contention that

The task of teaching a subject to a child at any particular age is one of representing the structure of that subject in terms of the child's way of viewing things. The task can be thought of as one of translation. General hypothesis that has just been stated is premised on the considered judgment that any idea can be presented honestly and usefully in the thought forms of children of school age, and that these first representations can later be made more powerful and precise the more easily by virtue of this early learning.[24]

Attention to Transfer

The next phase of the *structure within lessons* is to account for transfer. Consider again the reading of pictures. If students have experienced success in developing inferential statements from pictures they have "read" while being guided through the process as suggested above, then they are ready to try the procedure without the aid of carefully structured guides. They still need some coaching so that they can transfer from highly structured material to more independent application of the skill, and this coaching is part of the attention to transfer. The teacher helps students recall experiences they have had relative to the particular skill or idea in question. He discusses with them how the skill "worked" in those previous situations, and then he discusses the appropriateness of that process to the situation they now face. He suggests to them that they set up the same kind of structure that was provided for them when they originally applied the skill.

Recall of prior uses of the skill and discussion of its appropriateness to the new situation ensure transfer and lead students to ultimate independence. The attention to transfer is profitable only when a pattern has been explored sufficiently and students have been carefully guided in its use so that they have an understanding which can be transferred.

Modification of Pattern

For students truly to be independent it is necessary that they be allowed to perform tasks differently than they have been taught if their own method is efficient and produces the desired results. It may be, for example, that a student can discover another way to approach the task of reading for inference. If so, he should be allowed to adapt the skill to suit his personal style and personal need. To insist that students perform a task in precisely the same manner that the teacher prescribes is to produce stereotyped robots, not individual thinkers and learners. Certainly students must follow required procedure in the first phase of the structure within lessons so that they are exposed to a pattern and learn how it works. They are then in a position to modify it. Without the first phase, students have nothing to modify and their "independent" modifications may not be modifications at all but only the results of nondirected self-discovery, a much less efficient way to learn.

Ironically, teachers who reject the use of reading and reasoning guides

[24] Bruner, *The Process of Education*, p. 33.

because they might encourage dependence, themselves foster dependence. They focus on informational recall and also insist that students perform tasks or make use of ideas in precisely the same manner they were taught. Only when students are allowed to develop a personal style with respect to any skill or understanding, are they truly independent. The *structure within lessons,* part of the *structure of lessons* of the Instructional Framework, allows such development but in a logical sequence: after students have been shown *how* to perform a task, how to transfer it to new but similar situations, they devise their own method and become truly independent.

INSTRUCTIONAL FRAMEWORK AND THE DIRECTED READING ACTIVITY

Readers familiar with the literature about reading instruction may think the Instructional Framework is merely a renaming of the Directed Reading Activity. Such is not the case. The DRA was designed principally for the development of a reading lesson from a reading textbook, though it is also recommended for use in content areas. The IF is designed mainly for use with content texts, though it could be used with reading texts.

The DRA is a 3-step procedure, as is the IF, but there are fundamental differences. The components of the IF were presented above. The phases of the DRA are: 1) building background and purpose by introducing new vocabulary, reviewing previous lessons where appropriate, drawing on students' experience background, previewing material to determine how it should be read; 2) silent reading and study to accomplish the established purposes; 3) follow-up questioning, testing, and discussing what was read to determine understandings derived related to content and process.

Both the IF and DRA are similar in their first phases. The major difference exists in phase two. The IF guides students as they read and react, as they gather information and develop concepts. The DRA allows time for reading and encourages students to apply skills discussed in phase one. However the "structure within" the lesson is not provided in the DRA as it is in the IF. Therefore, there is the assumption that a level of independence already has been attained by the readers. Phase three of the DRA builds on that assumption.

Phase two of the IF *guides* the student in the application of skills and the development of concepts. Then, in phase three, the IF allows for independent application of both skills and concepts. Both in phase two and three students have opportunity to explore ideas, under close guidance in phase two and in independent activity in phase three, whereas this activity is reserved to phase three of the DRA.

In effect, phase three of the IF incorporates phases two and three of the DRA, making phase two of the IF, the guided reading (structure *within* lessons), a unique phase. The independent application of skills and concepts is similar to what occurs in the DRA's phase two with its independent reading and phase three with its relatively unstructured discussion of information and ideas in the story.

The structure within lessons—phase two of the IF—stands apart from the DRA. It is the critical factor in teaching reading through course content.

Many have been critical of the DRA

On the instructional front, all teachers must understand how reading as a cognitive process is akin to thinking. Reading must be taught in such a way that the precept of versatility becomes a reality. . . . Yet classroom practices, saddled by out-moded and ill-conceived directed reading activities presented and re-presented by stereotyped basic reader programs, violate these principles. Children can think. They can read critically and reflectively and creatively at all levels—if they are taught to do so. Efficient cognitive skills can be taught. However, in the all-too-typical schools the minimal, parrot-like demands placed upon children actually deprive them of opportunity to do so.[25]

The Instructional Framework avoids the conditions which prompted such criticism of the DRA.

BENEFITS

What benefits accrue to the students and the teacher by making use of the Instuctional Framework and, particularly, the structured materials that are recommended? They can be summarized under three headings: 1) individualization of instruction; 2) student interaction; 3) functional analysis.

Individualization of Instruction

Faced with a class ranging across several grade-equivalent levels of ability and achievement, a teacher finds it difficult to meet the needs of each individual. Hjermstad makes the point more strongly: "Adjusting classroom instruction to accommodate each individual's level of reading skill in each reading selection is, of course, impossible." [26] He continues on a hopeful note, however: "by identifying the essential skills to be taught in vocabulary, comprehension, and rate, an approach can be established that will give every . . . lesson a firm, continuing, flexible basis." [27] Hjermstad does

[25] Russell G. Stauffer, "Time for Amendment," *The Reading Teacher,* May, 1967, p. 685.

[26] Fritz Hjermstad, "Identifying Significant Reading Skills in Grades One through Fourteen," in *Reading: Seventy-Five Years of Progress* (Chicago: University of Chicago Press, 1966), p. 43.

[27] *Ibid.*

not identify this approach or how it is applied; however, what he suggests is possible through the guidance phase of the Instructional Framework.

Materials which provide structure *within* lessons, are designed to guide students in the development of specific skills and concepts. These materials can be constructed to account for differences in students' levels of ability and achievement. As was stated in chapter 2, a given skill or concept can be applied at many levels of sophistication. If the materials which accompany the reading selection are properly designed, each student will be provided sufficient guidance to respond to the selection at a level appropriate to his needs. Chapters 5 and 6 include sample materials which demonstrate the possibilities for meeting the learning needs of each individual in a class.

"Comprehending and recalling materials they [students] have read is much more than a matter of the right vocabulary load." [28] It *is* a matter of adjusting the structure within which students are guided in their application of the skill so that the level of sophistication at which the skill is to be used is appropriate to their capabilities at the moment.

Of course, no one is ever going to claim that it is possible to meet the needs of every single individual in every classroom every day. However, we can come close and, certainly, it is possible to come much closer to that ideal than we have in the past. Chapter 9 discusses this matter in more detail.

Grouping

Though it is virtually impossible to meet the needs of each student every day, one can approximate this goal by grouping students within a class. Reading guides provided for each group take into account the general level of ability and achievement of the group. There is sufficient latitude within the guide to accommodate the narrower range of ability and achievement that would be present in a subgroup of a class. Each student responds to material which closely approximates his need for skill development. He has the advantage of working with other students within the structure provided by the guides so that what he cannot do by himself he can do with the assistance of other members of the group.

Reasoning guides, those guides that assist students in the development of concepts, work in the same manner. The structure of the guides provides the components of the concept confined by the structure of the guide. Sufficient latitude is allowed to accommodate individual differences within the groups for, as Bruner says,

[28] Donald D. Durrell, *Improving Reading Instruction* (New York: Harcourt, Brace, and World, 1956), p. 287–88.

. . . the merit of a structure depends upon its power for *simplifying informa-tion,* for *generating new propositions,* and for *increasing the manipulability of a body of knowledge,* structure must always be related to the status and gifts of the learner.[29]

Grouping is discussed in greater detail in chapter 9 and was touched on in chapter 2. However, it is useful to review and anticipate some of the discussion at this juncture.

ACTIVE STUDENT INVOLVEMENT   Someone referred to people "who sit behind their eyes. . . ."[30] This is quite characteristic of students in a classroom where passive receptivity by students and active presentation by the teacher is the order of the day. If one were to classify the students' conscious state, one could label it the "conference state" and place it one step above the catatonic. This state is characteristic of people participating in situations in which they are "talked to" and have little opportunity to respond in any active manner. Symptoms are the glazed eye, the head fixed in position to face the speaker, the occasional nod and smile of automatic response. One finds these symptoms among adults who attend church, art lectures, presentations of philosophical treatises; particularly it is found among teachers who attend faculty meetings, in-service sessions after school, and evening courses at the university! People do, indeed, often just sit be-hind their eyes, with much that is unrelated to the topic under considera-tion going on behind those eyes. And students in elementary and secondary schools are no different from adults in this respect.

Imagine the typical high school student who rushes to school each morn-ing, enters his first period class where he is talked to for forty minutes. He has four minutes to go to his next class where he is talked to for another forty minutes, and so on through the day until, if he takes five subjects, he has been talked to for a total of three and one-half hours with little opportunity to respond as an active participant. If this continues year after year a student is reduced to the state of intellectual curiosity that motivates him only to discover what the teacher has in mind, what the teacher ex-pects to be given back on examination papers, and then to deliver what is expected. The natural curiosity he possessed at birth is stultified and diminished. To renew that curiosity or to "channel curiosity into more powerful intellectual pursuits requires . . . that there be . . . [a] . . . transition from the passive, receptive, episodic form of curiosity to the sustained and active form."[31] There certainly is no question about whether or not students desire and respond to situations in which they can pursue points of interest brought on by their natural curiosity. Indeed, there is

[29] Bruner, *Toward a Theory of Instruction,* p. 41.
[30] Attributed to Emerson.
[31] William H. Allen, "Audio-Visual Communication," in *Encyclopedia of Educa-tional Research* (New York, The Macmillan Co., 1960), p. 117.

"considerable research that indicates the extent to which even non-human primates will put forth effort for a chance to encounter something novel on which to exercise curiosity." [32] How much greater the desire that students must have to exercise their curiosity!

Reading and reasoning guides which help students acquire and apply skills and concepts, also provide for student interaction, student involvement in the learning process. These structures provide what Bruner calls for when he says that "the young learner should, we think, be given the chance to solve problems, to conjecture, to quarrel. . . ." [33] Through these structures, as already discussed, the components of skills and concepts are presented. Students are allowed to bring to these structures their present knowledge and experience, and to share both with other members of the group. Each student's contribution is accepted and respected as the content is explored and the skills developed and reinforced.

The teaching acts that develop content, elaborate and add to the content or problem under consideration. Response is made to the data placed in the situation by the children. It is believed that children involved in content have something to say. They are encouraged in this by the teacher who respects their efforts.[34]

This is not to suggest that intraclass grouping is the panacea for all educational ills or even just for the problems related to the involvement of students in the learning process. Much research must be conducted. To the extent that grouping or not grouping students in a classroom for guided activity reflects autocratic or democratic teacher behavior, there is evidence that cognitive gain is largely unaffected by having students work together in groups. "The majority of investigators who have attempted to measure differences in achievement report no particular advantage for either approach." [35] However, where studies [36] have been conducted in which the "democratic approach" has been expressed definitely through the use of reading and reasoning guides, there has been a significant cognitive growth. There is no evidence of the effect of this approach on affective gains. One can be relatively certain, however, that "at least as many (students) feel dissatisfied, frustrated, or anxious in a nondirective classroom as consider it valuable." [37] Whether this reflects the natural state or conditioning brought on by years of experience in directive classrooms, one cannot be certain.

[32] Bruner, *Toward a Theory of Instruction,* p. 115.

[33] *Ibid.,* p. 155.

[34] Hughes, "What is Teaching," p. 251–59.

[35] George G. Stern, "Measuring Noncognitive Variables in Research on Teaching," in *Handbook of Research on Teaching* (Chicago: Rand McNally & Co., 1963), p. 426.

[36] Herber, "Teaching Reading and Physics Simultaneously," pp. 84–85.

[37] Stern, "Measuring Noncognitive Variables," p. 428.

SHIFTING RESPONSIBILITY FROM THE TEACHER TO THE LEARNER　　As students become independent learners, the responsibility for learning is assumed more by them and less by the teacher. Some students are always ready to assume more responsibility for their learning. Stern reports that "Student-centered instruction was preferred by students who reject traditional sources of authority, have strong needs for demonstrating personal independence, and are characterized by high drive for academic achievement." [38] Hughes believes, however, that "dependence is always present in some degree in any teacher-pupil relationship." [39] The teacher's problem is to stimulate independent activity among students so they carry the burden of learning and he becomes a guide for that learning.

Manning's study revealed what is generally observed by anyone who notes the predominant form of classroom activity. Covering grades one through twelve he found four times more teacher directed behavior than nondirective. He also observed that the intensity and frequency of teacher directed behavior increased with grade level. He drew the implication that schools apparently do little to foster self-direction among students. [40]

How can the teacher change students from passive to active participants in the learning process for his subject? "An act of indirect influence expands freedom of action and usually makes a student less dependent on the teacher . . ." [41] even though "teachers find it difficult to stimulate self-directed problem solving among highly dependent-prone students." [42] Reading and reasoning guides allow students the freedom to explore ideas and develop skills while under the indirect influence of the teacher, provided through the guide he designed. Students become actively engaged in learning; they have a structure to provide security if they need it, yet the structure has sufficient latitude so that they can express independence in their thinking and activity, if they are so inclined. The teacher can observe students' responses and make some judgments relative to their growth and the need for clarification, redirection, enrichment, and so on. As Hughes suggests, "An indirect approach stimulates verbal participation by students and discloses to the teacher students' perceptions of the situation." [43] This suggests another major benefit to be derived from the use of the Instructional Framework, the reading and reasoning guides it assumes, and the opportunities thus provided for intraclass grouping: functional analysis of students' needs.

[38] *Ibid.*

[39] Flanders, "Teacher Influence," p. 49.

[40] Norman E. Wallen and Robert M. W. Travers, "Analysis and Investigation of Teaching Methods," in *Handbook of Research on Teaching* (Chicago: Rand McNally, American Educational Research Association, 1963).

[41] Flanders, "Teacher Influence," p. 48.

[42] *Ibid.,* p. 50.

[43] *Ibid.,* p. 63.

Functional Analysis

When carefully guided and differentiated instruction is provided in a classroom, teachers have excellent opportunity to observe daily progress of students. When instruction is adjusted for ability and achievement levels in a lesson, the teacher can continue to modify the level of required response in subsequent activities, according to how well the student performs the present task. Thus the content teacher conducts an ongoing analysis of his student's needs rather than an elaborate formal testing program.

Obviously there is more to diagnosis and evaluation than this, and the topics are treated in detail in chapter 9. However, it is important to note that when instruction is differentiated it automatically follows that there is ongoing analysis of students' progress. We cannot have differentiated instruction that is flexible and current to the needs of students without constant assessment. And such instruction automatically provides the basis for such assessment. "If children are not listened to, how can one know what concepts are developed or what interpretations are made?" [44] Interaction among students within groups makes this knowledge available to teachers.

SUMMARY

The Instructional Framework is a structure *of* lessons. Of critical importance is the structure *within* lessons, reading and reasoning guides that simulate the application of skills and development of concepts for students. Within such structure students develop proficiency until they are able to function independently.

We can serve individual differences in the content classroom and also exercise indirect influence as students enjoy interaction within the structure provided by the guide. The interaction provides the basis for ongoing, functional analysis of students' needs.

Through the Instructional Framework, with its structure *of* and structures *within* lessons, desirable experiences are simulated. As students go through the simulated experiences they develop patterns of behavior that ultimately lead them to function independently.

[44] Hughes, "What is Teaching," p. 251–59.

REACTION GUIDE

Inference

Directions: Several statements are listed below, some of which are directly stated in this chapter, others implied. Place an "I" on the line before the items which represent inferences you can draw from this chapter. Mark with a "D" items which represent direct statements from the text.

_____ 1. Teachers generally neglect to prepare students to do their assigned reading.

_____ 2. The Instructional Framework and the Directed Reading Activity are not the same.

_____ 3. The DRA is appropriate for reading lessons.

_____ 4. Students read with greater comprehension when they have a purpose for reading.

_____ 5. The preparation phases of the DRA and IF are essentially the same.

_____ 6. Content teachers are often reluctant to incorporate the Instructional Framework because it takes too much time away from the course.

_____ 7. There are strong feelings against the DRA as an instructional procedure.

_____ 8. Being guided in the use of a skill is much different than being tested to see if one has used it correctly.

_____ 9. Teachers can simulate the use of a skill so that students develop a "feeling for" it.

_____ 10. Teachers frequently engage in more testing of reading skills than teaching of same.

_____ 11. Carefully structuring students' responses to show them *how* to respond is neither "handholding" nor "spoonfeeding."

_____ 12. A few "extra" moments spent preparing students for an assignment returns dividends in their increased achievement in reading and responding to the material.

_____ 13. There are some who believe students should set their own purposes for reading, hence, the IF is detrimental to their development of independence in the use of skills.

_____ 14. When a teacher says to his students, "By the way, be sure to read the next chapter for tomorrow!" *as they leave the room, after the bell has rung,* he is not adequately preparing students to read that assignment.

_____15. The structure, through which one provides guidance in the *use* of reading and reasoning skills, is very flexible and takes many forms.

Generalization
Check those generalizations you can support as a result of relating this chapter to your teaching/learning experiences.

_____ 1. An activity can be "taken apart" and its "pieces" studied separately.

_____ 2. Any skill is operational over a great range of sophistication.

_____ 3. When a person is *prepared* to function in a certain task, he does so with greater efficiency than when he is unprepared.

_____ 4. Unless a teacher prepares a student for a reading assignment, he will begin the task unprepared.

_____ 5. Testing can also serve to teach but testing is not generally thought of as being the same as teaching.

_____ 6. Reading and reasoning skills can be "simulated" so students can consciously experience how they "feel."

_____ 7. There must be a structure *of* lessons as well as a structure *within* lessons in any subject.

_____ 8. One can, but need not, jeopardize the substance of what is read by emphasizing the skills needed to read it.

_____ 9. Testing and teaching can occur simultaneously when guided instruction is individualized.

4

PREPARATION FOR INSTRUCTION

VOCABULARY

Several terms, each representing a complex concept, are introduced. Each is defined directly and by context:

— major concepts
— technical vocabulary
— organizational pattern
— skills and processes
— levels of comprehension

IDEA DIRECTION

This chapter recommends a "self-preparation" procedure for teachers, and speculates on its effectiveness. Principles related to this preparation, and their application, are developed throughout the remainder of the book.

READING DIRECTION

You should look for relationships between the products of this recommended procedure and the process described in chapter 3.

Much has been written about the need to prepare teachers to teach reading in their subject areas. Preservice education of teachers should include this preparation with periodic inservice refresher courses required. For our purpose, however, "preparation" relates to activities in which teachers should engage before they assign a reading selection from texts. If basic texts are used both as vehicles for developing subject-related skills and as sources of information, the procedures described below certainly should be followed.

Many factors are involved in the preparation of a lesson; analyzing the material to be assigned is of particular importance. Before a content teacher gives a reading assignment in his text, he should carefully examine that selection to identify: 1) the major ideas which students should acquire as a result of their reading; 2) the technical vocabulary which holds potential difficulty for students as they read the text; 3) the skills which students will need to apply in order to *identify, understand,* and *apply* the important ideas in that particular selection.

Identification of Major Concepts

Content teachers question the necessity to identify the major ideas contained in their texts. They know what they want their students to learn; it is not necessary to examine a text to discover what should be learned. The curriculum is not dictated by a text!

"If one can first answer the question, 'What is worth knowing about?' then it is not difficult to distinguish between the aspects of it that are worth teaching and learning and those that are not." [1] This is true, but this point of view precisely expresses the problem which prompts the suggestion for analysis of the text.

There is no question that the curriculum evolves from sources other than the textbooks required in the course. Years of research and years of teacher education combine to establish priorities and curriculum goals. The text used is only *one* source of information; students learn through many other sources. Therefore, the sources support the course objective; course objectives are not determined by the sources. However, textbooks are legitimate and valuable sources of information, which students should learn to use, and which teachers find necessary to use as teaching instruments.

Subject area teachers are well acquainted with content in their areas of

[1] Jerome S. Bruner, *On Knowing* (New York: Atheneum Publishers, 1965), pp. 121–22.

specialization and know the major concepts their students should develop. They plan each new unit with those concepts in mind. They give reading assignments so that students' understanding of these concepts will be developed, reinforced, and extended. But here is where problems arise. Teachers attribute ideas, which sometimes are not actually there, to a given selection in a text. Drawing upon their thorough knowledge of the content, teachers unconsciously supply information to fill in the gaps in exposition written and read by experts in their fields. As a result, teachers assume that students will develop certain understandings from their reading when, in reality, the components of those understandings are partially or completely missing from the text.

The teacher does not sense these gaps because he subconsciously supplies the missing information. Students do not have the background or conditioning to be able to supply the missing information. Indeed, students frequently are not sufficiently sophisticated in the subject to realize when there are gaps. As a result, they may develop partial concepts, confused impressions, erroneous conclusions, which little resemble the major ideas the teacher assumes they should acquire. In other words, students are occasionally set to the task of reading the text to discover ideas that are in the teacher's mind, but are not in the text.

This understandable phenomenon is constantly at work. When subject area specialists examine their resource materials to determine the ideas they actually contain, it becomes clear how they have "read into" these sources non-existent information (in terms of actual content of the text).

The reason for the presence of these gaps in textbooks is understandable. Texts are written by scholars who have a high level of understanding in their discipline. They draw on this personal wealth of information as they write their texts. Frequently they make assumptions in the development of concepts, assuming for students a prior level of understanding which is not warranted. These concepts are so elementary to specialists, it seems hardly necessary to develop them. However, students are frequently uninitiated in the subject, or at least in the particular unit being read, and the assumptions made by the experts become knowledge gaps for the students. Indeed, on one occasion the examination of a new chemistry text revealed that concepts presented in early chapters were based on information which was not developed until later chapters. Because the authors and their editors possessed such a thorough knowledge of the subject, this reversed development, and the basic assumptions which caused it, had not been detected. Though not a problem to the specialists—authors and editors—it did prove a problem to the "uninitiated" reader.

So the teacher prepares to give the reading assignment by determining the ideas actually present in the material that is to be read. He plays the role of one who knows relatively little about the subject, placing himself in the position of the student who reads the material with an understanding only of those concepts which have been developed in the subject up to that point. As a hypothetical "student" the teacher has limited facility with the language of the subject and has neither extensive experience in the subject nor depth of understanding which comes from years of study. Endeavoring to push from his mind most of what he knows about the subject, the teacher looks at the reading selection and asks himself, "What ideas that students can perceive and use are actually here in this material?"

This is one of the most difficult tasks to ask of a content teacher. However, if he makes such an analysis, he finds it eliminates much frustration— his students' and his own. His expectations of what concepts the students should obtain from their reading are based on knowledge of material actually in the text, not on assumptions of what should be there. Obviously, students respond to what is in the reading selection rather than to what teachers assume is there. Procedures for developing, reinforcing, and extending an understanding of these concepts are discussed in chapter 7.

Identification of the Technical Vocabulary

If students are to engage in the communication of ideas related to any content area they must have facility with the language of that subject. In order to listen and read, as well as write and speak, with understanding, students must know the technical language of a content area. Students can communicate only those ideas for which they have words to convey meaning.

The responsibility of the subject area teacher to teach this technical language is quite clear. "Teachers must select texts that are written to assist learning and study them to familiarize themselves with the language barriers which pupils will meet." [2] To improve his students' communication in the subject, to help them read the source materials successfully, he must help them develop competence and facility with that language. Without this understanding, students' reading is little more than word calling. Little understanding, communication, or retention result.

Several practical questions arise in reference to the matter of selecting, teaching and reinforcing this technical vocabulary. They are identified and treated in chapter 8. In the present discussion it is sufficient to say that the teacher should be aware of the vocabulary which may be difficult for his students and then prepare them to handle it successfully.

Skills or Processes to be Applied

When the teacher has determined the major ideas to be acquired from the reading, and the technical vocabulary through which these ideas are

[2] David H. Russell and Henry R. Fea, "Research on Teaching," in *Handbook of Research on Teaching* (Chicago: Rand McNally & Co., American Educational Research Association, 1963).

communicated, he is ready to examine the text to determine the organizational pattern used by the author and the skills students must apply to acquire information and develop the ideas in the text. Many subject area teachers find this analysis for patterns and skills difficult because they are not familiar with the nomenclature of reading.

A subject-matter teacher . . . needs only ask himself . . . "What competencies must my students have to carry out the learning tasks in this course as I teach it?" . . . forget the labels and think of the tasks that the students must perform. Those are the skills that must be taught or reviewed regardless of the factors that may emerge from an elaborate study.[3]

With practice, subject area teachers can become very efficient in this analysis.

As the subject area teacher looks at the structure of the selection he asks, "Does the text follow a sequential development? Does it develop a cause-effect relationship? Does it draw comparisons?" Then he asks, "must students, within the organizational patterns, use specific skills such as inference, deduction, drawing conclusions?" Whatever the pattern or skill, whatever label one chooses to affix to a process, students must be shown how to recognize the patterns and how to use the skills to gain information from the materials they are required to read. These skills and processes are discussed in chapter 6.

After reading chapter 5, Levels of Comprehension, one can see how useful the levels are when applied to the analysis of the text. It might be useful to read pages 62–63 at this point and then return to complete this chapter.

Priorities

There is no special priority that teachers should place on one of these factors over the other two. All are equal in importance. Nor is there a special order to be followed in identifying these three factors, though it does seem logical to identify the major ideas first to delimit the vocabulary to be selected for emphasis.

There are priorities, however, *within* each of these factors, in keeping with the principle of "in-depth study" of selected concepts within a curriculum rather than a general survey of all concepts.

For example, among all of the ideas that are presented in a given section of a text, there are those select few that are judged by the teacher to be of primary importance. Priority is given to those few as the lesson is developed. Such delimiting makes reading much more manageable for the students.

---

[3] A. Sterl Artley, "Influence of Specific Factors on Growth in Interpretation," in *Reading: Seventy-Five Years of Progress* (Chicago: University of Chicago Press, 1966), p. 73.

They learn that it is possible to sift through a morass of material and focus on a few major concepts—and they learn how to do it well. The teacher does not have to require memorization of excessive detail. As he explores the significant concepts with students he develops their study techniques related to development of concepts. At the same time students move one step closer to independence in their own pursuit of the discipline.

Chapter 8 discusses priorities in selecting technical vocabulary to be emphasized in a unit of study. It is clear that a teacher cannot emphasize all of the words, with the limitation of time to say nothing of energy. After specific criteria are applied and words selected, he has a critical list of technical words representing major concepts and/or supporting information for the unit. These words can be taught in such a way that students learn skills for acquiring vocabulary while they learn the new words.

The teacher must also establish priorities in selecting levels of comprehension, organizational patterns, or specific skills to be emphasized. In nearly all sections of a text he can find all comprehension levels, a variety of patterns, and many skills. He need emphasize only those that will aid his students in understanding the most important or "priority" ideas. This procedure builds skills and content simultaneously.

SUMMARY

To perform a function well, we must prepare for it. Chapter 3 explored the preparation of students for the reading act. This chapter has explored the self-preparation teachers engage in to make certain their instruction meets the needs of students and is focused on the content as it really exists in the assigned resources.

Essential to the preparation is the identification of basic concepts to be studied, technical vocabulary conveying those concepts, and processes students need in order to discover the concepts.

Flexible teachers, who prepare in this way, have a positive influence and raise the level of their students' receptivity to learning.

REACTION GUIDE

Statements 1 through 5 represent certain teaching situations. Following each statement a series of observations is listed. Based on your understanding of the text to this point, evaluate each of the responses according to the criteria given below. Fill in the letter of the criterion you select on the line in front of each item.

S—sufficient substantiation
I—insufficient evidence
U—unrelated to the situation

1. A math textbook selection committee rejects a text because they judge the vocabulary load to be too heavy for tenth grade college-bound students.

_____ a. The teachers are unacquainted with the "new math."

_____ b. The committee has assumed students should know most of the vocabulary in the text.

_____ c. The administration has been pressed by the PTA to "upgrade the curriculum."

_____ d. Teachers assume students' texts should be written at their independent-reading level.

_____ e. The teachers really want to keep their old text.

2. From a question a student asks, a world history teacher discovers that 20% of his students do not know the word "famine" as used in their unit on India.

_____ a. The teacher did not identify this word as potentially difficult for his students.

_____ b. The teacher did not preview his text for potentially difficult words.

_____ c. This was a class of low achievers.

_____ d. Some students can study a country and not understand factors which are basic to its culture.

_____ e. The teacher used information from a question to analyze students' vocabulary needs.

3. An American history teacher is frustrated because his students do not perceive the complexities of the interaction between Americans and British prior to the Revolutionary War.

_____ a. The students do not recognize a cause-effect organizational pattern in the material they read.

_____ b. The teacher believes greater understanding comes through lectures than through reading.

_____ c. The teacher assumed that students could perceive cause-effect relationships on their own.

_____ d. The teacher did not preview the material to determine *how* the students should go about reading it.

_____ e. Students would rather listen to a lecture than read a text.

4. A physics teacher is surprised to find his students unable to see the major ideas developed by the authors of the text he assigns.

_____ a. These students are good "word callers."

_____ b. The ideas the teacher has in mind may not be developed in the text.

_____ c. The teacher assumed students could see relationships which they overlooked or avoided.

_____ d. The teacher did not preview the text to discover ideas it actually developed.

_____ e. This was a course in classical physics.

5. A biology teacher is at a loss because, "My students don't know the words I use to explain the words I want them to know!"

_____ a. This was a class of low achievers.

_____ b. Biology texts are highly saturated with technical vocabulary.

_____ c. This teacher enjoyed teaching honors students.

_____ d. The teacher assumed greater knowledge for his students than he should have.

_____ e. The teacher previewed the text, found too many words his students didn't know, and resorted to other media.

_____ f. These students weren't interested in biology.

5

LEVELS OF
COMPREHENSION

VOCABULARY

The following terms, each of which is probed in depth, are critical to an understanding of this chapter:
- literal
- interpretive
- applied
- intrinsic concepts
- extrinsic concepts

IDEA DIRECTION

This chapter explores ways to meet the reading achievement needs of individual students in content classes without jeopardizing the substantive part of the courses. Ideas presented are illustrated by materials designed for adult use. The chapter will have more meaning if you use the materials as suggested.

READING DIRECTION

Look for information presented and problems posed in previous chapters as you read this chapter. You will have to switch roles as you read various sections—sometimes you will read *about* a procedure, other times you will actually *experience* the procedure yourself.

"What are the reading skills that should be taught in each of the content areas? Are the skills different in each area or are they quite similar? Are they clearly identifiable? What do you call them? Why not teach 'comprehension' and 'understanding' and forget all of the fancy nomenclature?"

When a content teacher reflects on how he can improve his students' reading of the texts in his subject, he generally will raise these questions. They are good questions, which need to be answered, because within the answers lies much of the solution to teaching reading in content areas.

The first thing a content teacher should do is to postpone his worry about specific skills. It is much more useful if he concerns himself at first only with "levels of comprehension." Concern with specific skills can come later after he has mastered the concept of "levels of comprehension" and has used it successfully in his classroom.

LEVELS OF COMPREHENSION

What are levels of comprehension? There is general agreement with Smith that comprehension is a generic term which embraces many specific labels for "thought getting processes." [1] Moreover, there seems to be general agreement that comprehension can take place at different levels of cognition.[2] It is useful to think of these levels as 1) literal; 2) interpretive; 3) applied. Each level requires the product of the previous level or levels in order to function. Obviously, the literal level can stand alone.

Brief Overview

The literal level of comprehension applied to a content textbook produces knowledge of what the author said. Students who function at this level decode words, determine what each means in the given content, and recognize that there is some relationship among the words. That relationship repre-

[1] Nila Banton Smith, *Reading Instruction for Today's Children* (Englewood Cliffs: Prentice-Hall, Inc., 1963), p. 264.

[2] David H. Russell, *Children's Thinking* (Waltham, Mass.: Ginn and Co., 1956); Helen M. Robinson, "The Major Aspects of Reading," in *Reading: Seventy-Five Years of Progress* (Chicago: University of Chicago Press, 1966); Guy L. Bond and Eva Bond Wagner, *Teaching the Child to Read* (New York: The Macmillan Company, 1966); Jerome S. Bruner, *The Process of Education* (New York: Random House, Inc., 1960); Emerald V. Dechant, *Improving the Teaching of Reading* (Englewood Cliffs: Prentice-Hall, Inc., 1964).

sents what the author has said. It is quite possible for students to identify what an author has said, and even memorize and repeat it in class, without understanding what the author meant by his statements.

The interpretive level of comprehension is applied to what the author said in order to derive meaning from his statement. The reader looks for relationships among statements within the material he has read. From these intrinsic relationships he derives various meanings. The intrinsic relationships he perceives are colored and influenced by his previous knowledge of and experience with the topic in question. However, the reader is confined by the text and determines meaning primarily as he perceives intratext relationships.

The applied level of comprehension takes the product of the literal, what the author has said, and the interpretive, what the author meant by what he said, and applies it in some pragmatic or theoretical exercise. Possibly he might apply this product to other knowledge he already possesses, thereby deepening his understanding. At the applied level the reader selects intrinsic relationships produced at the interpretive level of comprehension and places them in juxtaposition to concepts which are the product of previous knowledge and experience. Out of this juxtaposition the reader perceives a new relationship—an extrinsic relationship—which has a scope larger than the meanings imposed by the context of the reading selection, producing new ideas which extend beyond those immediately identifiable in the reading selection.

Consider the following illustration of levels of comprehension. First read the brief selection on seagulls. Then examine the statements which follow the selection and label each with the level of comprehension you believe it represents—literal, interpretive, applied.

For years millions of hungry seagulls have flown inland and seriously damaged Swedish crops and gardens. Experts at first tried to reduce the number of gulls by destroying their eggs but found that the gulls merely laid more eggs.

Now, armed with saucepans and cooking stoves, the experts boil the eggs and carefully replace them in the nests. The gulls, not knowing the eggs will never hatch, sit on them hopefully until it is too late to try again.

_____1. Man's ingenuity insures his survival.
_____2. Seagulls are seriously damaging Swedish crops and gardens so attempts are being made to reduce the number of gulls.
_____3. Seagulls don't recognize hard-boiled eggs even when they are sitting on them.
_____4. The Swedes have found a way to control the seagull plague.
_____5. A good way to keep seagulls from multiplying is to make it impossible for their eggs to hatch.
_____6. If at first you don't succeed, try, try again.

Before reading on, you would find it profitable to compare your responses to those of your colleagues. The purpose of the comparison is to find differences and, if there are any, to resolve them through discussion. Then compare the results of your discussion with the following opinion.

Statements 2 and 5 represent a literal level of comprehension. Essentially the author of the selection has made those two statements. Both merely reflect what the author has said, not what he meant by what he said. Neither has been produced by turning information back in on itself to form an interpretive relationship.

Statements 3 and 4 represent a response at the interpretive level of comprehension. Beyond being a feeble attempt at humor, statement 3 represents a conclusion one can draw by relating two sets of information presented in the two sentences in the second paragraph: a) that the gulls' eggs are hardboiled; b) that the gulls hope for a hatching that will never happen. Statement 4 is an inferential summary drawn from a relationship among the stated problem, the first attempted solution, and the second attempt.

Statements 1 and 6 represent a response at the applied level of comprehension. The reader, for example, might draw the inferential summary identified above and represented in statement 4, and place that in juxtaposition to ideas and experiences he has had in reference to efforts man has made to overcome adversities of nature. Statement 1 could well be the end product of that thought process. The double entendre of statement 6 could relate to statement 3 extended in its effort toward humor or it could relate to statement 4, the inferential summary, expressing in another manner the idea of man's persistence in modifying his environment so that it is favorable to his needs and desires.

Admittedly, the paragraph is rather "thin" for such exegesis; however, the analysis does illustrate what occurs when one reads material at various levels of comprehension. The content teacher can make use of the fact that students can and do respond to the content of reading selections at these various levels of comprehension. The two major objectives in the use of levels of comprehension are discussed later in this chapter. The question to consider now is how to help students become aware of these levels so that they can use them effectively.

"Structure within lessons" was discussed in chapter 3. The teacher needs to guide students if they are to become aware of the levels of comprehension. It is useful to devise a structure to guide students' responses at each of the levels of comprehension. The guide can have three separate sections, each containing statements representative of one of the levels of comprehension; or the guide can be a single section with each of the three levels represented by appropriate statements in that section. In the latter case, statements for each level could be signalled by asterisks of the corresponding number: * = level one; ** = level two; *** = level three. (Examine the guide on page 91.)

Part of the structure should include a coding of the reading selection so students can more easily identify information and relationships basic to the various levels of comprehension. This is done simply by numbering sentences and/or paragraphs so they are easily identified when relationships among them are noted. An appropriate sequence should be planned so that students move progressively along the continuum of independence, in the exercise of levels of comprehension, until they reach the point where they can be independent of external structures as they apply the level or levels of comprehension their abilities allow.

Before designing guides for students it is useful for the content teacher to: 1) experience what it is like to be guided in reading at the three levels of comprehension and guided in justifying statements representative of the three levels; 2) experience the coding of a selection to justify statements representative of the three levels of comprehension; 3) experience the coding of a selection and the construction of statements which incorporate the coding and represent the three levels. Having had this sequentially developed experience in the use of the three levels of comprehension, the teacher is better prepared to design a sequence for the students in his content class and construct guides to make it work.

The method and design presented here is the same as a content teacher can apply to his own texts. The difference is in degree of sophistication, depending on the ability of the students and the difficulty load of the material. The difference is not in kind; the structure is essentially the same whether used with third graders or advanced graduate students.

Within each step of the sequence described above, there will be repeated analyses of the levels of comprehension, from the point of view of the independence possible at that particular phase of the sequence.

Complete Guidance

The following selection on study skills is taken from a professional text on reading instruction.[3] Immediately below is a guide for reading this selection at the *literal level* of comprehension. First read the statements. Then as you read the selection, refer back to the statements in the guide and check those that you believe say what the author *said* in the selection (not what you believe he *meant* by what he said). Number the sentences so you can refer to them more easily when showing relationships in subsequent exercises as well as when identifying information at the literal level of comprehension.

[3] Ned D. Marksheffel, *Better Reading in the Secondary School* (New York: The Ronald Press Company, 1966).

LITERAL

_____ 1. Study skills cannot be defined.

_____ 2. Students' grades improve when students are taught how to study.

_____ 3. Students of above average ability do not need practice in study skills.

_____ 4. Research in study skills is inconclusive.

_____ 5. Study skills must be taught.

_____ 6. A study skills program should be flexible. ✓

_____ 7. Study skills and learning skills are the same.

_____ 8. Self-examination and confession raise efficiency in use of study skills.

_____ 9. Good and poor students differ in the way they study.

_____10. Students aren't honest with teachers.

_____11. Many students do not study as well as they know how.

_____12. Students develop efficiency only through guided practice.

_____13. A good study skills program balances motivation with guided application of skills.

READING SELECTION

What Does Research Tell Us About Study Skills?

The specific techniques that should be taught in study skills courses are not clearly defined at this time. Methods or techniques stressed are numerous and mainly based upon "expert opinion" . . . and psychological principles of learning. Despite the lack of unanimity of skills taught, a large number of research reports . . . indicate that teaching students how to study is beneficial and is reflected in better student adjustment and improved grades. One intensive investigation of study skills courses at the college level . . . revealed that when student participation was voluntary, quite impressive gains were made. In all reports of courses that included follow-up studies of students' achievement, it was noted that the gains they made during the courses were maintained. Glock and Mallman . . . , however, after studying a group of high school students with above-average grades reported that required study skills courses for these kinds of students were not advisable.

Research, as spotty, contradictory, and inconclusive as it is in this area, indicates that the teaching of study skills is helpful for improving the learning of a large number of students. This is particularly true when students volunteer to take the courses, when they are motivated to improve their skills, and when they are not above average in achievement.

Reprinted by permission of the publisher from Ned D. Marksheffel, *Better Reading in the Secondary School—Principles and Procedures for Teachers.* (New York: The Ronald Press, 1966), pp. 216–18. Copyright © 1966.

Are Study Skills Learned Without Guidance?

Study skills must be taught. Few students learn how to study efficiently without directed practice and guidance by a teacher. And there are basic study skills that students must learn and use for successful classroom learning.

Any program of study skills should be flexible and based upon student needs. A rigid, systematized program in which all students do a prescribed number of specific exercises without due consideration of individual differences in achievement cannot help but be a failure. To consider study skills primarily as a set of mechanical procedures is to limit one's view of study, and to oversimplify; study skills, when properly taught, include a systematic, sequential approach to learning.

A functional study skills program should provide teachers with sufficient time to test, diagnose, evaluate, and give students guidance both individually and in small groups. There should be provision for discussions about motivation, self-motivation, anxiety, and students' goals. There is little doubt that many students may become self-motivated and develop an interest in learning when they are given an opportunity to talk with a teacher about their objectives, interests, weaknesses, and strengths.

On the other hand, a highly motivated and interested student may achieve little learning in school unless he has developed the required learning skills. Such a student, however, may be taught how to learn and to develop the skills in which he is weak. Thus it appears logical to assume that a study skills program must be organized in such a way that individual and group needs may be met, whether they be in the area of attitudes or skills, or both.

A reasonable approach to determining the kinds of skills that should be taught might appear to be that of determining how good and poor students differ in the ways they approach school learning tasks. Although there has been some research in this particular area, Strang . . . notes that such research is inconclusive because there have been no accurate means devised to determine how good and poor students differ. Answers obtained from giving questionnaires and checklists to students have proved to be interesting but for many reasons the results are questionable. It is well known, for example, that most students tend to answer surveys and checklists in the way they think the researcher wants them to answer unless they are positive that they are in a completely free and anonymous situation. In one study . . . , the researchers asked students who were studying what skills they were using and found that those questioned were using many different and often unique approaches.

Many students have been taught a number of basic study skills before they enter high school or college, but for various reasons fail to use them properly. For some, the major reason for not using study techniques appears to be a lack of sufficient practice in using previously learned skills. The efficient use of study skills requires guided practice until such use becomes habitual. Others lack understanding of when to apply the skills they apparently know. It is, for example, easier to underline a sentence that appears to be important than it is to recognize how the sentence fits into the total organizational pattern of the content that is being studied. Such indiscriminate practices may prove to be more confusing than helpful. Most study skills courses are based upon the premise that students will benefit more from an orderly plan of learning than they will from a hit-or-miss approach. Some courses place heavy emphasis on improving students' attitudes, motivations, and interests while others emphasize a particular technique or plan. Experience indicates that overemphasis on either the psychological aspects of learning or the skills is not the most fruitful approach. A successful study skills program is one in which a competent teacher has time to meet with students, provide extrinsic motivation when it is needed, supply students with numerous interesting materials at their own reading levels, and teach them the skills they need for learning.

Now that you have completed the level one guide, compare your answers with your colleagues'. Where there are differences, try to resolve them by reference to the selection. When you have finished your discussion, go on to the next level.

INTERPRETIVE LEVEL   You have read the selection and are familiar with its content. Immediately below is a guide for responding to the selection at the interpretive level. Check each statement you believe represents what the author meant by what he said. Refer back to the text to find bits of information which, when considered together, would form a relationship represented by the statement. Use your coding to note the relationship on the line before each statement you accept.

_____ 1. Those who determine the content of study skills programs justify their selections by logic, experience, and common sense more than by empirical research.

_____ 2. Motivation toward study of above average students is the same whether the students are in high school or college.

_____ 3. Study skills courses should be required for below average students but not for above average.

_____ 4. Researchers in the area of study skills insist upon taking action according to their findings even though their findings are inconclusive or unsupportable.

_____ 5. There is an insistence that study skills be taught even though there is uncertainty as to what the skills should be.

_____ 6. The secret for proper study is to have a system tailored to one's personal needs rather than to possess knowledge of a set of specific skills.

_____ 7. Self-motivation is not self-generated.

_____ 8. Self-motivation and proficiency in skills contribute about equally to a student's success in study.

_____ 9. Assessment of students' true proficiency in study depends on the threat projected by the teacher image.

_____10. There is a difference between intellectualizing about skills and applying them.

Now that you have completed the level two guide, compare your answers with your colleagues'. Where there are differences, try to resolve them by reference to the selection. When you have finished your discussion, go on to the next level.

APPLIED LEVEL   By now you are quite familiar with the content of the selection. Immediately below is a guide for responding to the selection at the applied level. Check each statement you believe can be supported by the text when the author's meanings are related to ideas from other sources, ideas not necessarily expressed in the selection itself. Look for the intrinsic relationships you developed at the interpretive level and place them in juxtaposition to other ideas and experiences you have had in reference to this topic.

_____ 1. Instruction in use of study skills provided for bright, average, and slow students should differ in degree, not in kind.
_____ 2. Good students are born, not made.
_____ 3. One cannot teach flexibility in a rigid instructional system.
_____ 4. What one does does not necessarily reflect what one knows.
_____ 5. Simulation is appropriate in the development of study skills even as it is in astronautics.

Now that you have completed the level three guide, compare your answers with your colleagues'. Where there are differences, try to resolve them by reference to the selection and identification of ideas and experiences outside the selection on which you drew when making your choices.

Discussion of Responses

Having completed and discussed your responses to the guides for each level of comprehension, examine the following suggested responses. Compare your coding of the article and the decisions you and your colleagues resolved with those that follow. This is not to say that the coding and responses are *the* correct answers, since personal opinion and experience influence some of the responses. However, these materials provide another basis of comparison and, therefore, are helpful.

Relate your experience with these materials to what you can provide your students as they read the material you require of them in your subject. Supplying guide material for each level; allowing intragroup analysis, discussion, and resolution; giving them your coding and response as a basis for comparison and discussion—all combine to promote reading competence and understanding of content.

Here, then, is the same article, coded for ease of reference. You will note that only significant statements are numbered. This is optional but the usual procedure after you have developed skill in sorting out significant information for emphasis in a reading guide.

READING SELECTION

What Does Research Tell Us About Study Skills?

1 { The specific techniques that should be taught in study skills courses are not clearly defined at this time. Methods or techniques stressed are numerous and mainly based upon "expert opinion" (3, p. 243) and psychological principles }2 of learning. Despite the lack of unanimity of skills taught, a large number of research reports (3, p. 243; 13, p. 335; 14, pp. 675–68) indicate that teaching }3 students how to study is beneficial and is reflected in better student adjustment and improved grades. One intensive investigation of study skills courses at the college level (3, p. 250) revealed that when student participation was voluntary, }4 quite impressive gains were made. In all reports of courses that included fol- low-up studies of students' achievement, it was noted that the gains they made during the courses were maintained. Glock and Mallman (4, p. 289), however, after studying a group of high school students with above-average grades re- }5 ported that required study skills courses for these kinds of students were not advisable.

Research, as spotty, contradictory, and inconclusive as it is in this area. indi- }6 cates that the teaching of study skills is helpful for improving the learning of a large number of students. This is particularly true when students volunteer to take the courses, when they are motivated to improve their skills, and when the are not above average in achievement.

Are Study Skills Learned Without Guidance?

7 { Study skills must be taught. Few students learn how to study efficiently without directed practice and guidance by a teacher. And there are basic study skills that 8 { students must learn and use for successful classroom learning.

Any program of study skills should be flexible and based upon student needs. A rigid, systematized program in which all students do a prescribed number of specific exercises without due consideration of individual differences in achieve- }9 ment cannot help but be a failure. To consider study skills primarily as a set of mechanical procedures is to limit one's view of study, and to oversimplify; study skills, when properly taught, include a systematic, sequential approach to learning.

A functional study skills program should provide teachers with sufficient time to test, diagnose, evaluate, and give students guidance both individually and in small groups. There should be provision for discussions about motivation, self-motivation, anxiety, and students' goals. There is little doubt that many students may become self-motivated and develop an interest in learning when they are given an opportunity to talk with a teacher about their objectives, interests, weaknesses, and strengths.

On the other hand, a highly motivated and interested student may achieve little learning in school unless he has developed the required learning skills. Such a student, however, may be taught how to learn and to develop the skills in which he is weak. Thus it appears logical to assume that a study skills program must be organized in such a way that individual and group needs may be met, whether they be in the area of attitudes or skills, or both.

A reasonable approach to determining the kinds of skills that should be taught might appear to be that of determining how good and poor students differ in the ways they approach school learning tasks. Although there has been some research in this particular area, Strang (14, p. 676) notes that such research is inconclusive because there have been no accurate means devised to determine how good and poor students differ. Answers obtained from giving questionnaires and checklists to students have proved to be interesting but for many reasons the results are questionable. It is well known, for example, that most students tend to answer surveys and checklists in the way they think the researcher wants them to answer unless they are positive that they are in a completely free and anonymous situation. In one study (1, pp. 92–128), the researchers asked students who were studying what skills they were using and found that those questioned were using many different and often unique approaches.

Many students have been taught a number of basic study skills before they enter high school or college but for various reasons fail to use them properly. For some, the major reason for not using study techniques appears to be a lack of sufficient practice in using previously learned skills. The efficient use of study skills requires guided practice until such use becomes habitual. Others lack understanding of when to apply the skills they apparently know. It is, for example, easier to underline a sentence that appears to be important than it is to recognize how the sentence fits into the total organizational pattern of the content that is being studied. Such indiscriminate practices may prove to be more confusing than helpful. Most study skills courses are based upon the premise that students will benefit more from an orderly plan of learning than they will from a hit-or-miss approach. Some courses place heavy emphasis on improving students' attitudes, motivations, and interests while others emphasize a particular technique or plan. Experience indicates that overemphasis on either the psychological aspects of learning or the skills is not the most fruitful approach. A successful study skills program is one in which a competent teacher

20 { has time to meet with students, provide extrinsic motivation when it is needed, supply students with numerous interesting materials at their own reading levels, and teach them the skills they need for learning.

LITERAL LEVEL   Suggested responses to the guide for the literal level are identified below.

_____ 1. Study skills cannot be defined.
_____ 2. Students' grades improve when students are taught how to study.
_____ 3. Students of above average ability do not need practice in study skills.
_6_ 4. Research on study skills is inconclusive.
_7_ 5. Study skills must be taught.
_9_ 6. A study skills program should be flexible.
_____ 7. Study skills and learning skills are the same.
_____ 8. Self-examination and confession raise efficiency in use of study skills.
_13_ 9. Good and poor students differ in the way they study.
_____ 10. Students aren't honest with teachers.
_16,17_ 11. Many students do not study as well as they know how.
_17_ 12. Students develop efficiency through guided practice.
_20_ 13. A good study skills program balances motivation with guided application of skills.

Note that statements 1, 2, 3, 7, 8, and 10 are not checked. The remaining ones have been accepted as representing what the author said in the article. Code numbers from the article are placed before each accepted statement, indicating the part of the article that states the same thing as the statement.

Statement 1 is rejected because it is an inference, not an actual statement. The author says that study skills *are not clearly defined* rather than they "cannot" be.

The author says nothing about improvement of grades, only improvement of skills. We can assume grade improvement, but this assumption or inference cannot be attributed to a direct statement by the author. Therefore, statement 2 is rejected.

Statement 3 is rejected because code number 4 says they do need practice—and on a volunteer basis. Statement 7 is rejected. Code number 11 refers to learning skills in a manner which might imply the two are synonymous, but there is no actual statement that equates the two. Statement 8 is rejected because it is only implied in code number 10, not directly stated. Statement 10 is rejected because, though code number 15 definitely implies it, no direct comment is made about students' honesty with teachers.

The balance of the statements are accepted and the code numbers are given. Each statement says what the author says in his article. There are no inferences drawn, no assumptions, no extrapolations.

INTERPRETIVE   Suggested responses to the guide for the interpretive level are identified below.

1,2,3,6 1. Those who determine the content of study skills programs justify their selections by logic, experience, and common sense more than by empirical research.

4,5 2. Motivation toward study of above average students is the same whether the students are in high school or college.

_____ 3. Study skills courses should be required for below average students but not for above average.

1,2,3,6,8 4. Researchers in the area of study skills insist upon taking action according to their findings even though their findings are inconclusive or unsupportable.

1,6,8 5. There is an insistence that study skills be taught even though there is uncertainty as to what the skills should be.

3,9 6. The secret for proper study is to have a system tailored to one's personal needs rather than to possess knowledge of a set of specific skills.

10,11,16 7. Self-motivation is not self-generated.

10,11,12,16,19 8. Self-motivation and proficiency in skills contribute about equally to a student's success in study.

14,15 9. Assessment of students' true proficiency in study depends on the threat projected by the teacher image.

16,17 10. There is a difference between intellectualizing about skills and applying them.

Statement 1 is accepted because it summarizes the relationship between code numbers 1, 2, 3, and 6. Key words within these segments paint the picture: "specific techniques . . . not clearly defined"; "expert opinion"; "lack of unanimity of skills taught"; "research . . . spotty, contradictory, and inconclusive."

Statement 2 is acceptable *if* one assumes that college students are "above average." Code numbers 4 and 5 combine to imply what statement 2 infers. But since the article does not state that college students are above average, we have to assume it if we accept the inference of item 2.

Statement 3 is rejected even though we can draw this conclusion if the inference in item 3 is carried out to its logical end. That is, though there is a clear statement that above average students should not be required to take courses because they do better in volunteer courses (and a clear inference that above average students in high school and college are equally motivated), it is only by gross assumptions that one can infer that below average students should be required to take study skills courses. The "reach" required is more than the content really supports.

Statement 4 is accepted. Adding code number 8 to the support of statement 1, discussed above, makes the difference necessary to support statement 4. The key words ". . . students must learn and use . . ." support the conclusion drawn by item 4.

Statement 5 is accepted because it says essentially the same thing as statement 4 and is supported by the same code numbers.

Statement 6 is proper interpretation of the combination of code numbers 1 and 9. The key words tell the story: "teaching students how to study is beneficial"; "program . . . should be . . . based upon students' needs"; "consideration of individual differences."

Statement 7 is accepted. Code number 10 implies that students' self-motivation is generated by talking with teachers about themselves. Code number 11 obliquely adds to the inference in its statement that students must have more than motivation—they also need skill. Code 16 embellishes the inference by stating that students often do not use what they know.

Statement 8 is accepted, supported by code 10, 11, and 16 as explained above. Added to those numbers are code 12 and 19. Twelve points out that students' needs might be in the area of attitudes and/or skills. Nineteen calls for a balance between skills and motivation. The relationship among all the code numbers is the inference expressed in statement 8.

Statement 9 expresses a conclusion one can draw from the combination of code numbers 14 and 15: that inaccuracies in student assessment are due to the practice of students responding as they think the assessor wants to hear it. The logical inference is given in statement 9: that a student's security with a teacher determines the objectivity of his response.

Statement 10 clearly interprets what code numbers 16 and 17 say. Note the key words: "students have been taught . . . skills . . . but . . . fail to use them"; "lack of understanding of when to apply skills they . . . know."

APPLIED   Suggested responses to the guide for the applied level are identified below.

4, 5, 7, 8, 9, 13, 18, 20 + Bruner ___ 1. Instruction in use of study skills provided for bright, average and slow students should differ in degree, not in kind.

_____ 2. Good students are born, not made.

9, 14, 15, 18, 20
+ Flanders _____ 3. One cannot teach flexibility in a rigid instructional system.

14, 15, 16, 17 +
Romans 7:15 + 19 ___ 4. What one does, does not necessarily reflect what
one knows.

7, 9, 18, 20 +
Cybernetics _____ 5. Simulation is appropriate in the development of
study skills even as it is in astronautics.

Statements 1, 3, and 4 are accepted. Statement 2 is rejected.

Statement 1 combines the code numbers as indicated. When the resulting relationship is considered in light of Bruner's ideas of the structure of
curriculum and instruction, the full meaning of item 1 is realized.

Statement 2 is rejected, because the relationships among code numbers
4, 7, 16, and 17, supported by everyday classroom experience, suggest
the opposite.

Statement 3 is accepted in spite of the negative connotation of the word
"rigid." Code numbers 9, 14, 15, 18, and 20 form a relationship which
is supported by Flander's findings concerning flexibility in instruction. The
word "cannot" balances the word "rigid," making the statement acceptable.

Statement 4 is accepted. When the combination of code numbers 14, 15,
16, 17 is applied to St. Paul's letter to the Romans in the *New Testament,*
[*Romans* 7:15 ff.—"For that which I do I allow (understand) not; for
what I would, that do I not; but what I hate, that do I."], a relationship
results which is well expressed by statement 4.

Statement 5 is also accepted. The emphasis on guidance in the development of skills is clear when one combines code numbers 7, 9, 18, and 20.
When this relationship is applied to texts such as *Cybernetics,* statements
such as number 5 logically follow.

Partial Guidance

The following selection is an editorial by James Reston that appeared
in *The New York Times,* July 7, 1967. The editorial and guides related
to it are used to illustrate the next step in the sequence of building understanding and independence in the application of levels of comprehension.
This phase is labeled partial guidance because though the guides are given,
the responses are not coded and analyzed within the text. The previous
phase, you will recall, provided both the guides and coded analysis of
possible responses. This phase requests you to code your own statements,

drawing on the experience you had in responding to the coding provided for you in the first phase.

Here is the procedure you should follow if you intend to continue through this sequence. First read the statements for the literal level and then read the editorial. Check the statements in the guide that you believe say what the author said. Use the sentence numbers to identify parts of the editorial that support each of the statements you select.

Literal Level

1. *Opening Section*

_____ a. Secretary Rusk knows how President Johnson feels.

_____ b. Diplomatic reports do not reveal improvement of relations with the Soviet Union.

_____ c. The Moscow Government is replacing equipment the Arabs lost in the Israeli War.

_____ d. Mr. Rusk revealed that reports show a discouraging trend in diplomacy.

2. *The Moscow Split*

_____ a. President Podgorny argued the case for Soviet personnel being available to insure best use of Soviet equipment.

_____ b. The Soviet Government wishes to substitute western influence in the Arab world with its own.

_____ c. American officials were hopeful that relations between USSR and U.S. would improve after Glassboro, but the improvement appears to be one-sided.

_____ d. Soviet Government officials are divided on what Middle East policy the Soviet Government should follow.

_____ e. The Soviet Government believes it can out-maneuver the U.S. Government in the distribution of arms to Middle Eastern nations.

3. *Expensive Expansion*

_____ a. USSR spent great sums of money in Indonesia.

_____ b. USSR encouraged the Arab's confinement of and pressure on Israel.

_____ c. U.S. believed USSR wanted Israel to be weaker than the Arab nations, but would work toward the solution of the problems posed by refugees and unsettled boundaries.

_____ d. The Soviet Government is masking its true desire for cooperation with U.S. by verbal blasts at U.S. foreign policy.

4. *The Priorities*

_____ a. Both U.S. and USSR have choices they can and must make.

_____ b. Moscow policy on the Mideast remains the same as it was before Glassboro or the Middle East crisis.

_____ c. Moscow appears to be using the Arab's weakness to make its influence in the Middle East the dominating one.

_____ d. Moscow precipitated the Middle East crisis, knowing the Arabs would lose, counting on subsequent Arab dependence as the opportunity to get rid of Western influence in these countries.

READING SELECTION

Washington: The Diplomatic Reports from Moscow

By James Reston

WASHINGTON, July 6—In his foreign policy review in Chicago this week Secretary of State Rusk said President Johnson was "deeply intent on trying to improve our relations with the Soviet Union," but the diplomatic reports out of Moscow and elsewhere are extremely discouraging on this question.

One reliable report, for example, insists that the Moscow Government has already committed itself to replace half the aircraft and a quarter of the armor lost by the Arab states in the Israeli war, and that already over 100 Soviet planes have been delivered to the United Arab Republic alone.

The Moscow Split

Another indicates that President Podgorny of the U.S.S.R., during his trips to Cairo and Damascus, argued that closer military liaison with the Soviet Union was essential to make effective use of the new Soviet equipment. A third says Soviet military missions have already arrived in Syria and Egypt and that negotiations for Soviet military bases at Alexandria and elsewhere in the Arab world are now taking place.

All this apparently was decided upon in Moscow even before Premier Aleksei Kosygin got back to Moscow with his personal report on the conversations with President Johnson. Thus the Glassboro talks between the two leaders may have raised hopes here of better relations between the two countries and boosted Mr. Johnson's standing in the popularity polls in this country, but there is no evidence of a *détente* on the other side.

There have been quite a few reports since the start of the Middle East crisis of divisions within the Soviet Council of Ministers on Soviet Middle East policy. On the question of avoiding the risk of a direct confrontation with the United States in the war there, and on the question of agreeing to talks between Mr. Kosygin and Mr. Johnson, the "moderates" apparently prevailed.

But there is a great difference between avoiding a big war and reaching a *détente*. Even the so-called "moderates" in the Soviet Council of Ministers seem to favor one more expensive round of the Middle Eastern arms race.

The hope in the Johnson Administration was quite different. Officials here, looking at the Soviet reverses in Cuba, the Congo, Indonesia, Greece and the Middle East over the past five years, had begun to wonder whether this expensive process of competitive influence-peddling could not be reduced or eliminated and replaced by parallel if not cooperative policies of economic aid in these contested areas.

Expensive Expansion

Indonesia alone cost the Soviet Government over $1 billion and ended in a ghastly massacre of the Communists and their supporters. In the Middle East, the Soviet Union encouraged if it did not direct the Arab encirclement of Israel and supplied between $3 billion and $4 billion of arms to carry it out.

The Johnson Administration never believed that Moscow would leave the balance of power in Israel's favor after the war, but it did hope for cooperation in getting at the causes of war in the Middle East and helping in the settlement of boundaries and refugees.

This is the kind of *détente* Secretary Rusk and President Johnson were hoping for, but the trend of events is not going that way. Leonid Brezhnev, the General Secretary of the Soviet Communist party, while arguing that the "moderates" were right in limiting the Middle Eastern war, added this week that "the arrogance and perfidy of imperialist reaction necessitate an even greater concern" for the strengthening of the Soviet armed forces. And, if anything, the attacks on U.S. Vietnamese and Middle Eastern policy are becoming more vicious, while the Johnson-Kosygin talks are virtually ignored in the Soviet press.

The Priorities

Thus the battle over priorities in Moscow remains about the same. The officials at the two extremes—those who wanted to take greater risks of war and those who wanted to give first priority to the internal development and modernization of the Soviet state—have lost, and the cold war continues on all fronts.

In fact, Moscow seems to be regarding the weakness of the Arab states as an opportunity to wipe out all Western influence from the part of the world and establish itself as the dominant force over the oil and communications lines of the area. This would not be *détente* but defeat for the West, which may be what Moscow had in mind all along.

After you have selected and coded the statements you believe represent what the author said, compare your responses with those of your colleagues. Try to resolve differences. Obviously, only Reston himself could give the absolute answers. However, exchange of your responses and discussion of differences will undoubtedly bring you close to the author's intention. Be careful not to accept implications as literal statements.

When you have completed your comparisons and resolved your major differences, go on to the next level.

You have already read the selection and are familiar with its content. Immediately below is a guide for responding to the editorial at the interpretive level. Check each statement you believe represents what Reston meant by what he said. Refer back to the text to identify the information which, when combined, forms the relationships represented by the statements. Use the sentence numbers to code the combinations for each statement.

1. *Opening Statement*

_____ a. The Soviet replacement of arms lost by the Arab nations during the Israeli War signals deteriorating Soviet-American relations.

_____ b. Israel started the Middle East War.

_____ c. The Soviets place greater faith in air power than in "land armor."

2. *The Moscow Split*

_____ a. Arab soldiers need to learn how to use Russian-made equipment.

_____ b. Moscow is viewing the Arab nations' present vulnerability as an opportunity for its own military expansion and entrenchment.

_____ c. Some in the Soviet Government favor military confrontation with U.S.

_____ d. Washington misinterpreted the effect that Russian setbacks in various countries in the world would have on its military assistance program.

_____ e. Premier Kosygin's discussions with President Johnson were an empty gesture, unrelated to decisions already reached by the Soviet Government.

3. *Expensive Expansion*

_____ a. The Soviet Government has experienced grievous setbacks in its efforts to expand politically and militarily.

_____ b. The solution to causes of war in the Middle East and its effect on the victims is of greater importance than the war itself, according to Washington's view.

_____ c. Soviet people know little about the Johnson-Kosygin talks but much about U.S. support of Israel.

_____ d. Israeli-Soviet relations have deteriorated badly in recent months.

4. *The Priorities*

_____ a. Russian political and military objectives remain approximately the same in the Middle East as they were before the Israeli War.

_____ b. There are those in the Soviet Government who believe the time has come to consolidate gains and build up present holdings rather than continually to expand USSR political and military influence.

_____ c. Moscow precipitated the Middle East crisis, knowing the Arabs would lose, counting on subsequent Arab dependence as the opportunity to get rid of Western influence in these countries.

After you have selected and coded the statements you believe represent Reston's intended meaning, compare your responses with those of your colleagues. Again, where you have differences, try to resolve them. Interpretation depends on the information one selects to combine into sets from which meaning is derived. Your experience and knowledge of the subject will necessarily influence what you determine to be possible sets. Only the author can say for certain what he means and, of course, his own experience and knowledge of the subject can lead him to combine different pieces of information than a reader might, given a different background of experience and understanding.

Applied Level

The guide for responding to the editorial at the applied level is given immediately below. Check those statements which represent ideas not necessarily stated in the editorial but which could be supported by the extrinsic relationship formed from the combination of Reston's meanings, determined through the interpretive procedure, with ideas from other sources (ideas which lie outside the editorial itself).

Go through the list of statements and identify those which you believe express ideas you can support. By code, identify the intrinsic relationships to support a specific statement. After you complete the guide, discuss it with your colleagues. Be certain to focus on the application of the meanings in the editorial to ideas from other sources.

_____ 1. Moscow acts; Washington hopes.

_____ 2. Russia is willing to experience financial loss and its satellites' military losses in order to achieve political gain.

_____ 3. It is better not to negotiate at all than to negotiate and fail to resolve problems.

_____ 4. The Middle-East crises changed Russian opportunities, not objectives.

_____ 5. Washington reacts to negative or positive Soviet actions, and develops hopes. Moscow precipitates action, feeds hopes, and pursues objectives.

_____ 6. The summit meeting at Glassboro was futile because, though both principals were committed to a specific position, only Mr. Johnson was free to alter his course of action.

Independence

The next step in the sequence to develop a feeling for reading at different levels of comprehension (and also to explore a procedure for guiding students through the same process), is to formulate statements that would represent responses to a selection at each of the three levels. These statements, when organized into guides, could assist another person in his response to the selection.

It will be useful for you to review the purposes for the three levels and the evolution of the statements representative of each of the levels. Also, it will be useful to read the discussion on pages 117–118 of criteria one can use in the creation of statements for guides for the literal and interpretive levels. Read and code the selection by John Gardner, former Secretary of Health, Education, and Welfare. Write and code statements which represent what Gardner is saying in the article. Next, write and code statements that represent what Gardner means by what he is saying. Finally, write and code statements that represent an application of Gardner's ideas beyond the selection itself. Group each set of questions under the appropriate heading: literal; interpretive; applied. Add distractors to each section to make the exercise more discriminating. After you have completed your guides and have compared them with your colleagues', you may wish to make a comparison with the set that follows the selection.

READING SELECTION

Self-Renewal

Do-It-Yourself Jailbirds

"Keep on growing," the commencement speakers say. "Don't go to seed. Let this be a beginning, not an ending."

It is a good theme. Yet a high proportion of the young people who hear the speeches pay no heed, and by the time they are middle-aged they are absolutely mummified. Even some of the people who make the speeches are mummified. Why?

Unfortunately the commencement speakers never tell us why their advice to keep on learning is so hard to follow. The people interested in adult education

Reprinted by permission of the publisher from John W. Gardner, *Self-Renewal: The Individual and the Innovative Society* (New York: Harper & Row, Publishers, 1964), pp. 8–20. Copyright © 1964 by the author.

have struggled heroically to increase the *opportunities* for self-development, and they have succeeded marvelously. Now they had better turn to the thing that is really blocking self-development—the individual's own intricately designed, self-constructed prison, or to put it another way, the individual's incapacity for self-renewal.

A prison is not quite the appropriate image because the individual does not stop learning in all aspects of his life simultaneously. Many young people have stopped learning in the religious or spiritual dimensions of their lives long before they graduate from college. Some settle into rigid and unchanging political and economic views by the time they are twenty-five or thirty. By their mid-thirties most will have stopped acquiring new skills or new attitudes in any central aspect of their lives.

As we mature we progressively narrow the scope and variety of our lives. Of all the interests we might pursue, we settle on a few. Of all the people with whom we might associate, we select a small number. We become caught in a web of fixed relationships. We develop set ways of doing things.

As the years go by we view our familiar surroundings with less and less freshness of perception. We no longer look with a wakeful, perceiving eye at the faces of people we see every day, nor at any other features of our everyday world.

That is why travel is a vivid experience for most of us. At home we have lost the capacity to see what is before us. Travel shakes us out of our apathy, and we regain an attentiveness that heightens every experience. The exhilaration of travel has many sources, but surely one of them is that we recapture in some measure the unspoiled awareness of children.

It is not unusual to find that the major changes in life—marriage, a move to a new city, a change of jobs or a national emergency—break the patterns of our lives and reveal to us quite suddenly how much we had been imprisoned by the comfortable web we had woven around ourselves. Unlike the jailbird, we don't know that we've been imprisoned until after we've broken out.

It was a characteristic experience during the Second World War that men and women who had been forced to break the pattern of their lives often discovered within themselves resources and abilities they had not known to exist. How ironic that it should take war and disaster to bring about self-renewal on a large scale! It is an expensive way to accomplish it.

When we have learned to achieve such self-renewal without wars and other disasters, we shall have discovered one of the most important secrets a society can learn, a secret that will unlock new resources of vitality throughout the society. And we shall have done something to avert the hardening of the arteries that attacks so many societies. Men who have lost their adaptiveness naturally resist change. The most stubborn protector of his own vested interest is the man who has lost the capacity for self-renewal.

Self-Development

No one knows why some individuals seem capable of self-renewal while others do not. But we have some important clues to what the self-renewing man is like, and what we might do to foster renewal.

For the self-renewing man the development of his own potentialities and the process of self-discovery never end. It is a sad but unarguable fact that most human beings go through their lives only partially aware of the full range of their abilities. As a boy in California I spent a good deal of time in the Mother Lode country, and like every boy of my age I listened raptly to the tales told by the old-time prospectors in that area, some of them veterans of the Klondike gold rush. Every one of them had at least one good campfire story of a lost gold mine. The details varied: the original discoverer had died in the mine, or had gone crazy, or had been killed in a shooting scrape, or had just walked off thinking the mine worthless. But the central theme was constant: riches left untapped. I have come to believe that those tales offer a paradigm of education as most of us experience it. The mine is worked for a little while and then abandoned.

The development of abilities is at least in part a dialogue between the individual and his environment. If he has it to give and the environment demands it, the ability will develop. Any small boy with real ability to wield his fists is likely to discover that ability fairly early. The little girl with the gift for charming grown-ups will have no trouble discovering that talent. But most abilities are not so readily evoked by the common circumstances of life. The "mute, inglorious Miltons" are more numerous than one might suppose, particularly in an age in which even an articulate Milton might go unnoticed, certainly unrewarded. Most of us have potentialities that have never been developed simply because the circumstances of our lives never called them forth.

Exploration of the full range of his own potentialities is not something that the self-renewing man leaves to the chances of life. It is something he pursues systematically, or at least avidly, to the end of his days. He looks forward to an endless and unpredictable dialogue between his potentialities and the claims of life—not only the claims he encounters but the claims he invents. And by potentialities I mean not just skills, but the full range of his capacities for sensing, wondering, learning, understanding, loving and aspiring.

The ultimate goal of the educational system is to shift to the individual the burden of pursuing his own education. This will not be a widely shared pursuit until we get over our odd conviction that education is what goes on in school buildings and nowhere else. Not only does education continue when schooling ends, but it is not confined to what may be studied in adult education courses. The world is an incomparable classroom, and life is a memorable teacher for those who aren't afraid of her.

The society can do much to encourage such self-development. The most important thing it can do is to remove the obstacles to individual fulfillment. This means doing away with the gross inequalities of opportunity imposed on some of our citizens by race prejudice and economic hardship. And it means a continuous and effective operation of "talent salvage" to assist young people to achieve the promise that is in them. The benefits are not only to the individual but to the society. The renewing society must be continuously refreshed by a stream of new talent from all segments or strata of society. Nothing is more decisive for social renewal than the mobility of talent.

Self-Knowledge

But the discovery of talent is only one side, perhaps the easier side, of self-development: the other side is self-knowledge. The maxim "Know thyself"—so ancient . . . so deceptively simple . . . so difficult to follow—has gained in richness of meaning as we learn more about man's nature. Even today only the wisest of men have some inkling of all that is implied in that gnomic saying. Research in psychology and psychiatry has shown the extent to which mental health is bound up in a reasonably objective view of the self, in accessibility of the self to consciousness, and in acceptance of the self. Erikson has helped us to understand how crucial and how perilous is the young person's search for identity.

We cannot explore here the full implications of these views. Nor can we even begin to examine the various psychological conditions that facilitate or obstruct self-renewal. It would be interesting to examine the manner in which life's blows and brutalities cause a tough scar tissue to form over naturally responsive spirits. It would be useful to examine the processes by which fears and anxieties cut us off from some of life's deepest experiences—a kind of imprisonment that is no less so for being "protective custody." But these topics would take us far afield.

Josh Billings said, "It is not only the most difficult thing to know oneself, but the most inconvenient one, too." Human beings have always employed an enormous variety of clever devices for running away from themselves, and the modern world is particularly rich in such stratagems. We can keep ourselves so busy, fill our lives with so many diversions, stuff our heads with so much knowledge, involve ourselves with so many people and cover so much ground that we never have time to probe the fearful and wonderful world within. More often than not we don't want to know ourselves, don't want to depend on ourselves, don't want to live with ourselves. By middle life most of us are accomplished fugitives from ourselves.

A long, long time ago George Herbert said:

> By all means use some times to be alone.
> Salute thyself: see what thy soul doth wear.

That is good self-renewal doctrine. The individual who has become a stranger to himself has lost the capacity for genuine self-renewal. He can no longer return for sustenance to the springs of his own being.

Niebuhr has written:

The conquest of self is in a sense the inevitable consequence of true self-knowledge. If the self-centered self is shattered by a genuine awareness of its situation, there is the power of a new life in the experience.

Courage to Fail

One of the reasons why mature people are apt to learn less than young people is that they are willing to risk less. Learning is a risky business, and they do not like failure. In infancy, when the child is learning at a truly phenomenal rate—a rate he will never again achieve—he is also experiencing a shattering number of failures. Watch him. See the innumerable things he tries and fails. And see how little the failures discourage him. With each year that passes he will be less blithe about failure. By adolescence the willingness of young people to risk failure has diminished greatly. And all too often parents push them further along that road by instilling fear, by punishing failure or by making success seem too precious. By middle age most of us carry in our heads a tremendous catalogue of things we have no intention of trying again because we tried them once and failed—or tried them once and did less well than our self-esteem demanded.

One of the virtues of formal schooling is that it requires the student to test himself in a great variety of activities that are not of his own choosing. But the adult can usually select the kinds of activity on which he allows himself to be tested, and he takes full advantage of that freedom of choice. He tends increasingly to confine himself to the things he does well and to avoid the things in which he has failed or has never tried.

We pay a heavy price for our fear of failure. It is a powerful obstacle to growth. It assures the progressive narrowing of the personality and prevents exploration and experimentation. There is no learning without some difficulty and fumbling. If you want to keep on learning, you must keep on risking failure— all your life. It's as simple as that. When Max Planck was awarded the Nobel Prize he said:

Looking back . . . over the long and labyrinthine path which finally led to the discovery [of the quantum theory], I am vividly reminded of Goethe's saying that men will always be making mistakes as long as they are striving after something.

Love

Another characteristic of the self-renewing man is that he has mutually fruitful relations with other human beings. He is capable of accepting love and capable of giving it—both more difficult achievements than is commonly thought. He is capable of depending on others and of being depended upon. He can see life through another's eyes and feel it through another's heart.

And what has this to do with self-renewal? The man or woman who cannot achieve these relationships is imprisoned, cut off from a great part of the world of experience. The joy and suffering of those we love are part of our own experience. We feel their triumphs and defeats, their hopes and fears, their anger and pity, and our lives are richer for it.

But vicarious experience is a minor consequence of love. Love and friendship dissolve the rigidities of the isolated self, force new perspectives, alter judgments and keep in working order the emotional substratum on which all profound comprehension of human affairs must rest.

Motivation

The self-renewing man is highly motivated. The walls that hem a man in as he grows older form channels of least resistance. If he stays in the channels, all is easy. To get out requires some extra drive, enthusiasm or energy.

This is in some degree a matter of sheerly physical energy. No matter how intellectual or spiritual one's interests may be, there is an immensely important physical element in one's capacity to learn, grow, recover from defeats, surmount obstacles and live life with vitality and resilience. Anyone interested in leading a creative life will have the deepest respect and concern for the marvelously intricate organism that he is.

But aside from staying in good health, is it really possible to do anything about one's own motivation? The answer is "Perhaps."

Everyone has noted the astonishing sources of energy that seem available to those who enjoy what they are doing or find meaning in what they are doing. The self-renewing man knows that if he has no great conviction about what he is doing he had better find something that he can have great conviction about. Obviously all of us cannot spend all of our time pursuing our deepest convictions. But everyone, either in his career or as a part-time activity, should be doing *something* about which he cares deeply. And if he is to escape the prison of the self, it must be something not essentially egocentric in nature.

How many times have we seen people leave work that they care deeply about to do something that does not interest them because it will bring more money or higher status or greater power? How many times have we seen middle-aged people caught in a pattern of activities they don't care about at all—playing bridge with people they don't really like, going to cocktail parties that bore them, doing things because "it's the thing to do." Such people would be re-freshed and renewed if they could wipe the slate clean and do *one little thing* that they really cared about deeply, one little thing that they could do with burning conviction.

The conventions and artificialities of life, to say nothing of habit, routine and simple momentum, carry us so far from the sources of our interest and convic-tion that we all need a few primer lessons in how to get back in tune with our own being.

When Emerson said, "Once we had wooden chalices and golden priests; now we have golden chalices and wooden priests," he was saying something funda-mental about the relation of men to their institutions. We are forever "building the church and killing the creed." Form triumphs over spirit. A social institu-tion is created out of human ardor and conviction. As its assets expand, the ardor wanes. The buildings grow bigger and the spirit thins out.

Institutions are renewed by individuals who refuse to be satisfied with the outer husks of things. And self-renewal requires somewhat the same impatience with empty forms.

The man who wants to get back to the sources of his own vitality cuts through the false fronts of life and tries to understand the things that he really believes in and can put his heart into.

In this the self-renewing man remembers the mythical giant, Antaeus, who was invincible in wrestling as long as he remained in contact with the earth. He is worth recalling in our intricately organized, ververbalized civilization. We drift further and further from the realities of life. Words become more real than the things they signify. The powerful factors in our lives become less and less things that can be touched and felt, more and more statistical indices and verbal abstractions. It is wisdom to cut through such abstractions and artificialities in a periodic return to the solid earth of direct experience.

Of course, one can overdo the business of complaining about the artificialities of our civilization. A symphony orchestra is as artificial as television. Penicillin is as artificial as neon lights. Most of the artificialities are designed to serve us in some important way. But the wise man turns his back on them occasionally and seeks to renew himself with the things he can see, hear and feel—direct contact with nature, face-to-face relations with his fellow man, fashioning some-thing with his own hands.

Some people think of motivation as a rather mysterious ingredient (initiative, ambition, the will to win) that is put into individuals to make them run, as gasolne is put into a car. Naturally, they are immensely curious as to the nature of that mysterious ingredient and eager to get more of it—particularly when they think the social tank is leaking, as they do today.

But motivation isn't a fuel that gets injected into the system. It is an attribute of individuals, in part linked to their physical vitality, in part a resultant of social forces—patterns of child-rearing, the tone of the educational system, presence or absence of opportunity, the tendency of the society to release or smother available energy, social attitudes toward dedication or commitment and the vitality of the society's shared values.

In our own society the most popular explanation for lowered motivation is "too much prosperity." There is something to be said for the diagnosis. The old boxing adage that a hungry fighter is hard to beat is not without basis. And it is true that most individuals (and societies) deeply committed to the accomplishment of vital purposes are characterized by a certain austerity. But poverty doesn't always bring high motivation; some of the most impoverished populations in the world are the most lethargic. And prosperity doesn't always dampen motivation; indeed, a prosperous society—by virtue of its capacity to extend the range of individual opportunity—may release energies which would otherwise have lain dormant. Certain kinds of creativity require a reasonable margin of abundance. People under severe deprivation are not free to experiment and to try new ways of doing things. In all creative achievement there is a certain recklessness or gambling quality that is often suppressed in a society close to the margin of survival.

In short, although it pleases our puritanical streak to believe that prosperity has blunted our drive, the loss of motivation from this cause is greatly overestimated.

One may argue, as Toynbee does, that a society needs challenge. It is true. But no society has ever mastered its environment and itself to the extent that no challenge remained. Many have gone to sleep because they failed to understand the challenge that was undeniably there. In a sense, societies create their own challenges.

David McClelland makes an interesting case for the view that child-rearing practices determine the level of motivation in a society. We don't know enough to say with confidence what kinds of child-rearing practices will contribute to high levels of motivation; but qualified experts believe that such an outcome will be favored if the family sets standards for the child's performance, encourages habits of self-reliance and avoids excesses of authoritarianism.

The relation of education to the level of motivation in the society is more direct than most people recognize. The goals the young person sets for himself are very heavily affected by the framework of expectations with which adults surround him. The educational system provides the young person with a sense of what society expects of him in the way of performance. If it is lax in its demands, then he will believe that such are the expectations of his society. If much is expected of him, the chances are that he will expect much of himself. This is why it is important that a society create an atmosphere that encourages effort, striving and vigorous performance. In its early days—when it is struggling upward—such effort is apt to be highly rewarded. As the society becomes more successful it often demands less in terms of vigorous effort.

Directions: Refer to the specific section of the reading indicated by the numbers in parentheses for each question. Work with others in your group to answer the questions. (Numbers refer to page and paragraph.)

_____ 1. A person's incapacity for self-renewal blocks his self-development. (82, 0)

_____ 2. Self-development is limited by self-imposed restriction. (82, 1)

_____ 3. Only freed prisoners realize how it feels to be imprisoned. (82, 5)

_____ 4. People who lose their capacity for self-renewal resist change. (82, 7)

_____ 5. Self-renewal is possible for some people and not for others and the reasons are quite clear. (82, 8)

_____ 6. Interaction between an individual and his environment will help to develop his ability. (83, 1)

_____ 7. The goal of formal education is to make the individual responsible for his own education. (83, 3)

_____ 8. People employ multiple strategies to avoid self knowledge. (84, 2)

_____ 9. One can become entangled in a domestic and social web without knowing it. (82, 2)

Directions: Below are references to specific sections of the text. Following each reference is a list of statements. Read the statements for a section first; then read the section. Check those statements which you can support as "correct" interpretations or inferences related to the section. Work with others in your group.

1. (82, 1 to 82, 6)

_____ 1. Attending college does not necessarily assure learning.

_____ 2. A person should continue learning all of his life.

_____ 3. Learning takes place only under pressure.

2. (82, 1 to 82, 6)

_____ 1. Poor learners should be jailed.

_____ 2. People often are unaware that they are unaware of life around them.

_____ 3. Major changes in life reveal stagnation in a person's life.

3. (82, 6 to 83, 1)

_____ 1. Change is good in itself; it needs no other reason.

_____ 2. People resist change because it makes them uncomfortable.

_____ 3. A person who accepts change has no standards.

4. (83, 1 to 83, 3)

_____ 1. People generally do only what is required of them.

_____ 2. Circumstances of life generally shape the individual rather than the reverse.

_____ 3. A person should not live "under the circumstances."

5. (83, 3 to 84, 1)

_____ 1. A person does not need to be in a classroom in order to experience learning.

_____ 2. A teacher or parent need not be talking in order for children to learn.

_____ 3. Fear of knowledge limits learning.

6. (84, 1 to 84, 3)

_____ 1. Introspection is painful.

_____ 2. Running away from self is a hard task.

_____ 3. It is easier to listen to information about others than to discover information about yourself.

7. (84, 3 to 84, 5)

_____ 1. Failure is too uncomfortable to risk.

_____ 2. "If at first you don't succeed, try, try again," is not a realistic statement.

_____ 3. Society's insistence on continued success limits risk taking.

Directions: Read the selection from the text. Working alone, check those generalizations you can support from the text and discussions about ideas developed in the text. Compare your selections with others in your group. Where you have differences, see if you can resolve them.

_____ 1. Change for its own sake has little value.

_____ 2. Resisting change to protect the *status quo* or to avoid discomfort is shortsighted.

_____ 3. Only those who have been imprisoned know the value of free education.

_____ 4. Activity for others is often used to avoid reflection about one's self.

_____ 5. Success, not failure, develops mature people.

_____ 6. Fear of failure is a learned condition, not a natural one.

_____ 7. We do best what interests us most.

_____ 8. We do better in those activities and responsibilities in which we have greater interest.

_____ 9. The accomplishments of an individual reflect the expectation-environment in which he exists.

_____10. The self-expectations of an individual are conditioned by society's expectations for that individual.

Use of Levels of Comprehension

SERVING A RANGE OF ACHIEVEMENT   The content teacher most frequently faces a class whose students range in achievement over several
"grade levels," all of whom have the same text available to them. Arguments concerning the value of multilevel texts notwithstanding, a great
many content teachers are in precisely this situation. Until (and even when)
the situation changes, and multilevel materials are available and used, the
concept of "levels of comprehension" is extremely useful for meeting the
range of achievement in a class.

Students in an average class will range in reading skill from good to
poor. Since any content material can be responded to at all three levels
of comprehension, a teacher can serve the range by having groups of students respond to the material at the level of comprehension appropriate
to each. The poorer readers can be guided to read at the literal level of
comprehension; the "average" or adequate readers to respond at the interpretive level; and the good or superior readers at the "applied" level.
Each group completes its own work and resolves differences it may have.
The teacher subsequently leads a full class discussion and draws information and ideas from each group as he develops the overall concept appropriate to the part of the curriculum being studied. Thus, each student
experiences success with the group activity he has been assigned, working
at the level at which he is capable of responding. Each group experiences
success as it contributes to the total class discussion. Independently, students learn from one another within groups and among groups. Therefore,
even though one person has not read at all three levels of comprehension
and, perhaps, has not read the entire selection, he is able to benefit from
the work of other students as each group reports the results of its work.

There are many variations on this point. For example, within each level
of comprehension there can be a range of sophistication, depending on the
material being read and the needs of the students. Because of limited
achievement, all students in a given class may require help in reading successfully at the literal level. Yet, within that class, some students will
require more aid than others. The following guide is a solution to the
problems. Some students are guided to the page, column, and paragraph
where they can find the information; others are guided only to the page
and column; others only to the page. Even this relatively little distinction
makes a considerable difference in the students' success. No one in the
class is reading at the interpretive level, except to the extent to which some
of the questions go beyond the "what" to the "why." Even there, however,
the "why" is definite information given in the text and does not have to

be ferreted out by an interpretive process. As students grow in their achievement, the teacher can guide their response at higher levels.

DIFFERENTIATED GUIDE AT THE LITERAL LEVEL OF COMPREHENSION

Grade Seven   Chapter Three: "Your Country's Story"

DIRECTED READING FOR DETAIL

Directions: There are several important details in this section of chapter three. *As you read,* answer the questions *you have been* assigned. Sometimes the page, column, and paragraph are given to identify the location of the answer.

* * 1. Who were the Pilgrims? (54, 1, 1)
* ** 2. Why did the Pilgrims leave England? (54, 55)
* *** 3. To what two places did the Pilgrims go after leaving England?
* * 4. Who were the Puritans? (59, 1, 2)
* ** 5. Why did the Puritans leave England? (59)
* *** 6. What advantage did the Puritans have that the Pilgrims didn't? (59)
* * 7. Who founded Rhode Island? (59, 2, 2)
* ** 8. Why was Rhode Island founded? (59, 2)
* *** 9. What cautious act by the founder saved the colonies from trouble? (59)
* * 10. Who settled Connecticut? (60, 1, 1)
* ** 11. Why was Connecticut settled? (60, 1)
* *** 12. What arrangements made in the settling of Connecticut caused problems in later years?
* * 13. Who settled New Hampshire? (60, 1)
* ** 14. Why did the settlers of New Hampshire pick that area? (60)
* *** 15. Why did the settlers of New Hampshire eventually change their occupations?

Some teachers object to having students read only at the literal level, believing that if they do they will not know the meaning of what they read. This may be true, but if the teacher uses the information students contribute from their literal response to the selection, he can develop their understanding of meanings through oral exchange. Other teachers are fearful that if they guide students to page, column, and paragraph, they "will not read the whole story," (as one English teacher complained). Of course this is true, but one must ask if the students could read *any* of the "story" if they did not have this help. If the answer is "no," then one has two choices: 1) guide students' response at the needed level; 2) get material appropriate to the students' level. If the latter is not available—as is often the case—one can use the former procedure and watch students grow because of the success they experience.

Where low vocabulary materials are available, the teacher still needs to guide students' response. Because the material is easier—presumably with respect to concept load as well as vocabulary—slower students can respond to it at the interpretive level rather than just the literal. To be certain this occurs with multilevel materials, the teacher guides each group at the comprehension level appropriate to the sophistication of the material and the students' own achievement level. Whether a single text or multitexts are used, the responsibility of the teacher remains the same: provide guidance at the level (or levels) of comprehension appropriate to the students in the class. Many sample guides are given in the Appendix for single and multiple texts.

UNDERSTANDING THE COMPREHENSION PROCESS   The full process of comprehension incorporates all three levels that have been discussed in this chapter. It is possible, as has been pointed out, for a student to function with only part of the whole. However, when students are able to function at all three levels, it is useful to have them respond to a selection, periodically, at all three levels of comprehension, in much the same manner you did when reading the material on pages 75–81. This process develops an appreciation and understanding of what must be done when you endeavor to "comprehend" what you read. You must identify the pertinent information (literal) which represents what the author is saying to the reader; you look for relationships (interpretive) among those pieces of information to determine, from those relationships (intrinsic concepts), what the author means by what he says; you look for ideas in your experience or from other readings with which these new (intrinsic) concepts have some relationship. Relating these "intrinsic" concepts to the other ideas (applied) you form "extrinsic" concepts which enlarge your perception and understanding of the content of the course being studied.

When students are "walked through" this full process periodically, by responding to reading guides provided by the teacher, they benefit from the experience. Because the full process can be applied at many levels of sophistication, it is appropriate to lower grades as well as to higher, to lower ability groups as well as higher. When students are so limited in achievement that they cannot profitably consider levels of comprehension beyond the literal, attempts to "walk them through" the full process is rather fruitless. Relatively speaking, however, few students are in this position of limited achievement to the extent that adjustments in sophistication are useless.

The following guide, used with an average tenth grade World History class, illustrates the use of all three levels of comprehension with a single class. Note, however, that the students start their work at the interpretive level. The relationships they are to examine first are really alternative interpretations of interaction between listed countries. They go back to the literal level by identifying the place in the selection that contains the information by which they judge their interpretations to be correct. They then move on to the applied level which, in this case, is a reaction to generalizations.

Students worked on the material in groups, in class. The teacher directed the concluding discussion, focusing on the generalizations students had some difficulty resolving. He drew from all groups in the total discussion; but much of the understanding had already been developed within the group work.

READING GUIDE FOR THREE LEVELS OF COMPREHENSION

Grade Ten: World History   *Our World,* Prentice-Hall,
"Industrial Revolution and Imperialism"

Directions: Examine the statements on list entitled "Relationships" on p. 94. These state relationships between countries. Following are listed three major countries which were expanding their empires. Next to each of these three countries are listed other nations which experienced certain kinds of relationships with these expanding powers.

Draw from the list of stated relationships to indicate the kind of relationship which took place during this time of expansion. Write the number on the lines between the countries to represent the relationship you believe existed. Base your judgment on what you read in the text; of course, you may draw on your knowledge from other sources as well. Indicate the location in the text where you would find support for your view.

Expanding Power	Relationship	Affected Power	Reference
	_____	Japan	_____
RUSSIA	_____	China	_____
	_____	Britain	_____
	_____	Germany	_____

Expanding Power	Relationship	Affected Power	Reference
JAPAN	⎧ _____	China	_____
	⎨ _____	Russia	_____
	⎪ _____	France	_____
	⎩ _____	Britain	_____
FRANCE	⎧ _____	China	_____
	⎨ _____	Africa	_____
	⎪ _____	Britain	_____
	⎪ _____	Italy	_____
	⎩ _____	Germany	_____

RELATIONSHIPS

1. Boundaries were expanded.
2. Ports were needed for exports and imports.
3. Spoils did not entirely belong to the victor.
4. Concessions were reached.
5. Suspicious rivals going against common, more dangerous, rival.
6. Need for natural resources created Industrial Revolution.
7. Expansion changed to acquisition.
8. Territory was leased.
9. Gains through negotiation were lost through war.
10. Action taken, in acquiring land, independent of other imperialistic nations.
11. Surprise provides strategic advantage.
12. The "tables were turned" in the act of domination.
13. War is not always essential to expansion.
14. Power lies in resources and organization, not necessarily in size.
15. Joining an enemy's enemy allows a country to attack *the* enemy.

GENERALIZATIONS

Directions: Check those generalizations which you can support from material in the text, in supplementary materials, and class discussions. Work alone first, then compare your responses with others in your group and resolve any differences you might find.

_____ 1. Wounded oriental pride led Japan to aggression against Russia.

_____ 2. Britain and Russia found it more advantageous to fight Germany than one another.

_____ 3. China was a pawn rather than a power, bartered and bargained over rather than respected.

_____ 4. Alliances among nations are formed only if advantageous to all parties.

_____ 5. Treaties reached between countries are not mutually beneficial.

_____ 6. What is gained through war may well be lost through negotiations.

_____ 7. Rulers of a large nation defeated by a small nation have a considerable amount of explaining to do.

_____ 8. Factors of *drive, ambition, need,* and *imagination* create a world power from a backward nation.

_____ 9. Small nations are victorious because they are more aggressive and do not rely on their size alone for protection or progress.

_____10. Some nations seek gain by concession and accommodation rather than by aggression.

READING SELECTION

Competition Increases in Empire Building

1. *The Russian Empire Expands Toward Seas and Oceans.* The British built their empire by acquiring scattered territories, but the Russians built theirs by expanding their own boundaries. For centuries landlocked Russia sought to expand to the Baltic, Black, and Mediterranean seas, to the Far Eastern Pacific ports, and to the Middle Eastern Persian Gulf. About 1700, Peter the Great had won a window on the Baltic. His explorer, Bering (page 280), had laid the basis for Russia's claim to Alaska. About 1800, Catherine the Great had won a Black Sea window. Russia's nineteenth- and twentieth-century wars directed toward control of the Dardanelles are other examples of the Russian drive for warm-water ports.

2. Toward the end of the nineteenth century, the Industrial Revolution got started in Russia. As a result, Russia began to develop its own natural resources and to reach out to control mining, railroad, and other economic concessions outside its borders. In a push to the Middle East and central Asia, Russia was approaching India. This seemed a threat to British control there. However, at this time both Russia and Britain feared Germany more than they feared each other. Instead of going to war, therefore, in 1907 Britain and Russia partitioned Persia into three spheres of influence. The north was to be open only to Russian businessmen, the south only to British, and the central area to both. Afghanistan was to be a buffer state under British domination to protect the frontier of India from Russian expansion.

3. In a push to the Far East, Russia had come to actual blows with Japan.

Reprinted by permission of the publisher from Nathaniel Platt and Muriel Drummond, *Our World Through the Ages,* 3rd Ed. (Englewood Cliffs, N. J.: Prentice-Hall, Inc., © 1967), pp. 461–64.

They both hoped to obtain, at China's expense, Manchuria, the Liao-tung Peninsula on which Port Arthur is situated, and the peninsula of Korea. When Japan defeated China in 1894, Russia, among other powers, stepped in to prevent Japan from retaining all its gains. However, Russia itself obtained from China a lease on Port Arthur, concessions in Korea, and the privilege of completing the Trans-Siberian Railroad through Manchuria to the sometimes frozen port of Vladivostok. This stretch of the Trans-Siberian Railroad is known as the Chinese Eastern Railway. Russia also got the right to construct another branch railroad, the South Manchurian Railway, to connect ice-free Port Arthur with the main line in the north. Japan's anger over these efforts of Russia to dominate Manchuria led to the Russo-Japanese War of 1904. By the Treaty of Portsmouth which ended the war, Russia was forced to give up the southern half of the island of Sakhalin, its concessions in Korea, and its lease on Port Arthur. But Russia retained its railroads in northern Manchuria.

4. Russia's interest in the Balkans (page 280)—its desire to obtain warm-water ports there—was considered by the British a threat to their lifeline to India and by the Germans a threat to their plan to build a Berlin-to-Baghdad Railroad. However, Russia joined its rival, Britain, in World War I with the major object of winning Constantinople and the Dardanelles from Turkey, Germany's ally. Even today Russia continues its expansionist policies (Chapter 27).

5. *Japan Imitates European Imperialists.* Almost overnight Japan had changed from a backward feudal country to a highly industrialized nation. In 1894, small modernized Japan attacked and defeated huge but backward China. The jubilant Japanese then acquired in the peace treaty the island of Formosa and the Liao-tung Peninsula. They made Korea a Japanese sphere of influence. After Russia, France, and Germany forced Japan to surrender some of its acquisitions, they and Britain helped themselves to some Chinese territory, spheres of influence, and concessions. In addition to Russia's gains, France expanded its territory in Indo-China; Britain, its territory in Burma: and Germany, its foothold on the Shantung Peninsula. Japan was especially angry at Russia for dominating fertile and mineral-rich Manchuria.

6. To strengthen its position, Japan signed an alliance in 1902 with Britain, Russia's rival in the Middle East. Then in 1904, suddenly and without declaring war, Japan torpedoed many Russian battleships at Port Arthur. In the months that followed, little, efficient Japan defeated the overconfident Russian giant on land and sea. The President of the United States, Theodore Roosevelt arranged for the peace treaty ending the Russo-Japanese War, the terms of which we have just studied. In 1910, Japan annexed Korea outright and expanded its political and economical control in Manchuria.

7. By defeating a big European nation, Japan came to be counted among the world powers. This was the first evidence in modern times that an Asiatic power could be a competitor of rather than a victim of Western imperialists. In the years that followed, Japan continued its imperialistic expansion. But at the close of World War II (1945), Japan was stripped of all its imperialistic gains.

8. *France Loses One Empire But Builds Another.* In the eighteenth century, France had lost out to Britain in colonial competition for Canada and India. But by the early twentieth century, France had almost caught up to Britain in the extent, although not in the value, of its empire. In 1830, France invaded Algeria in North Africa. The French excuse was that the ruler of that Turkish dependency had insulted France by slapping the French consul with a fly-swatter. Historians recognize, however, that King Charles X thought that this invasion might distract the minds of the French people from his undemocratic policies

at home. He hoped, too, that it might revive the lost prestige of the Bourbon family. Once France had annexed Algeria,[1] it was easy for French business-men, military officials, and politicians to push eastward into Tunisia and west-ward into Morocco.

9. Both France and Italy had flooded the ruler of Tunisia with loans in the hope of influencing his government and winning concessions. When Britain got France's support for its seizure of the island of Cyprus from Turkey in 1876, however, Britain in return backed France's claims to Tunisia. This type of bar-gaining is common among imperialistic nations. A few years later, France in-vaded Tunisia. Italy was so enraged at this that it joined Germany and Austria in a so-called *Triple Alliance* (1882).

10. Relations between France and Britain in Africa were not entirely friendly. Britain wanted to build a Cape-to-Cairo Railroad, while France desired an east-west band of territory stretching from the Red Sea to the Atlantic Ocean. When these conflicting lines of expansion met in the Egyptian Sudan, the two coun-tries almost came to blows at Fashoda. By another bargain, this Fashoda inci-dent was settled peacefully. France was to recognize Britain's claims to the Sudan in return for British backing for French expansion in Morocco. By this time, France had enjoyed considerable industrialization, and the nearness, the good harbors, the natural resources, and the markets of North Africa looked increasingly attractive. French insistence on acquiring Morocco in the face of German opposition almost caused World War I to break out before it did (page 536). It was with Britain's backing that France was able to make Morocco a French protectorate in 1912.

11. In 1884, a meeting had been held at Berlin in which the imperialistic powers had laid down the rules for contestants in the race for African territory. One rule stated that a country must actually occupy a territory before annex-ing it. Thus the French occupied and then annexed what is today the French Congo, French West Africa, French Somaliland, and the island of Madagascar.

12. But France did not confine its empire to Africa. About 1850, France joined Britain in forcing China to open its ports to trade. By 1867, France had ac-quired Indo-China. When Japan exposed China's weakness in the Chino-Japanese War of 1894, France, like other European powers, carved out spheres of influence in China. The French Empire also included such Pacific islands as Tahiti and Caledonia, acquired in the nineteenth century, and such Caribbean possessions as French Guiana and the island of Martinique, acquired in the seventeenth century. After World War II, the French Empire, like other em-pires, was faced with many uprisings among colonial peoples.

SUMMARY

You have applied "levels of comprehension" to materials written mainly for adults and you have examined materials used with students. You can provide the same kind of material—and experience—for students enrolled in your subject. The Appendix to this text, pages 217–275, includes addi-tional examples of such material. These guides were designed by, for, and/or with content teachers and were used in regular classrooms. Your

---

[1] Algeria is governed as part of France, sending delegates to the French Parliament just as French provinces at home do.

perusal of them will be useful since they can serve as patterns for you to follow in constructing your own material. When considering the use of the guides, always keep in mind that they fit into an overall lesson structure; that they do not constitute the total lesson or total unit. The guides serve as structure within, as discussed in chapter 3.

"Levels of comprehension" is a gross treatment of comprehension, precisely the reason that the "levels" concept is useful to content teachers. There is no concern with nomenclature. Depending on the level at which they function, students read to find out "what the author said," "what he meant," "how to use the ideas." By well-designed questions that guide their responses, students are aided in the development of their gross skills and in their understanding of the content.

The levels concept can be used to serve the range of achievement of students in a single class in response to a single text. Each separate group can respond to the text at the different level of comprehension and subsequently contribute its findings to the total class discussion. Thus, the relative needs of each student are met within the framework of a regular content class. If multiple texts or multilevel texts are used, material to guide students' levels of response are just as useful.

The "levels" concept also can be used to reinforce an understanding of the process of comprehension: one takes in information (literal), determines what it means (interpretive), and makes use of the ideas that have been developed (applied). Periodically taking students through the entire process aids their understanding of comprehension and builds an appreciation of all they should consider while reading their texts. Obviously, use of the "levels" concept to build appreciation of the total process of comprehension should be reserved for those students who can function at all three levels.

After a content teacher becomes comfortable with an emphasis on "levels of comprehension," he can refine his guidance and assist students in perceiving and using "organizational patterns" and "specific skills." The nature and use of each is discussed in the next chapter.

REACTION GUIDE

Literal

Check statements from the following list that represent what the author actually said in this chapter.

_____ 1. It is possible to meet the learning needs of one student even though he is in a group.

___ 2. A successful learning experience provides incentive to learn more.

___ 3. Generally speaking, content teachers are not familiar with procedures for teaching reading.

___ 4. Self-sufficient learners are taught how to achieve at that level; it doesn't just happen.

___ 5. There are four levels of comprehension: literal; interpretive; applied; creative.

___ 6. Levels of meaning correspond with levels of comprehension.

___ 7. Multitexts, multilevel texts, multilevel guides provide for a range of ability and achievement.

___ 8. Readability formulas do not represent true reading levels of content texts.

___ 9. Students need to be shown how to read assigned material.

___10. Controlling students' levels of response to a reading selection is more important than controlling the level of vocabulary in which the selection is written.

Interpretive

Statements 1–10 interpret various parts of the chapter you just concluded. Immediately following these directions are criteria by which to judge these statements. Place the letter of the criterion you select for each statement on the line in column A. In column B place a check on the line before the statements you accept.

> C. Correct interpretation of the content
> I. Incorrect interpretation of the content
> U. Unrelated to the chapter

A   B

___ ___ 1. Most content teachers are unprepared to teach reading skills as part of their subject.

___ ___ 2. Emphasizing reading skills in a content area may jeopardize an understanding of the subject itself.

___ ___ 3. When a student cannot read beyond the literal level of comprehension, he should not be required to read independently above that level until he is taught how to do so.

___ ___ 4. Better teaching at the elementary level would insure better reading achievement in content areas at the secondary level.

___ ___ 5. Multiple labels for comprehension levels suggest lack of definitive studies which precisely delimit comprehension.

___ ___ 6. Each comprehension level has its own set of skills, separate and unrelated from those related to the other levels.

A   B

_____ _____ 7. A "meaning level" is another term for a "comprehension level."

_____ _____ 8. Multilevel guides used with basic texts best serve the reading achievement needs of individual students, as opposed to multitexts and multiple sources.

_____ _____ 9. Multilevel guides can be used with multilevel texts or multiple sources as successfully as with single texts.

_____ _____10. The surest solution to reading problems is to substitute other media as means for conveying information and just abandon reading instruction.

Applied

Several statements are given in each of two sections listed below. The first section lists "solutions" to problems related to the use of texts and resource materials in subject area classes. The second section lists "Problems or Conditions" faced by content teachers.

On the line before each "Problem or Condition" indicate the letter (letters) of the "Solutions" which should be used by the teacher involved. More than one solution may fit a problem or condition. You may indicate order in the application of solutions by the order in which you place the letters on the line.

Solutions

A. All students read from the same text with no differentiations in assignments.

B. All students read same text but with questions on different levels of difficulty assigned to groups of students.

C. Students read multilevel materials, each one given a book according to his achievement level not accompanied by guides.

D. Students real multi-source materials, each one given a book according to his interests.

E. Students guided in the application of specific skills related to the assignment in the text or texts.

F. Students guided in manipulating and using ideas related to the assignment in the text or texts.

Problems or Conditions

_____ 1. Ninth grade science class which is very homogeneous in ability and achievement.

_____ 2. Eighth grade history class which is very homogeneous in ability and achievement, but with no one a remedial reader.

_____ 3. Regents class in eleventh grade English.

_____ 4. Low-achieving sixth grade class (I.Q. range of 80–95) in social studies.

_____ 5. Honors class in physics.

_____ 6. Developmental reading class in grade ten.

_____ 7. A home economics class with a wide range of ability but narrow and low range of reading achievement.

_____ 8. A business education class, heterogeneously grouped on ability and achievement.

_____ 9. A Problems of Democracy class required for all seniors.

_____10. A geometry class in a small high school.

6

PATTERNS, SKILLS, AND TRANSFORMATION

Two terms of special importance are introduced in this chapter:
- external organization
- internal organization

Several other important terms in this chapter were introduced earlier in the text. It would be helpful to review them at this time:
- transformation
- reading guides
- structure

IDEA DIRECTION

The substantive part of this chapter was mentioned briefly in earlier chapters. Now it is examined in detail. A review of earlier references will provide a context for this discussion.

READING DIRECTION

There is a relationship among the three elements in this chapter title; also among "Patterns and Skills" and the "Levels of Comprehension" of the preceding chapter. It will be helpful to look for this as you read.

Chapter 5 is devoted to a discussion of levels of comprehension. The concept of the levels is important because it simplifies the content teacher's task. Cumbersome nomenclature is avoided; procedures are looked at in gross sets rather than in infinitesimal parts. Much can be accomplished for the student by the teacher—as well as for the teacher himself—through an emphasis on levels of comprehension.

Assuming familiarity with the concept of levels and security about incorporating it into one's teaching, the next consideration is the use of organizational patterns.

ORGANIZATIONAL PATTERNS

There are two organizational structures by which any written material can be identified: external and internal. External organization is a gross characterization, focusing on format and physical features. Graphic aids appear in most expository text: tables of contents; indices; appendices; chapter headings; divisions and subdivisions shown by boldface type, underlinings or italics; maps; charts; pictures; graphs. These contribute to the external (gross) structure of written material. Students can gather clues from such aids to tell what priorities the authors place on ideas and information they present in their material.

Moreover, students learn to identify the nature of the content merely by viewing the external peculiarities (organization) of the material. Formula and problems written in numerical form are identified as having to do with math and/or science. Poetry and drama are revealed by their format as is exposition characteristic of science, history, economics, and so on. "Word problems" in science and math are easily identified by form as are technical materials in distributive education and the crafts.

This aspect of external organization, features unique to each subject area, seems so obvious as to be absolutely unnecessary to "teach." Perhaps so, but many understandings appear obvious after they have been understood and have become a part of our set of reflex understandings. They are not obvious to the person struggling to acquire the insight. Sometimes a teacher must run the risk of laboring the obvious in order to avoid the risk of assumptive teaching.

Awareness of such clues, of course, prepares students to read "math" when they encounter material with the external organization that triggers that association, and that corresponding set will occur when they see material in science, literature, and social studies. This point is discussed more in detail under the heading "Transformation" later in this chapter.

External organization related to graphic aids and the structure of the text is less obvious. Jewett, Shepherd, and Summers [1] give valuable suggestions for helping students derive maximum value from such aids. Their comprehensive comments are of practical benefit and are worthwhile for you to investigate. They point out clearly that competence with these aspects of external organization is a learned skill. Students who acquire such skill are able to use their texts with greater efficiency.

Again, we are confronted with the obvious. Is it possible that students read their texts and do not use graphic aids? Unfortunately, unless the value and usefulness is pointed out to them, students ignore these aids. Many students view maps, charts, graphs, and pictures as filler which reduces the number of words they must cover when reading from page x to page y. Unfortunately, many do not see these aids as devices by which authors clarify their exposition, unless taught to do so. And since this is an area in which "assumptive teaching" clearly occurs (who can believe that students don't use maps to clarify exposition!), relatively few students receive adequate instruction.

Aiding students in this area is a relatively simple matter and this aid can be a regular part of the curriculum. Early in the school year, students can be led through an examination of their texts and resource materials. Special features related to format and graphic aids can be pointed out at that time. Subsequently, as each assignment is given in these materials, teachers can point out (or draw from students) the particular graphic aids that are pertinent to the concepts to be acquired from the reading. As necessary—students' response being the determiner—teachers can give specific instruction in how to make proper use of the aids. Such incidental, functional instruction promotes students' competence with the external organization of materials.

Internal Organization

More subtle and, consequently, more difficult to teach and learn is the internal organization of material. Authors generally follow some organizational structure as they write. Some writers evidence little organization but that, in itself, is a type of structure which can be discerned by students prepared to look for such clues.

Several authors concerned with reading and study skills have identified

[1] Harold L. Herber, ed., *Developing Study Skills in Secondary Schools* (Newark, Del.: International Reading Association, 1965).

organizational structures characteristic of expository material.[2] Though there is not a common agreement on those which are of greatest importance, the following appear with regularity in text materials used in content classes: cause/effect; comparison/contrast; time order; enumerative order. "Main idea" also is listed by these sources as an organizational pattern. True, it is a pattern—but it is of a different magnitude than the others. Its construct is so broad that it subsumes each of the other patterns. For example, a *cause* might be the "main idea" of a paragraph and the *effects,* the "details"; or a *comparison* might be the "main idea" and *contrasts,* the "details"; or a stated *objective* might be the "main idea" and the *enumeration* of steps leading to that objective, the "detail"; and so on. There are occasions, however, when the relationship between the statement of the central topic, or "main idea" and supporting information, "detail," does not subsume one of these four basic patterns. In such cases, the broader label, "main idea/detail," is applied.

It is helpful, at this juncture, to recall the interpretive level of comprehension. Reading at this level, the student searches for relationships within the text so as to form "intrinsic concepts." These relationships fall into patterns that are identifiable. The organizational patterns listed above describe the structure of various "relationships" one can perceive when formulating intrinsic concepts at the interpretive level of comprehension. This is why one can refer to "organizational patterns" being contained within levels of comprehension.

Organizational patterns are found within the applied level of comprehension also. You will recall that we associate intrinsic concepts, formulated through the interpretive level, with concepts previously established through direct experiences outside the text and/or reading from other sources. By this association a new, third concept is developed. This extrinsic concept, so-called because it is formulated outside of the selection itself, is developed through a specific relationship among ideas. The relationship that occurs can be characterized by the manner in which it occurs, its organizational peculiarity, and that characterization can be labeled with one of the names given above. Thus within both the interpretive and applied levels of comprehension, we can perceive organizational patterns by analyzing the nature of the relationships we find when formulating intrinsic and extrinsic concepts.

Organizational patterns do not occur within the literal level of compre-

[2] Ruth Strang, Constance M. McCullough, and Arthur E. Traxler, *The Improvement of Reading* (New York: McGraw-Hill, 1967); Henry A. Bamman, Ursula Hogan, and Charles E. Greene, *Reading Instruction in the Secondary Schools* (New York: David McKay Company, ĩnc., 1967); Nila B. Smith, *Reading Instruction for Today's Children* (Englewood Cliffs: Prentice-Hall, Inc., 1963); Olive S. Niles, "Organization Perceived," in *Developing Study Skills in Secondary Schools* (Newark, Del.: International Reading Association, 1965).

hension in the same sense that they do within the interpretive and the applied levels. When responding at the literal level, we search only for what the author says, for the basic information. However, after students are sufficiently familiar with organizational patterns to identify those that are inherent in given selections, they can use this knowledge to distinguish between important and unimportant information. Students will learn to focus on information that contributes to the organizational patterns which formulate the intrinsic and extrinsic concepts. This understanding gives them an objective criterion by which to select information to commit to memory and thus gives them one more tool for developing independence in study.

There are implications concerning the use of organizational patterns to construct reading guides for the literal level of comprehension. These are discussed on pages 117–118.

We should understand that organizational patterns characterize entire works as well as single paragraphs. For example, a full chapter in history may be organized in an enumerative order, another in a cause-effect pattern. At the same time, single paragraphs within those chapters may be similarly organized.

We should also understand that there can be, and often is, a mixing of these organizational patterns within both single paragraphs and longer selections. For example, within a chapter organized sequentially, there may be several paragraphs with cause/effect or comparison/contrast organization. Though there is frequently such a mixture, we generally find a predominant pattern within paragraphs or longer selections. Teachers assisting students in the successful reading of expository material can focus on the most obvious pattern in the selection and ignore the others as far as that particular assignment is concerned. Students can be taught to focus on the dominant pattern and use it as an aid to understanding relationships within the material as well as an aid for recall after the reading has been completed.

We should also consider the place of various literary genres in the discussion of internal organization. Each of the genres has external characteristics, as discussed above. As is true of expository material, literary genres, other than the essay, have identifying internal structure: the novel, short story, biography, autobiography, types of poetry, types of drama. Texts devoted to the teaching of literature [3] discuss in more detail than is possible here patterns peculiar to the several genre. A teacher interested in literature should secure these texts and read carefully the appropriate sections of each.

[3] Dwight Burton, *Literature Study in the High School* (New York: Holt, Rinehart, & Winston, Inc., 1959); Walter Loban, Margaret Ryan, and James R. Squire, *Teaching Language and Literature* (New York: Harcourt, Brace, & World, Inc., 1961); J. N. Hook, *The Teaching of High School English* (New York: The Ronald Press Company, 1965).

Guiding Students' Use of Organizational Patterns

Part of the teacher's preparation for a lesson discussed in chapter 4 is to examine the intended reading assignment to determine how the students should read it; what process they should use to derive maximum understanding. After the teacher identifies one of the organizational patterns, he has two specific tasks. First, he should discuss this pattern as part of the structure of his total lesson (cf. chapter 3) so that students are aware of the process they are to apply. Second, he should provide guidance for the students (particularly if they are relatively unfamiliar with the pattern and its application) so that as they read the selection they develop a conscious understanding of the process. The purpose of the guide is not to test to see if students use the pattern correctly. Rather, it is to make certain that students develop a feeling for the process so that ultimately they will be able to use the pattern independently.

The guide is a simulator. The process is analyzed, taken apart, and the parts placed before the student. He is shown how to put them back together again and, through the experience, he develops an understanding of the process itself.

The reading guide below illustrates how one teacher guided his low achieving seventh graders in using the cause/effect pattern as they read their history text. At first glance, it looks like nothing more than a simple matching exercise; but it is much more than that.

READING GUIDE: CAUSE AND EFFECT PATTERN

Effects

a. Growth of farming
b. Needed skilled labor
c. Beginning of slavery
d. People become indentured servants
e. Needed farmers
f. Growth of industry

Causes

  * 22. Rich soil in South (59, 1, 0) _____
 ** 23. Farming not profitable in North (58, 2) _____
 ** 24. Cheap land, high wages (63, 2) _____
*** 25. Northern colonies were industrial (63) _____
*** 26. Southern colonies were agricultural (63) _____
*** 27. Lack of help on farms (63) _____

Specific cause and effect relationships were identified in the text. These were taken apart; causes were placed in one list, effects in another. Students were asked to associate causes and effects in accordance with relationships among details contained in the text.

There was a range of achievement in the class and so the teacher designed the guide to accommodate the levels of sophistication represented in that range. The difficulty level of each item was signaled with one, two, or three asterisks, ranging from "easy" to "hard." Statements of cause signaled with a single asterisk were almost word for word quotes from the text. In addition, the page, column, and paragraph were provided to identify where this cause could be found in the text. The student assigned that item then was to search through the list of effects and find the one most nearly associated with the cause he was considering. When studying each of the alternatives in reference to the stated cause given in the guide and found in the text, the student was led through the process of manipulating cause/effect relationships. He selected the effect he believed belonged to the cause he was considering. Later, he checked with other students in his group to compare answers; and where they had differences, they attempted to resolve them, adding further reinforcement to his understanding of the cause/effect organizational structure.

Meanwhile, more able students examined those causes in the list signaled by two or three asterisks, depending on their need and level of sophistication. The guide was designed so that these items were not direct quotations from the text but paraphrasings or interpreted statements of cause. In addition, the items were followed by less direction, that is, some were followed by page and column number, others only by page, and still others by no reference. This created a guide, or a portion of a guide, appropriate for each student in the class. The group analysis and resolution of differences allowed students to learn from one another and to engage actively rather than passively in the learning process.

This same format can be used with students of higher ability and achievement. The amount of aid and direction can be lessened according to the level of independence the students have attained. Even more importantly, the items within the guide itself can be adjusted to the competence of the students. Statements identifying both causes and effects can be more inferential in nature rather than direct statements from the text. Thus students may not only develop the feeling for the organizational structure of cause/effect, but also the subtleties of implication.

There are those who say such guides are no different than many exercises appearing on outmoded workbooks. Not so. Workbook materials generally are used to "test" comprehension rather than guide its development. There is the assumption that students already can read the material and apply the skill required by the exercise. The guide illustrated above does not make such an assumption. Rather it is assumed that the students have difficulty reading the text and, therefore, must be guided carefully so as to experience success at the level that their present competence will allow. Perhaps the student will not read the entire selection if he responds only to those items assigned to him; but the items are assigned to him precisely because he has difficulties in reading the material. What he cannot read himself he learns from other students who can, as all students engage in group and then in full-class discussion.

An English teacher objected to this approach and its use, saying she "resented it" and would never use it. When asked what she resented, she replied, "If students read only for the items assigned to them, they will not be reading the entire selection." When asked if the students could read the material without such aid, she said, "No, they cannot." That being the case, it was suggested that she use the procedure, helping students experience success at their level of competence, allowing them to learn from one another as each group contributes information and ideas it acquires by doing its assigned task. But she replied that she couldn't do it. "Why?" "I'd resent it!" "Why?" "They wouldn't read the entire selection." "Can they read it anyway?" "No." "Then why not use the procedure?" "I couldn't." "Why?" "I'd resent . . . !" There seems to be the widespread fear that unless a student actually reads a selection himself the content has no value for him, and that his fellow students have nothing to offer him even when they read and discuss with him the selection he himself cannot read. Reading is only one way of learning. We should utilize others even while we apply procedures to provide students with successful reading experiences appropriate to their levels of competence.

When students' confidence is buoyed by repeated successes in this guided experience, it is possible for them to use this confidence and build a degree of independence. After students use the guide to read about the Pilgrims, for example, applying the cause/effect pattern, they are ready to use the organizational pattern within a less controlling structure. The next time an assigned selection requires reading for a cause/effect relationship, the teacher will remind his students of how they read the selection on the Pilgrims. Then, rather than distributing a guide of the type previously examined, the teacher will give oral directions to the students, assigning each group in the class the task of determining specific causes or effects or both. The task assigned to each group is adjusted to its competence, but is built on the previous experience the group has had with the organizational pattern. If some students still need it, the teacher will identify specific places in the text where they can locate the assigned cause/effect relationships. The idea is to provide guidance as long as necessary for students to gain sufficient confidence and skill to function independently.

The following reading guide illustrates how another teacher guided his

eleven grade honor students in history in the use of the cause/effect as
they read a rather complicated selection from their history text. In previous
years with comparable groups, the teacher had assumed that the students
could read the text with no difficulty—but he always had to lecture on the
content because they failed to grasp the significant ideas from their reading. The teacher was correct in his assumption that the students could
read well. They scored well on standardized reading tests; they had no
trouble reading at the literal level of comprehension and relatively little
at the interpretive. However, they had not been guided sufficiently in the
use of the organizational patterns at the interpretive level and, as a consequence, were missing ideas contained in complicated passages.

So the teacher constructed the guide and gave it to students as homework to complete as they read the text. He discussed the cause/effect patterns and told the students they would be applying that structure as they
read the selection. The guide was to simulate the experience for them.

Each student completed the guide alone. In class the next day, students
were divided into groups. Their assignment was to compare their responses
and, where they had differences, attempt to resolve them. And there were
differences.

When the lively discussion was over, the teacher focused his comments
only on those items the students were having difficulty resolving. He summarized and then moved on to the next unit. His lecture from previous
years was unnecessary. His students had learned the content and apparently
they had learned how to apply the cause/effect organizational pattern
where it was appropriate to do so.

Now, consider the guide this teacher prepared. The content it treats is
the interaction between the British and the Americans prior to the Revolutionary War. This interaction contributed to the state of war. The teacher
wanted students to see how this inexorable movement toward war, the
escalation of the 1770's, actually took place.

READING GUIDE: CAUSE AND EFFECT

Bragdon and McCutchen, Chapter II, "The Road to Revolution"

III. CAUSE AND EFFECT: In history it is very difficult to be sure that
one event is the direct cause or effect of another. We can, however,
by applying common sense to a series of events, at least tentatively
conclude that one has helped cause another. In the following two lists,
place the letter or number representing a probable *cause* in the blank
beside the appropriate *result*. More than one cause may be indicated
for a result; one cause may be important to several results. You will

quickly notice that a result may in turn become a cause of something else. (p. 36–46) Dotted lines are guides to time periods. Some items may be irrelevent or false. Look anywhere in the opposite column for causes of actions or policies, they are not necessarily found within the same dotted lines.

American actions or policies	British actions or policies
_____ 1. American custom of smuggling, 1760's.	_____ a. Writs of Assistance, 1763.
	_____ b. End of Salutary Neglect.
_____ 2. Failure of Americans to fully support French and Indian War.	_____ c. Sugar Act of 1764, with duties to be paid in gold and silver.
_____ 3. Peace of Paris, 1763.	_____ d. Trials in Admiralty Courts without juries.
_____ 4. High cost to Britain of administering the colonies.	_____ e. Proclamation of 1763.
_____ 5. American desire to settle the Ohio Valley.	_____ f. Stamp Act, fees to be paid in gold and silver.
_____ 6. Shortage of gold and silver in the colonies.	_____ g. Stationing of 10,000 British troops in America.
	_____ h. Lord Grenville appointed Minister of Finance.

. . . .

_____ 7. Americans violated law in settling West of the Appalachians.	_____ i. Fights new war with France in Europe.
	_____ j. Townshend duties.
_____ 8. Boycott of British goods, 1865.	_____ k. British governors and judges to be paid from British revenue.
_____ 9. Continued smuggling, 1864.	
_____ 10. Colonial alliance with Spain.	_____ l. Suspension of colonial legislatures of New York and Massachusetts.
_____ 11. Formal protests to Britain by colonial legislatures.	_____ m. Repeal of the Stamp Act and passage of Declaratory Act.
_____ 12. Cooperation of nine colonies at Stamp Act Congress, 1765.	_____ n. Boycott of American goods.
_____ 13. Violence and riots, 1765.	

The left column lists American actions or policies; the right column lists British actions or policies. Looking at the upper left column, we see that the Americans took certain actions which can be identified as causes; looking at the upper right column, we see that the British reacted (or we identify effects) to the Americans' actions. But we know from history that the

Americans did not quit after the British reacted. They reacted to the British reaction to the Americans' action; thus the British "effects" became causes; so one matches the items in the lower left column to the items in the upper right. And reactions continued: the Americans' reactions (effects) to the British reactions (cause and also effect) to the Americans' actions (cause) in turn became causes for subsequent British reaction (effects), and so on through the entire selection. The original guide contains another page.

The teacher inserted items, suited to the students' ability, that were somewhat related but didn't really belong; and the students were to discard them. Also, the students could draw from any item in the opposite column when relating effects to causes. This latitude encouraged more critical and creative thinking; developed greater discrimination in reading and reasoning; provided greater excitement and probing and value in the group discussions. By selecting carefully the items to be incorporated in the guide and by structuring the guide so that it emphasized the concepts to be learned as well as the organizational pattern to be applied to the expository material, the teacher taught content and reading simultaneously.

The purpose of this guide was to simulate the complex organizational pattern. By manipulating the components of the pattern—assembling it, as it were—students developed competence with the pattern.

Note that there are no asterisks to signal items. Students were all competent readers, at least at the literal level, and were of comparable ability. This being true, it was not necessary to differentiate items for them. The subtle differences present among the students in terms of how they applied their ability was provided for in the very nature of the items in the guide. There was sufficient abstraction in the items so each student could apply, to the extent of his desire, the combination of ability and insight at his command. And it allowed the students to learn from one another because many students had insights that others did not have but discovered through the group discussions.

An English teacher designed the following guide for her students to use as they read a short story. She was teaching them the internal structure of the genre and gave them the guide to help them develop a feeling for it as they read. After they responded individually to the guide, they were to work together in groups, to resolve differences.

Note the level of sophistication of this material. It assumes reading skill at the literal and interpretive levels. The purpose is to simulate the organizational pattern of the genre. Students analyze what they read in reference to this structure and identify parts of the story that fit into various aspects of the genre.

Discussion of their work reinforces the simulation and the sensitivity to the internal organization of the short story. There is also a simultaneous appreciation and understanding of the story itself—a perception of the author's message as well as his craft.

READING GUIDE

Recognizing Plot: *Adventures in Appreciation,* Harcourt, "The Quiet Man"

SKILLS GUIDE—Grade 10

DIRECTIONS   Using the chart and the information on the chart, write the names of the parts of the plot on the dotted lines. Then read carefully the list of sentences taken from the story. Each sentence fits under a part of the plot on the diagram, but the sentences are not in correct order. Write the sentence numbers on the solid short lines, being sure to put them under the correct part of the plot. Try to put the sentences (as closely as possible) in chronological order.

The *exposition* is the beginning. It explains all that is necessary to understand the following action (setting, mood, main character, point of view, background).

The *complication* is that part which presents the problem or conflict implied in the beginning situation.

The *turning point* or crisis is that part in which the story or action takes a decisive turn.

The *climax* is the point of highest emotional intensity, the point of highest suspense.

The *resolution* is where the author unravels the complication and thus provides answers to the main question.

1. One evening before a market day, Ellen spoke to her husband: "Has Big Liam paid you my dowry yet, Shawn?"
2. A woman, loving her husband, may or may not be proud of him, but she will fight like a tiger if anyone, barring herself, belittles him.
3. Then he would smile to himself—a pitying smile—thinking of the poor devils, with dreams of fortune luring them, going out to sweat in Ironville, or to stand in a breadline.
4. Shawn Kelvin came home and found that he was the last of the Kelvins, and that the farm of his forefathers had added its few acres to that ranch of Big Liam O'Grady of Moyvalla.
5. And forthwith, Shawn Kelvin, with one easy sweep, threw the crumpled ball of notes into the heart of the flame.

6. "Mother of God!" she cried. "The trouble I had to make a man of him?"

7. Shawn Kelvin, a blithe young lad of twenty, went to the States to seek his fortune.

8. "It is a great pity that the father of my son is a Kelvin and a coward."

9. Shawn set out to demolish his enemy in the briefest space of time, and it took him five minutes to do it.

10. He realized that he was at the fork of life and a finger pointed unmistakably.

11. A quiet man under middle size, with strong shoulders, and deep-set blue eyes below brows darker than his dark hair—that was Shawn Kelvin.

12. But Big Liam O'Grady, for all his resolute promptness, did not win Kathy Carey to wife.

13. "Ask me again, Shawneen," he finished. . . .

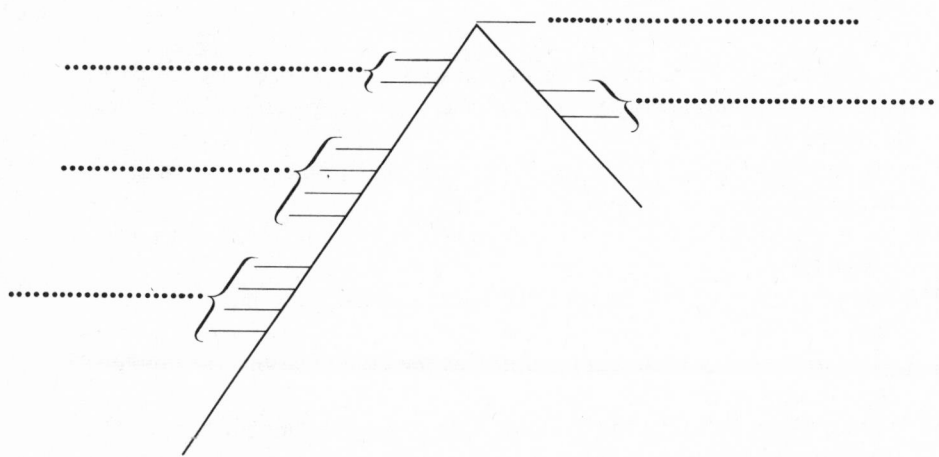

So that you might experience the use of a guide that simulates one of the organizational patterns found in expository material, the following is provided.

You are to read for comparison. Follow directions carefully. For part I, complete the guide as you read the editorial. Work alone on each part first before discussing it with your colleagues. The purpose of your discussion should be to resolve differences in your responses.

NEW YORK TIMES, APRIL 3, 1968   *Washington: A Time to Act or a*
Time to Wait? by James Reston.

COMPARISON

Part I

Directions: Listed below are sets of comparisons. Check each set you can
find in the editorial. Some are literal and some interpretive.

_____ 1. Nixon / Kennedy
_____ 2. Nixon / Kennedy / Humphrey
_____ 3. Knowledge in July / knowledge in November
_____ 4. Today's character / yesterday's reputation
_____ 5. Understanding at convention time / understanding at election
time.
_____ 6. Wit, haircuts, and delegation strength / ability to unify and
govern.
_____ 7. Questions producing answers / answers producing questions
_____ 8. Office seeking / office holding
_____ 9. Loyalty to man / fidelity to conscience.
_____10. Time brings knowledge / time brings understanding
_____11. Youth / middle age / old age
_____12. Benefits of defeat / disadvantages of victory

READING SELECTION

Washington: A Time to Act or a Time to Wait?

By James Reston

WASHINGTON, April 2—You can hardly pick up a newspaper these days
without reading that Richard Nixon and Robert Kennedy are the main survivors
and beneficiaries of Lyndon Johnson's latest explosion. Nixon, so the story goes,
now has the Republican nomination "sewed up" and Kennedy has the organization and the money to win on the Democratic side, and it may be so.
Nevertheless, the main lesson of the campaign so far is that both prophets and
voters should beware. We are passing through a period of profound intellectual
and political revision. Every week seems to bring some new surprise that
changes the question before the people, and we still do not have the whole cast
of characters.

The Main Question

In this situation it is hard enough to come up with the main question, let alone the answers. The candidates and parties have their own special problems and interests, but the overriding question for most voters is who can unify and govern this country from 1969 to 1973.

This is not the same as who has power among Southern delegates and what do you think of McCarthy's wit or Kennedy's haircut? The situation is changing with bewildering rapidity. We don't know at the moment whether we will need next year a President who can run a war or end a war, or one who can quell a rebellion at home or get the Congress to transfer appropriations from Vietnam to the cities. Maybe we won't know this in July or even November, but we'll know more than we do now.

Therefore, this is a time for a little watchful and judicious stalling. For one thing, all we have now are the names and numbers of some of the players. The nation is just getting acquainted with Senator McCarthy. It has a television impression of Vice President Humphrey, Richard Nixon, Nelson Rockefeller and Robert Kennedy, and very definite ideas about their reputations.

But the pictures in the American mind about these men could be very misleading. They are stereotypes out of the past. The reality of today is not the same as the reputation of yesterday. Time has not changed all the rest of us, and not affected Humphrey, Nixon, Rockefeller, Kennedy and McCarthy.

Middle age has been good to Nixon. Defeat, which the professional politicians hold against him politically, has been good for him personally. He is a much wiser and more tolerant man. Victory in the 1964 election, according to the conventional wisdom, has corrupted Hubert Humphrey and forced him to choose between loyalty to Lyndon Johnson and fidelity to his own conscience and beliefs, and there is something to this, but he too has come out of the struggle a wiser, if sadder man, and may very well be the best we have, regardless of what the polls and gossips say.

The Time Changes

The point is that we simply do not know the true quality of any of these men at this critical moment in our history. Kennedy is 42, McCarthy 52, Nixon 55, Humphrey 56, Rockefeller 59. All of them are different from what they were when their reputations were formed, some better, maybe some worse. It is almost impossible, for example, for men like Humphrey, Nixon and Kennedy not to be changed and improved and even ennobled by their proximity to the majesty of the White House, so there is a case to be made for looking at them anew—as they are now and not as we assume them to be out of the past.

The Uses of Adversity

This is what the long Presidential election campaign is for. If anything justifies its length, its expense, its punishment of the human mind and body, this is it. In the savage struggle, the endless exhausting travel, the chaotic press conferences, the dramatic speeches in howling halls and the pitiless questioning before the television lights, we find out something about the candidates involved.

It is almost a form of torture and there must be a better way to do it, but it does show us how the candidates are now, rather than how they were at some other day in the past. The pressure is almost unendurable, but so is the pressure in the White House.

Accordingly, this may very well be a time to wait and watch. In the next few months we will have a clearer picture of the world of the future and of the men who are available to help guide it.

READING GUIDE

Part II

Directions: Listed below are several statements which may or may not reflect applications of the comparisons you identified in part I of this guide. Write the numbers of comparisons you selected from part I on the lettered line before those items to which you believe they apply. Some lines may have more than one number; others may have none.

_____A. Political descendency of one person may trigger political ascendency for others.

_____B. Candidates should be selected on substantive views, not superficial characteristics.

_____C. People do not necessarily understand what they know.

_____D. Age is a critical issue to all political candidates.

_____E. Fidelity to conscience precludes fidelity to associates.

_____F. A man is a new person each day he lives and political candidates should be selected with this in mind.

_____G. Greatness can be "catching."

_____H. There are issues for which one knows neither what to ask nor how to answer.

_____ I. Pragmatic politics sometimes dictates allegiance to men rather than to conscience.

The Appendix contains several other illustrative guides for developing awareness and skill in the use of various organizational patterns. It is important to keep in mind that these are not tests; they are guides.

Organization Patterns and Guides for Levels of Comprehension

It is useful to know the organizational pattern inherent in a reading selection before beginning to develop reading guides for levels of comprehension. Knowing the pattern, we can create items for the literal level guide, focusing on information which contributes to the overall concept. In the knowledge of the pattern, we have some objective means of selecting information for students to focus on when they determine "what the author says." It is this information, then, that is related within the pattern to develop the intrinsic concepts.

Without knowledge of the pattern, we create random items for the literal level that may or may not contribute to the overall concept. With knowledge of the pattern, we create items that not only focus on information contributing to the overall concept but also set the stage for developing an awareness of the process by which the concepts are formed. Thus, we make certain that process is not separated from content.

Similarly, awareness of patterns gives us a criterion by which to create items for the interpretive level of comprehension. The items in the guide should state relationships that occur among bits of information within the selection. And these relationships occur, as stated above, in one of the various patterns. As the student responds to these items he is functionally developing a sensitivity to the pattern, even though the pattern has not been labeled.

Students need not be aware of patterns in order to respond to guides that structure their response at various levels of comprehension. The patterns are exercised functionally. Nevertheless, the *teachers* need to be aware of patterns in order to create the guides for levels of comprehension. Patterns provide criteria for the creation of items for the guides for levels; they preclude arbitrary items that neither provide focus on important concepts nor allow the functional exercise of patterns.

READING SKILLS

As discussed on page 105, we find organizational patterns within levels of comprehension. Can we also find specific reading skills that "stand alone" within levels of comprehension and/or within organizational patterns?

When we complete the chart on pages 123–127 and study its explication, we find very few skills that "stand alone" to be treated in isolation. Nevertheless we find a general tendency to discuss the teaching of reading skills as though each were a separate entity and could be taught in isolation from all others. For example, "interpretation" is often "taught" as though it were a unitary skill. Actually it is a generic term which covers several cognitive processes: inference, drawing conclusions, deducing, evaluating, and so on. Therefore, we should not teach "interpretation" as though it were a separate entity.

In teaching reading, the practice usually is to focus on so-called reading skills first, then on organizational patterns. Rarely, if ever, are "levels of comprehension" stressed, but where they are, they follow skills and patterns.

Because "levels" provide the "Gestalt," and patterns and skills are embodied therein, it is more useful to students to start with levels than skills.

Levels of comprehension allow students to read without becoming overly concerned with nomenclature and the various combinations of skills that function when they read. Working on levels builds students' confidence.

Sometimes we so burden students with an analysis of how they function that they falter just from the conscious effort to keep all of the parts working. One is reminded of the poem:

> The centipede was happy quite
> Until the toad in fun
> Said, "Pray, which leg goes after which?"
> And worked her mind to such a pitch,
> She lay distracted in the ditch
> Considering how to run.

Organizational patterns require more precision than levels of comprehension, but students are ready for them after they have developed confidence and are comfortable with levels. And the organizational patterns are relatively "clean." That is, it isn't necessary to keep in mind a variety of special terms for special skills. The straightforwardness of the patterns adds to students' confidence.

Then students are ready for work on specific skills. We find that the skills we can treat in isolation are either those that precede functioning at the literal level of comprehension or those appropriate to the interpretive level. Basic word analysis skills (or decoding skills) can be, and are, treated in isolation. For students learning how to decode words, there is need for work on letter sounds, on consonant blends, on grapheme-phoneme correspondence. But such emphasis, *except* where appropriate in vocabulary development as discussed in chapter 8, is reserved for early grades in school and for remedial instruction in later grades. This type of instruction is not the responsibility of the content teacher.

To identify the separate reading skills embodied in the interpretive level, it is useful to recall how organizational patterns are identified within that level. We study the relationships among specific details we have pulled together to form intrinsic concepts, and we label that relationship with a term describing its structure: cause/effect, time order, and so on.

We can probe somewhat deeper into those relationships to determine more precisely what cognitive processes are involved: inference; evaluation of argument; deduction; drawing conclusions, and so forth. These "skills" are descriptive of the relationships occurring within the organizational patterns which—in turn—are a description of the relationships occurring within the interpretive level of comprehension. For example, we might identify a cause/effect pattern within the interpretive level and on close examination discover that the cause/effect relationship is only implied, not directly stated. Therefore, we could emphasize inference rather than cause/effect pattern on the interpretive level of comprehension.

It should be clear that we could read for cause/effect, in this case, without having precise knowledge of how to read inferentially, even as we could read at the interpretive level of comprehension without having precise knowledge of the cause/effect organizational pattern.

We guide students' development of these specific skills in the same way we guide the development of proficiency at the interpretive level of comprehension. For example, the reading selection may be such that several conclusions should be drawn. As part of the lesson structure, the teacher discusses with the students how one draws a conclusion: one looks for logical relationships between or among specific ideas; he then formulates a statement which represents that relationship.

If the students have sufficient confidence in working at the interpretive level of comprehension so that they can more closely analyze what they are doing and without being confused by the nomenclature. We can construct a guide for them to use. Starting at a simple level, the guide might have students look for conclusions that the author himself draws, based on information he gives in his text. Then, at a more sophisticated level, students draw their own conclusions based on information the author gives in his selection. In either case, we do not guide students in the use of the skill merely by assigning them to "read the selection and list the conclusions the author draws" or "read the selection and list all of the conclusions you can draw from what the author states about _____." This is testing, not guiding.

A guide presents a list of statements to the students, some of which are conclusions the author has drawn (if the students are working on that level of sophistication). They read the alternatives, then read the selection with the alternatives in mind and identify which of the alternatives are conclusions drawn by the author. This gives students a mind set and an awareness of how to read for this purpose.

With this experience reinforced many times, students learn to conjure up alternatives out of their own experience in the subject and see which of them the author settles on in his writing. Again, this is a type of simulator which gives students a feeling for a specific skill. Whether students are reading for inference, deduction, recognition of assumption, evaluation of argument, or drawing conclusion, the procedure is the same.

Though discussed in reference to the interpretive level, it should be clear that these skills are found also within the applied level. As previously pointed out, we search for relationships to form extrinsic concepts. We can perceive the organizational patterns within those relationships, labeling them accordingly. Also, we can determine more precise cognitive processes (skills) involved in these relationships: inference, deduction, and so on. Development of these skills is guided in the same manner as discussed above.

To summarize, one gives labels for special skills *after* students become familiar with the process involved in the skill. This is the inductive principle which underlies the purpose in moving from levels, to patterns, to skills rather than the reverse.

TRANSFORMATION

The casual reader might assume that the heading for this section is introducing a discussion of "transfer." He would be wrong. Transfer makes possible a generalized use of knowledge and skills and creates greater economy in learning. As stated by Smith and Dechant, "No educator questions the importance of transfer of learning. If transfer were not possible, the learner would have to acquire new behavior for each new situation. . . . Transfer . . . is the application of our previous learnings to our current problems." [4]

Transfer is an important factor in reading instruction. Skills learned in reading classes at the elementary level are applied in other subjects at the elementary and secondary levels.

There seems to be some question, however, as to whether certain skills are transferable. Untold hours have been spent by well-intentioned teachers compiling lists of reading skills supposedly unique to each of the subject areas taught in schools. They believe some skills to be peculiar only to specific subjects and appropriate to no other. Therefore, there must be direct teaching of these skills in the appropriate courses. They compile lists of these skills presumably unique, or nearly so, to each content area to simplify the content teacher's task. If the teacher has available the list of skills appropriate to his subject, he can better meet his responsibility to teach them.

There is at least the implied belief that skills are transferred within subject areas, as students progress from grade to grade, but not among subjects within grades because of their uniqueness.

Given below is a compilation of skills suggested by many authors of professional texts on reading, many curriculum guides on reading instruction in content areas, and many journal articles. This process of examining lists of skills, coupled with experience in directing programs for teaching reading skills through content areas in secondary and elementary schools, causes serious doubt that each subject area has the considerable number of skills unique to itself, as has been supposed. Examination of these lists leads to the conclusion that uniqueness lies in semantics rather than in skills; different authors use different names for the same process. Go down the list of skills on this chart and see how many you can identify as being unique to one or even two areas. You will find very few.

[4] Henry P. Smith and Emerald V. Dechant, *Psychology in Teaching Reading* (Englewood Cliffs: Prentice-Hall, Inc., 1961), p. 68.

This chart is organized so one can classify the skills in some manner. Wherever possible, qualifiers included in the original lists were omitted. For example, "drawing conclusions" was shortened to "conclusions" and "reading to follow directions" was shortened to "following directions," and so forth. This was done so one could react with more objectivity to the categories included for classifying each item in the chart.

As you have time, complete this chart according to your own judgment and experience. The "areas" are social studies, English, math, science; "levels" refer to literal (1), interpretive (2), and applied (3); "organizational pattern" and "separate skill" were discussed above; "condition" refers to factors such as attitude, ability, predisposition, desire, interest; "category" refers to items of such breadth that several others are encompassed by them; "relationship to reading act" is to identify when the skill or process mainly functions—before (pre), during, or post (after) the reading act; "conglomerate" refers to items that are combinations of several other factors.

Go through the list and place check marks under each heading, as you believe it to be the case, for each item in the list. Based on previous discussions you perhaps would view "vocabulary" as a category; "interpretation" as a conglomerate. You may not find anything at all for "condition."

You may wish to read on and work on the chart over a period of time. After it is completed, you will find it valuable to compare your response with your colleagues'.

Uniqueness of each subject lies in the nature of the content and the materials used in each area, not in the skills applied to the materials. Skills required in one subject are generally appropriate to other subjects.

Therefore, if there is no uniqueness precluding transfer, presumably transfer does serve the development of reading skills in all content areas. This is almost (but not quite) true; almost, because the essential factor is unaccounted for—*transformation.*

Transformation is the adaptation of a skill or process to meet the demands of material peculiar to a content area. The need for this adaptation is clear when we accept the view that reading skills required in one subject are generally appropriate to all other subjects.

Does this mean that compiling lists of skills peculiar to each subject area is a waste of time? Yes, it means precisely that. *Very few* skills are unique to only one area. A more valuable exercise is to consider how to adapt skills which are common to all areas (and this appears to include most of the reading skills) so they suit the peculiarities of each subject. The concept of transformation more clearly delineates the responsibility of each content teacher for teaching his students how to read his subject matter. We must be aware, however, that there are two kinds of transformation: horizontal and vertical.

Factors	Areas				Level			Org. Pat.	Sep. Skill	Condi-tion *	Cate-gory	Rel. to Reading Act			Conglom-erate **	Other
	SS	E	M	SC	1	2	3					Pre.	During	Post		
1. vocabulary																
2. word analysis																
3. word recognition																
4. word meaning																
5. phonetic analysis																
6. structural analysis																
7. contextual analysis																
8. denotation																
9. connotation																
10. synonyms																
11. homonyms																
12. antonyms																
13. locational skills																
14. following directions																
15. use of dictionary																
16. use of maps																
17. use of charts																
18. use of graphs																
19. use of diagrams																
20. use of tables																
21. use of symbols																
22. use of illustration																

Factors	Areas				Level			Org. Pat.	Sep. Skill	Condi-tion *	Cate-gory	Rel. to Reading Act			Conglom-erate **	Other
	SS	E	M	SC	1	2	3					Pre.	During	Post		
23. use of pictures																
24. use of atlases																
25. use of globes																
26. use of numbers																
27. use of table of contents																
28. use of index																
29. use of appendix																
30. use of cross references																
31. use of abbreviation																
32. use of symbols																
33. critical analysis																
34. fact vs opinion																
35. explanations																
36. interpretations																
37. inferences																
38. conclusions																
39. arguments																
40. assumptions																
41. relationships																
42. generalizations																
43. judgments																

Factors	Areas				Level			Org. Pat.	Sep. Skill	Condition*	Category	Rel. to Reading Act			Conglomerate**	Other
	SS	E	M	SC	1	2	3					Pre.	During	Post		
44. propaganda																
45. problem solving																
46. inconsistencies																
47. relevancy																
48. authenticity																
49. validity																
50. importance																
51. evaluate																
52. concept development																
53. concept application																
54. bias																
55. prejudice																
56. prediction																
57. author's purpose																
58. point of view																
59. detail/fact																
60. reader's purpose																
61. recall																
62. creative reading																
63. synthesize																
64. imagery																
65. identification																

Factors	Areas				Level			Org. Pat.	Sep. Skill	Condi-tion *	Cate-gory	Rel. to Reading Act			Conglom-erate **	Other
	SS	E	M	SC	1	2	3					Pre.	During	Post		
66. plot																
67. theme																
68. character																
69. setting																
70. style																
71. tone																
72. allusions																
73. mood																
74. rhythm																
75. visualize																
76. sensory impression																
77. human values																
78. visualization																
79. generalize																
80. application																
81. symbolism																
82. figurative language																
83. organization																
84. main idea/detail																
85. cause/effect																
86. comparison/contrast																
87. time order																

Factors	Areas				Level			Org. Pat.	Sep. Skill	Condition *	Category	Rel. to Reading Act			Conglomerate **	Other
	SS	E	M	SC	1	2	3					Pre.	During	Post		
88. enumerative order																
89. outlining																
90. notetaking																
91. paraphrasing																
92. summarize																
93. rate																
94. flexibility																
95. preview																
96. survey																
97. skim																
98. scan																
99. accuracy																

* Factors such as attitude, ability, predisposition, desire, interest.
** Combinations of several factors.

Horizontal transformation is adapting a given skill as one moves from subject to subject within the same grade, adapting it to meet the demands of reading matter in each of the subjects. Though the same skill is applied, it has to be adapted because of the uniqueness of the material in each area. This is the significant point: it is not the skill that is unique, but the material to be studied. Because a different set of ideas, a different set of values, a different vocabulary are fed into this skill for each of the areas, students must adapt the process to meet the peculiarities of each subject.

For example, students must be able to handle one of the organizational patterns referred to previously—cause and effect. As is evident by examining the following paragraphs, we read for cause and effect one way in science, another in math, another in social studies, and another in literature.

READING SELECTION

Cause and Effect: Science

You know that an electric bell rings when you press down on a push button. The push button is a kind of switch. When you push it, it closes the circuit. Current flows through the wires, and the bell rings. It keeps ringing as long as you hold the push button down. It does not stop until you take your finger off the button. Then the circuit is opened, and the current no longer flows through the bell. The contact point and the spring work like a switch inside the bell. When the spring touches the contact point, the switch is closed. If you push the button now, current flows through the electromagnet, the armature is pulled toward the magnet and the hammer strikes the gong.

Reprinted by permission of the publisher from Glenn O. Blough, J. Stanley Marshall, James B. Bailey, Wilbur L. Beauchamp, *Science is Adventure* (Chicago: Scott, Foresman & Company, 1965), pp. 120–21. Copyright © 1966, 1965 by the publisher.

READING SELECTION

Cause and Effect: Mathematics

Since some rational numbers are whole numbers, the operations (addition, subtraction, multiplication, and division) with rational numbers are much like operations with whole numbers. . . .

Reprinted by permission of the publisher from Robert E. Eicholz and others, *Elementary School Mathematics, Book 5* (Menlo Park, Calif.: Addison-Wesley, copyright © 1964, 1968), pp. 238–39.

Since the whole numbers are rational numbers, the use of objects should also help you think about addition and subtraction of rational numbers.

READING SELECTION

Cause and Effect: Social Studies

The ruler ("khedive") of Egypt engaged in extravagant expenditures on public works and private pleasures. Needing money, he was forced to sell his Suez Canal stock to Britain and to borrow huge sums at interest rates as high as twenty-five per cent. His inability to pay his debts led to British and French interferences in Egypt's government. This brought about a nationalistic revolt in 1882. The French withdrew, but Britain suppressed the revolt and stationed British advisers and troops in Egypt. From 1883 to 1907, British Lord Cromer, who was in virtual control of Egypt, introduced many financial, legal, and other reforms. Together, the British and the Egyptians in 1898 suppressed a revolt in the Sudan, just south of Egypt, and thereafter maintained joint control there. This region then became known as the "Anglo-Egyptian Sudan."

Reprinted by permission of the publisher from Nathaniel Platt and Muriel Drummond, *Our World Through the Ages,* 3rd Ed. (Englewood Cliffs, N.J.: Prentice-Hall, Inc., © 1967), p. 461.

READING SELECTION

Cause and Effect: Literature

But the Pandora had been given the gift of curiosity. The more Epimetheus urged her to stay away from the box, the stronger became her desire to know what was in it. Wherever she went, whatever she did, the box was forever in her mind. At last the desire to open it was so great that she was no longer happy. She was so curious about what the box contained that she did nothing but sit in front of it hour after hour.

The organizational pattern, the process, is the same but idea sets are different in each. As the student moves from subject to subject, he must consciously adapt the skill to suit the set of ideas peculiar to each area. This is not accomplished by depending on transfer. It must be taught as transformation process. And the place where this can be taught effectively is in each classroom, by content teachers using methods and materials discussed in this text, as students move from subject to subject.

Reprinted by permission of the publisher from David H. Russell, Constance M. McCullough, Doris Gates, "Pandora," *Travels to Treasure* (Boston: Ginn and Company, 1961), pp. 305–6.

Vertical Transformation

There is another type of transformation, the vertical. As students progress through the grades, the concepts and materials which they are required to handle increase in sophistication at each grade level. As a student moves from grade to grade within a subject, he must be able to adapt his skills to handle the increased sophistication of materials to which his skills are applied.

To illustrate vertical transformation, consider again the use of the cause/effect organizational pattern. Whether applied to a simple or a complex set of materials in a content area, the process or the relationship set is the same. However, because the concept load is so much more sophisticated in the one, an adaptation in the skill or process is necessary in order to handle the material adequately. The two guides on pages 107 and 111 reflect the concept of vertical transformation quite clearly. Low-achieving students in grade seven were guided in their use of the cause/effect pattern as they read about the Pilgrims. Honors students in eleventh grade history were guided in their use of the cause/effect pattern as they read about events leading to the Revolutionary War. The process is the same; but the levels of sophistication apparent in each are quite different. A student moving from low-achieving status, or average, or honor in grade seven to low-achieving status, or average, or honor in grade eleven must learn how to adapt his skills to meet the increased sophistication required by the materials at each successive grade level. This is vertical transformation.

Neither vertical nor horizontal transformation can be assumed, whether applied to levels of comprehension, organizational patterns, or specific skills. Students at all levels of ability need to be shown how to adapt skills, must learn how it feels to make necessary modifications and adjustments as required by various subjects and grade levels.

SUMMARY

Students are successful readers when they can readily transform a repertoire of skills to meet the demands of various content areas and levels of sophistication. The first part of that repertoire is an awareness of levels of comprehension and how to function at each, according to one's competence. The inductive procedure of initially emphasizing the levels gives students the feeling of success, according to their needs, without burdening them with unnecessary nomenclature.

When secure in their use of levels of comprehension, students are able to consider the organizational patterns peculiar to expository material and/or literary genre. They learn to transform the patterns (a more difficult task than transforming the levels of comprehension), as they move from subject to subject and grade to grade. They become aware that the relationships they perceived in the interpretive and applied levels of comprehension were very much the same as the relationships they perceive when applying the organizational patterns. Then they discover that organizational patterns exist within the levels of comprehension! They were using them successfully before they knew what they were called. This discovery adds to their confidence.

In time, the students add specific skills to their repertoire and learn how to transform them as they move from subject to subject. They discover that the patterns embody certain skills. And the confidence they have gained by their success with levels of comprehension and patterns of organization encourage them to use the specific skills as appropriate.

Throughout their entire learning experience, students are guided by the teacher. The teacher does not assume they know what they came to him to learn. He uses reading guides to develop their understanding of levels of comprehension, organizational patterns, and specific skills. And because these guides relate to their required textbooks, they learn the content of the course while they learn how to read the material.

Teachers are aware that some students may never progress beyond successful use of levels of comprehension; other students may develop skill in using organizational patterns successfully and adapt them to the needs of each subject; some others might also be successful in the use and transformation of specific skills; but the teacher doesn't expect the same performance from every student. At least, all students are able to function at one of the levels of comprehension, so that each can contribute to class and group discussions and, thereby, be in a better frame of mind to learn from other students in the class.

When there is no guiding structure, the students are abandoned to their own resourcefulness to find a way to discover the content (a feat accomplished by many, but in an unnecessarily inefficient manner). How much better for students to expend energy *using* skills to explore content rather than *discovering* the skills by which the content eventually will be explored. Although we should fear too much structure, we should also fear the lack of it.[5]

REACTION GUIDE

Directions: Several analogies follow. Check those you believe reflect directly or inferentially the content of this chapter. Compare your response with your colleagues' and discuss how to resolve your differences.

[5] Roger Cartwright, "Promoting Student Thinking," *Journal of Educational Sociology* (September, 1962), pp. 33–41.

_____ 1. Levels are to patterns as patterns are to skills.

_____ 2. Skills are to patterns as patterns are to skills.

_____ 3. Skills are to levels as patterns are to skills.

_____ 4. Skills are to levels as skills are to patterns.

_____ 5. Cause-effect is to patterns as inference is to skills.

_____ 6. Relationships are to levels as processes are to patterns.

_____ 7. Vertical transformation is to grades as horizontal transformation is to subjects.

_____ 8. Structure is to genre as skills are to subjects.

_____ 9. Vertical transformation is to horizontal as subjects are to grades.

_____10. External structure is to patterns as skills are to subjects.

7

REASONING BEYOND READING

VOCABULARY

Be mindful of the following important terms as you read this chapter:
- — intuitive leap
- — heuristic concept
- — critical reasoning
- — creative reasoning

IDEA DIRECTION

Instruction in content areas includes reasoning as well as reading. This chapter does not suggest a dichotomy but does explore ways in which there can be "reasoning beyond reading."

READING DIRECTION

You should read to find interrelationships between the heuristic process and reasoning guides.

There are many students who read too well for their own good in most schools. They have no apparent reading difficulty in their subjects. They can discuss with good understanding what the authors presented in their writings. They see relationships between the content of their assignment and other reading they have done or various experiences they have had related to the topic.

Who, in their right minds, would ever consider these students to be in need of reading instruction? Probably no one. Then why the observation that they are reading too well for their own good? This implies that they need something they won't get because teachers think they already have it.

This statement is not really paradoxical. Many students *are* neglected because of their competence. They do read too well for their own good, given the criteria usually applied to select those who need assistance. In spite of their apparent reading competence, most of these students can benefit from instruction in reasoning. Many do not use their full potential because they have not learned how to apply their reasoning power creatively nor how to build and elaborate on concepts creatively. Teachers are satisfied with their performance, as compared with the performance of students who experience difficulty in understanding what they read, and do not see the considerable gap between their performance and their ability to perform. Not seeing the discrepancy, they do nothing to rectify it. Those students who do reach outstanding levels of achievement often do so by chance rather than by design. Somehow they evolve systems of study and creative application of their powers that allow them to function with their full potential. But thousands more brilliant students would realize their potential if instructional programs in content areas were designed to show them how to use that potential to the maximum.

This observation need not be limited to the unusually brilliant student. Many so-called average students also suffer from apparent competence. They have no obvious problem with their reading. They can identify what the authors say and can recite in class, responding to factual and interpretive questions. Why should the teacher be concerned about their reading? Perhaps he shouldn't; but what about their reasoning? Are these students using their full potential any more than the brilliant and gifted students discussed above? Probably not. And they are less able to evolve systems of study independently, they are less well-off than the brighter students, but are given no more assistance. Experience and research evidence suggest that much can be done to assist these students.[1]

Reasoning Beyond Reading

There is good reason for this chapter heading, even though it may seem strange in a textbook on reading instruction. Chapters 5 and 6 discussed how to assist students in reading their textbooks successfully. The students under consideration in this chapter are able to use specific reading skills. They are aware of the organizational patterns characteristic of expository material and can use these patterns to determine the author's intent and meaning, at least to a degree that satisfies their teachers, and can also use the patterns to produce well-organized material of their own. Moreover, they are able to read with competence at the literal, interpretive, and applied levels of comprehension, producing and applying intrinsic and extrinsic concepts to the delight of their teachers and to their own sense of satisfaction.

For students who have not attained this level of competence, the instructional need and the challenge to the teacher is quite clear. For students who *have* attained this level, the challenge, if one looks for it, is rather fuzzy. The challenge is to aid students' application of reasoning beyond the reading process; beyond critical reasoning to creative; beyond analytical development of concepts to the creative, the heuristic.

Creative Reasoning

Someone defined creative thinking as the ability to study two ideas, see a relationship, and develop a third. The processes often called critical thinking skills can become creative reasoning skills if extended, in the vertical transformation process, to their most sophisticated levels.

Critical thinking skills are not to be thought of as negative processes necessarily though one can be critical negatively if he desires. Rather, they are critical in that they are analytical processes, requiring careful scrutiny of the information being considered, a close study, an intensive examination. Take the critical processes measured by the *Watson-Glaser Critical Thinking Appraisal,*[2] for example. Each one can be applied with intensity and severity: Evaluation of Argument; Recognition of Assumption; Interpretation; Inference; Deduction. The internal consistency of information and ideas is examined in all of these processes. Also, ideas and information

[1] Harold L. Herber, "Teaching Reading and Physics Simultaneously," in *Improvement of Reading Through Classroom Practice* (Newark, Del.: International Reading Association, 1964), p. 84.

[2] Goodwin Watson and Edward Maynard Glaser, *Watson-Glaser Critical Thinking Appraisal* (New York: World Book Company, 1952).

from a variety of sources are compared or contrasted with the same analytical processes. All of this is critical analysis, critical reasoning. It assumes that students have developed a background of knowledge and experience sufficient to develop criteria by which to make the critical judgments required in each of the processes. Without criteria, reasoning is neither critical nor analytical; it is emotional; and emotion without analysis can be dangerous.

Creative reasoning generates new ideas out of the analysis of old ideas.[3] Intensive analysis of ideas using critical reasoning processes saturates students with ideas and information. If conditioned by an intellectual environment that allows it, if stimulated by an atmosphere that encourages them to seek out the value in their own reasoning, students will frequently make the "intuitive leap" as Bruner [4] calls it, that is characteristic of creative reasoning. This leap can bridge the gap between two ideas, and produce a third. This leap can carry students beyond the internal substance of an idea to the external application of its principle.

In many respects the creative reasoning process is descriptive of what occurs at the third level of comprehension. There, when seeking to generate extrinsic concepts, students seek to relate the intrinsic concepts to previously learned concepts which lie outside the reading selection. The result of this relationship can be the creation of (to the student, at least) a new idea. Certainly that is creative reasoning as we have defined it. However, the function at the applied level of comprehension assumes a working through, consciously perhaps, of the previous levels. It also starts from the reading of the selection assigned and is used to relate intrinsic concepts from the assigned selection to concepts outside the selection. This places limitations on the creativity of the reasoning, since the substance to which the reasoning is applied is restricted, being an examination and application of ideas produced by others.

Creative reasoning, as we have been discussing it, need not be prompted by a given reading selection. Contrary to those who would be guided to develop skill in functioning at the third level of comprehension, students in this category do not need assistance in reading at the applied level. Their reading skill, at all levels of comprehension, has been demonstrated. The guidance they are given is not directed to an understanding of process; they really have that. Rather, they are provided with experiences that are conducive to making the "intuitive leap" and, when they do so, they have

[3] Jerome S. Bruner, "What Social Scientists Say About Having an Idea," in *The Cognitive Processes* (Englewood Cliffs: Prentice-Hall, Inc., 1964), p. 293.

[4] Jerome S. Bruner, "The Act of Discovery," in *On Knowing* (New York: Atheneum Publishers, 1965), pp. 81–97.

the excitement of sharing the product of their creative reasoning with others in the class.

Heuristic Concepts

Concepts can be produced analytically or heuristically. Webster [5] defines a concept as a "generalization drawn from particulars." The "drawing from particulars" requires analysis to perceive likenesses and differences. This is part of the process described above in the discussion of critical reasoning contrasted to creative. Intrinsic and extrinsic concepts developed at the interpretive and applied levels of comprehension are the products of, in the main, critical, analytical reasoning rather than creative.

The term "heuristic" relates to discovery or guidance, having to do with ideas valuable for research but either unproved or incapable of proof. Bruner [6] uses the somewhat redundant term: "heuristic hunch" in much the same manner that he speaks of the "intuitive leap."

Heuristic concepts generally are not the end product of long and arduous analysis, of carefully relating ideas for the purpose of drawing generalizations. Rather they are the flashes of insight, the moments of deep perception into the nature of a problem, into the possibility of a solution, into the application of a principle. Frequently they are speculative, yet action can be taken on them.

Heuristic concepts presume excellent grounding in the fundamental disciplines related to the ideas being manipulated. That is, the student is not likely to have flashes of insight related to a field about which he has no knowledge.[7] He must first be grounded in the basic understandings of the discipline before he is able to generate heuristic ramifications.

The students about whom we are speaking are those who, because of their proficiency with various elements of comprehension, organizational patterns, and skills, usually have developed sufficient understanding of the discipline that they can successfully make intuitive leaps of their own.

The conundrum facing teachers is how to promote creative reasoning, the development of heuristic concepts. The process and the product, when considered together, are both highly personal. Many times they just "happen." However, environments can be created which encourage this type of activity and, with students responding to the environment, a higher incidence of such behavior is noted.

[5] *Webster's Seventh New Collegiate Dictionary* (Springfield, Mass.: G. & C. Merriam Company, 1963).

[6] Bruner, "After John Dewey, What?" *On Knowing* (New York: Atheneum Publishers, 1965), pp. 113–31.

[7] *Ibid.*, and Ruth Strang, Constance M. McCullough, and Arthur E. Traxler, *The Improvement of Reading* (New York: McGraw-Hill Book Company, 1967), p. 354.

Functional Development

Increase of this kind of reasoning process and product can be realized through functional emphasis. That is, since the process is so highly personal, there really are no "parts" to analyze, take apart, and assemble to learn the "heuristic hunch." The need is for situations or structures in which students have opportunity to pursue their own thoughts to see where they lead; to trace an implication to its logical conclusion; to cry "eureka" when a new thought strikes them; to share and elaborate on the idea with others in the group; to be free to modify it as new insights develop. The student does not learn the process by analyzing it; rather, he exercises it in an environment conducive to such behavior and gains confidence in the process as a result.[8] Many skills contribute to the process even as many ideas contribute to the product. But these skills are exercised functionally, not directly. The environment and structure are the important elements. The former is embodied in the teacher's attitude; the latter in Reasoning Guides.

Teacher Attitude

There is a widespread belief that one cannot teach creative reasoning or the development of heuristic concepts; that the capacity for such activity is the possession of the favored few that were born with it. If this is true, then the teacher's task is not to develop such powers in his students but to present, and have students learn, the product of the creative reasoning of those favored few. Instruction, then, is reduced to information dispensing and students learn how and where to find ideas rather than how to produce them.[9]

Fortunately, there are those teachers who do not subscribe to this view. They know that students can develop competence in such intellectual activity, if they (the teachers) provide the proper classroom environment. It takes a secure teacher to allow such activity—one who is not afraid to say "I don't know": one who will accept solutions to problems that differ from his own as long as they are valid; one who will applaud a flash of insight enthusiastically even while knowing he himself likely would never have produced the idea; one who will allow students to challenge his ideas and present alternatives, and does not always feel that he has to be right; one who believes the productive pursuit of an idea is more important than coverage of a prescribed segment of the curriculum in a prescribed period

---

[8] Bruner, "The Act of Discovery."
[9] Louis E. Rathes *et al., Teaching for Thinking* (Columbus: Charles E. Merrill Books, Inc., 1967), p. 115.

of time; one who can pose stimulating, open-ended questions that produce creative reasoning rather than carefully circumscribed, closed questions that require students to guess what is in his mind. This teacher perceives at least part of his role being to get out of his students' way so that they can pursue their own ideas within the structure he provides for them and learn from one another, and so that he can learn from them, too.[10] This is not laissez-faire education, as the Reasoning Guides will point out; but it is much less restrictive than the "I lecture—you listen; I ask—you answer" kind of instruction.

Reasoning Guides

Reasoning Guides are simulators of the heuristic process. They are created situations within which students respond to ideas. The statements or questions within the guides are sufficiently broad to stimulate a variety of hunches and insights. The guides are of such a nature that students are not bound to pursue a prescribed line of reasoning. The guides provide a suitable environment within which students learn a new kind of behavior— pursuit of their own ideas rather than the teacher's.

These guides are as appropriate for less able students as for the very able. They assume ability to read (and many students with average and below average ability can read adequately). The Reasoning Guides remain the same in principle and structure; the difference is in the type of questions or statements placed in the guide. They must be related to the background of experience and understanding of the students using them; appropriate to the intellectual range of the participants; sufficiently open-ended so every student can stretch himself to the maximum; coupled with the opportunity for discussion *among students* so that they can share the benefits of their own productive reasoning and thus learn from one another; coupled with the teacher's contribution that is as open to analysis, acceptance, modification, and rejection as the students'. For immutable laws and principles, the teacher can assume an authoritative role. For pursuit of creative reasoning and the heuristic concept, who is to say that a student's view is any less valid than the teacher's?

Three Reasoning Guides follow, one each from classes in history, science, and literature. They illustrate well what teachers are able to provide for their students when they put their minds to it. Each has been used many times with students covering a wide range of propensity for the intuitive leap; but on each occasion, the result is the same: extreme excitement and enthusiasm in the pursuit of an idea. Other examples of Reasoning Guides are given in the Appendix.

As you recall the discussion of "structure within" lessons presented in

[10] *Ibid.,* p. 3.

chapter 3, you will find the construction and use of Reasoning Guides follow the principles developed in that discussion.

Reasoning Guide for Literature

A teacher of eleventh grade honors English was concerned that her students were not deriving the potential benefit from exploring Thoreau's ideas as expressed in *Walden*. Her procedure in the past had been to have the students read the work; she would then present a lecture that explored Thoreau's ideas and how they related to our society as well as his. In other words, she assigned the reading, and then explained to students what it meant to them.

As a result of exploring the use of Reasoning Guides, she concluded that she would design a guide to help students discover for themselves what, if anything, Thoreau had to say to them.

She gave this Reasoning Guide to them as homework, to be completed either as or after they read the work. She applied the various elements of the Instructional Framework, described in chapter 3. The students were proficient in reading skills but they needed assistance in the creative pursuit of their own ideas when studying basic works in the curriculum.

The students came to class with the guide completed. They were assigned to groups and their task was to compare their responses. Where they discovered differences, they were to pursue them and see if they could be, or needed to be, resolved.

The teacher said this was one of her most exciting lessons. The discussion of differences in response proved very fruitful. Students explored the relevancy of Thoreau's ideas to their own society and developed some new insights on how literature in general, and this work in particular, comments on contemporary affairs, even though the authors may have lived centuries before.

Note the format of the guide. The teacher listed significant quotes from the work, then gave students specific directions as to what they were to do with the quotes and with the statements which followed. She created open-ended reaction situations to which students were to respond. They were designed to link Thoreau's ideas with students' experiences. Hopefully, students would see relationships between the two; and, hopefully, the thought thus stimulated would be pursued to a fruitful conclusion.

A guide such as this places side by side, as it were, an author's ideas and a student's experience with the hope that he will examine the juxtaposition of these two elements and make the intuitive leap that fuses them into new insight and understanding. The guide also allows the student to create his own response to the author's ideas, using his previous, more structured, experience as an example.

REASONING GUIDE

Adventures in American Literature—Thoreau: *Walden*

Directions: Here are some sentences from *Walden:*

A. "I went to the woods because I wished to live deliberately, to front only the essential facts of life, and see if I could not learn what it had to teach, and not, when I came to die, discover that I had not lived."

B. "Our life is frittered away by detail." "Simplify, simplify."

C. "It (the nation) lives too fast."

D. "What news!" "How much more important to know what that is which was never old."

E. "When we are unhurried and wise, we perceive that only great and worthy things have any permanent and absolute existence, that petty fears and petty pleasures are but the shadow of the reality."

F. "Time is but the stream I go a-fishing in."

I. Consider the following statements. Do you think Thoreau would have approved of them? In Column A answer *yes* or *no*.

II. In Column B write the letter indicating the quotation of Thoreau which you considered in deciding your answer.

III. For No. 10, write an original statement which you think Thoreau would have liked. This should be based on E.

A	B	
_____	_____	1. I have to stay up to listen to the 11 o'clock news.
_____	_____	2. I am going to give these extra hats to my cousin.
_____	_____	3. I have to attend three meetings today.
_____	_____	4. I'd rather take the side roads than the Thruway.
_____	_____	5. I have all the time in the world to watch the sunset.
_____	_____	6. I'm collecting pictures of my favorite actor. I now have 79 pictures.
_____	_____	7. The president of the company spent Monday in New York, Tuesday in Chicago, and Wednesday in San Francisco.
_____	_____	8. I'm going to budget some time for myself each day so that I'll have a little time to think.
_____	_____	9. My life will be ruined if I'm not elected to this club.
yes	E	10. _____
		_____
		_____

An honors seventh grade was studying Alexander Hamilton's contribution to the solvency of the new nation after the Revolutionary War. Based on previous experience with such classes, the teacher knew that students would have no difficulty reading the text and memorizing the plans and the purpose of each, as expressed by Hamilton and interpreted by the author of the text. The teacher was concerned about assimilation, about awareness of the significance of the plans for the new nation, of their contemporary relevance, and of their importance to the students themselves.

REASONING GUIDE: SOCIAL STUDIES

"Story of the American Nation": Chapter Nine

Directions: Alexander Hamilton developed five plans to solve the financial problems of the new nation. See if you can identify the plans by which the problems, listed below, might be solved. Write the letter of the plan on the line before the statement of the problem which it solves. More than one plan might be used to solve one problem.

PLANS

A. The national government must pay its war debts in full.
B. The national government must take over war debts of the states.
C. The national government must raise money with an import tax and a tax on whiskey.
D. The national government must issue coins and paper money for all the nation.
E. The national government must establish a bank to help deal with money problems.

PROBLEMS

_____ 1. A nation with poor credit finds it difficult to borrow money.
_____ 2. It is difficult to carry on trade when there is not a standard currency.
_____ 3. It is necessary to be able to borrow money in order to expand the economy.
_____ 4. The government requires income in order to operate properly.
_____ 5. If people are to have a voice in the government, they must support it in every way.
_____ 6. Any organization is only as strong as its weakest part.

_____ 7. Money must "work" to expand and grow even as people need to work to grow and prosper.

_____ 8. Businesses in one country need protection from competition in other countries.

_____ 9. People must have confidence in their government before they can support it fully.

_____10. If private citizens join the government in business it could be helpful to both parties.

Note the format of the guide. The teacher listed interpretations of Hamilton's plans rather than their names. He identified several situations with relevance contemporary to both Hamilton and the students. Students were to judge how the problems could be solved by combining solutions (Hamilton's plans) into various sets. Thus considerable latitude was allowed each student as he explored the relevancy of Hamilton's thinking to contemporary problems.

Students were assigned the reading selection from their text and the reasoning guide as homework, having been prepared for the activity as described in the discussion of the Instructional Framework. The next day they were divided into groups with their assignment being to compare responses and explore the validity of the differences. Students learned a great deal from one another. They were excited by being freed to pursue their own insights and those of their classmates. The teacher was used as a resource. He was careful not to play the role of the authority, but only an arbiter. Heuristic concepts were manifest everywhere. Students knew, consequently, not only *what* Hamilton's plans were, but how they worked and the essence of their value.

It is interesting to note that a teacher of eleventh grade honors American History used the identical format with his students when they studied this same part of our history. The statements and responses differed, reflecting the level of sophistication, but the purposes and the end product were the same. The discussion of vertical transformation is as appropriate for reasoning as it is for reading.

REASONING GUIDE: SOCIAL STUDIES

Bragdon and McCutchen: "Establishing the
New Government," Chapter VII

HAMILTON'S FINANCIAL PLAN: Much of the domestic history of Washington's administration related to Hamilton's program and the opposition to it. See if you can identify which of his five plans by which each of the problems listed below might be solved. Write the letter of the plan on the line before the statement of the problem which it might help solve. More than one plan might be used for a problem.

PLANS

A. The national government must pay its foreign debts in full promptly.
B. The national government must take over war debts of the states (assumption).
C. The national government must replace old bonds with new ones, thus planning to pay the domestic debt in full.
D. The national government must establish a central bank to help deal with money problems.
E. The national government must encourage the development of American industry.

PROBLEMS

_____ 1. The U.S. had poor credit with European nations because it was unable to repay its war debt.

_____ 2. It was difficult to carry on trade because there was not a standard currency.

_____ 3. It was difficult for the government to borrow money when needed.

_____ 4. The government required help in handling its financial affairs such as safe-keeping of its treasury.

_____ 5. People were often more interested in state government than in the national government.

_____ 6. Many former patriots were disgusted because the national government had never paid them for their wartime services.

_____ 7. Widely accepted bank notes were needed for interstate commerce.

_____ 8. Private citizens thought they needed protection from competition of other countries if they were to succeed in business.

_____ 9. People lacked confidence in their government and therefore did not support it fully.

_____10. Private citizens found it difficult to get established in business, especially because of difficulty in borrowing sound money.

Reasoning Guide in Physics

Students in PSSC physics were studying "wave motion." The text contained detailed and highly technical explanations of wave motion within various media. When pulses are introduced into a medium, certain phenomena occur, depending on the conditions of that medium and the nature of the pulse introduced. Other phenomena occur if pulses are introduced so they meet or if pulses are obstructed as they move through the medium. If we view the pulses by high-speed photography, we can generalize principles about the nature of the pulses and the medium from the behavior of the pulses. Also, by proper application of principles set forth in the text to observed phenomenon, we can generalize concepts which lie outside the discussions of the text or experiments in the laboratory.

The physics teacher requested help with his students precisely because they were not generalizing the concepts even though capable. He was receptive to creative reasoning, to the heuristic concept, but was experiencing difficulty in providing the vehicle that would trigger such activity. The following Reasoning Guide was provided for the students to use.

REASONING GUIDE: SCIENCE

PSSC Physics: Introduction to Waves

Directions: As you complete the reading of each section, answer the questions on the study guide related to that section.

Sections 16-1; 16-2

A. Since a wave is, itself, not a particle of matter, why is it that it can move from one point to another? Illustrate your answer.

B. Examine paragraph 2 on page 249 and answer the following two questions:

    1) Would there be any pulse at all if the light was in view of each driver?

    2) Would there be any pulse at all if some cars were around a curve?

C. What are the two assumptions in section 16-2, the first paragraph?

Section 16-3

D. "Total displacement of any point on a spring at any instant is exactly equal to the sum of displacements produced independently."

    1) What is needed to make this statement completely correct?

    2) When corrected, what principle does it become?

Section 16-4

Directions: You are to examine the answers to each of the statements in section E through I. If an answer is true, place a "T" on the line preceding it. If the answer is false, place an "F" on the line. If it is impossible to determine if the statement is true or false, due to insufficient data, place an "I" on the line.

E. If two pulses meet on a spring and there is one point which stands still at the instant of meeting, what can one say about the two pulses:

_____ 1. They are asymmetrical.

_____ 2. They are moving in opposite directions.

_____ 3. They are both moving at right angles to the spring.

_____ 4. Their displacements are in opposite directions on the spring.

_____ 5. They are traveling at the same speed.

_____ 6. They are produced by identical motion.

_____ 7. They are the same size.

_____ 8. They are the same shape.

F. If two pulses meet on a spring and there is an instant when the whole spring appears undisplaced, what can be said about the pulses:

_____ 1. Pulses are moving in opposite directions.

_____ 2. They are moving on a heavy spring.

_____ 3. Their displacements are on the same side of the spring.

_____ 4. They are of equal size.

_____ 5. They are of equal shape.

_____ 6. They travel at the same speed.

G. When two verticle pulses meet on a spring, what can be said about the pulses:

_____ 1. They are produced by the same source.

_____ 2. They are traveling in opposite directions.

_____ 3. The original shape of each will not be distorted after meeting.

_____ 4. The displacement of one pulse is up and the other is down.

_____ 5. They will pass through one another.

_____ 6. The total displacement at the point of meeting equals the sum of separate displacements of each pulse.

_____ 7. They are the same shape.

_____ 8. Any point on the spring moves at a right angle to a single pulse moving through it.

_____ 9. The right hand side of one pulse moves upward as the pulse moves from left to right.

_____10. They are the same size.

H. A pulse moves on a line made of two pieces of material, each having different density.

1) If the pulse moves from left to right and, at the junction of materials of differing density, it is completely reflected, what may one assume?

_____ a) It is a large pulse, generated by a strong source of power.

_____ b) The left side of the pulse moves upward before reflected.

_____ c) The reflected pulse displaces the opposite side of the medium than did the original.

_____ d) The medium is a spring.

_____ e) The pulse originated on the more flexible section of the medium.

2) If the pulse moves from right to left and, at the juncture of materials of differing density, it is partially reflected and partially transmitted, what may one assume?

_____ a) It is a small pulse, generated by a weak source of power.

_____ b) The transmitted pulse displaces in the opposite direction from the original.

_____ c) The reflected pulse displaces in the opposite direction from the original.

_____ d) The pulse originated on the more flexible section of the medium.

_____ e) The left side of the pulse moves upward before reflecting and transmitting.

_____ f) The reflected pulse is longer than the transmitted pulse.

3) If the pulse moves from left to right and at the juncture of materials of differing density it is completely transmitted, what may one assume?

I. If a reflected pulse meets a new pulse generated on the same side of the same medium, what may one assume?

_____ 1. One end of the medium is fixed.

_____ 2. The superposition principle will hold true.

_____ 3. There will be a point at the meeting which remains unmoved.

_____ 4. There will be a point at the meeting which appears to remain at rest.

_____ 5. Some of the original pulse was transmitted.

In illustration 16-2, what are the five essential elements that one must observe:

1)

2)

3)

4)

5)

Note that students were given certain phenomena and alternative responses or generalizations to use as the basis of their reaction. The described phenomena were situational interpretations of principles described and analyzed in their text. The alternative generalizations were possible relationships between the original descriptions and the subsequent phenomena. By responding to the alternatives and discussing their responses, they developed the feeling for creative reasoning. As they progressed through the guide, they were given more latitude so they could pursue their own insights and develop heuristic concepts.

Matched with a control group of comparable ability, achievement, and experience in the subject, the students using this Reasoning Guide scored significantly higher on the standardized test, published by Educational Testing Services, which measured an understanding of this unit of study.[11] This data supports other evidence from experiments in which students at all levels of ability are provided opportunity to pursue creative reasoning and develop heuristic concepts.

SUMMARY

Skills instruction in content areas should extend beyond reading processes to reasoning. Students can be guided in the development of their critical (analytical) reasoning. They can be provided an environment and structure which stimulates creative reasoning as well.

Teachers' attitudes provide the environment; Reasoning Guides provide the structure. Both can combine to produce students conditioned to generate and pursue the heuristic hunch.

REACTION GUIDE

Directions: Listed below are quotations from this chapter and statements which reflect practices, attitudes, beliefs frequently observed among students and teachers.

Place a check in Column A before each statement with which, you believe, the author of the text would agree. In Column B, enter the number of the listed quote (or quotes) by which you support your response. In Column C, place a check if *you* agree with the statement. Be prepared to discuss your responses with your colleagues, particularly focusing on points of disagreement with the author. Also attempt to resolve differences among yourselves indicated in Column C.

Quotations

1. For immutable laws and principles, the teacher can assume an authoritative role: for pursuit of creative reasoning and the heuristic concept, who is to say that a student's view is any less valid than the teacher's?
2. Reasoning Guides provide a suitable environment within which students learn a new kind of behavior—pursuit of their own ideas rather than the teacher's.

[11] Herber, "Teaching Reading and Physics Simultaneously."

3. In most schools there are many students who read too well for their own good.
4. The teacher's challenge is to aid students' application of reasoning beyond the reading process.
5. Creative reasoning generates new ideas out of the analysis of old ideas.
6. Heuristic concepts presume excellent grounding in the fundamental disciplines related to the ideas being manipulated.
7. One does not learn the heuristic process by analyzing it; rather, one exercises it in an environment conducive to such behavior and gains confidence in the process as a result.
8. Students can develop competence in creative reasoning if teachers provide the proper classroom environment.
9. Reasoning Guides are simulators of the heuristic process.

Statements

A	B	C	
____	____	____	1. My students are very creative. They don't need to read the texts.
____	____	____	2. Students won't develop insight into this concept unless I tell it to them.
____	____	____	3. Why worry about this class? No one scores below the 94th percentile on the standardized reading test we use in the district!
____	____	____	4. Related to the reading act, one reasons before, during, and after.
____	____	____	5. Unless students already possess ideas, they can't create new ones.
____	____	____	6. "Psyching out" the teacher to insure an "A" may produce critical reasoning but rarely creative.
____	____	____	7. One cannot make something from nothing.
____	____	____	8. Functional exercise of creative reasoning requires a conducive environment.
____	____	____	9. Squelched students and insecure teachers are highly correlated.
____	____	____	10. Students should be given the right to be wrong.

8

TECHNICAL VOCABULARY AND LANGUAGE DEVELOPMENT

VOCABULARY

The following terms are presented and studied in detail:
— word analysis
— word recognition
— word meaning
— word power
— structural analysis
— phonetic analysis

IDEA DIRECTION

A seemingly impossible task faces the content teacher: to teach more words than he has time to teach. This chapter suggests vocabulary development procedures that provide a practicable solution to the problem.

READING DIRECTION

Several categories and classifications and procedures related to vocabulary development are incorporated in this chapter. As you read, be certain to look for relationships among them, but be certain to keep the function of each clearly in mind.

The following discussion of vocabulary development in content areas is based on three assumptions: 1) that each subject has its own special language which students must learn to use in order to read and react successfully to various sources related to the subject; 2) that it is impossible to teach every word a student will encounter in a given subject area at a given grade level; 3) that the technical language of a subject must be taught in spite of the fact that there are more words to teach than a teacher has time to teach.

Consider assumption number one, that each subject has its own special language. Basic concepts in any discipline are expressed in nomenclature with meaning peculiar to that discipline. If a person is to communicate his understanding of those concepts, it is necessary for him to have facility with the language in which the concepts are expressed.

This technical language of a subject generally causes communication problems for students. The language is new to them and the words have special meanings, and sometimes even different meanings within the same subject depending on concepts being studied. Then, to compound the problem, students find, as they progress through the grades within a given subject, that new meanings are applied to old and familiar words. Moreover, they are confronted daily with words they have never considered before, appearing in material they are required to read. Since they do not know the meanings of these words, they derive little benefit from their reading. Their teachers assume these students have reading problems when, in fact, they are having language problems; that is, they do not know the language of the subject and therefore cannot participate in the communication of its concepts.

Given the limitation of time and the extensiveness of the curriculum, it is not possible for a classroom teacher to teach every technical word that his students will encounter during their studies of his subject. The careful teaching of a single word might consume two to five minutes of class time. In subjects highly saturated with technical vocabulary, one unit could contain fifteen, twenty, or thirty words representing important concepts that the students must know. Teaching thirty words at three minutes each would consume one and a half hours. Considering the fact that a teacher meets with his students approximately 150 hours a year, devoting this much time just to teach the technical vocabulary for one unit is not realistic. And, it is not done.

However, even though time available for vocabulary is limited in a content area, it still remains that the technical language of a subject must be taught if students are to be successful in the communication of ideas in that subject. The solution, to be explored in this chapter, is to teach a few words in such a way that there is economy of time through transfer of skills. Teach three to five carefully chosen words so that word analysis, word recognition, and word meaning skills are developed. Consistency in this procedure develops students' competence to the point that they can apply skills independently to untaught words.

Types of Vocabulary

There is yet another reason for the necessity to teach vocabulary in a subject so as to aid students in their reading of required material. This reason has little to do with the fact that each subject has its own technical language. Rather, it is due to the fact that any vocabulary can be divided into types: listening, reading, writing, speaking. The relative facility students have with these vocabulary types shifts as students mature. A basic principle is involved here: it is easier to recognize a thought than to produce it. Listening and reading vocabularies are of the recognition type, produced by someone else who is communicating ideas to us. Speaking and writing vocabularies are the production type, used to produce the communication. Moreover, reading and writing are dependent on an external coding system; therefore, students generally demonstrate less facility with these than with speaking and listening, where the external coding is not essential. For most people (depending on their occupations and interests) the relationship of the listening, reading, and speaking vocabularies stabilizes, with listening and speaking larger than the reading. Again, one often hears words he does not use in his conversations, and he both hears and speaks words he might not recognize in print.

This points out the necessity for teachers to make certain that students' reading vocabularies grow consistently as they progress through the grades. Often students have technical words in their listening and speaking vocabularies but those same words are stumbling blocks to them in their reading. Merely calling students' attention to the configuration cf these familiar words as they are pronounced is sufficient for them to recognize the words subsequently, when they see them in print.

Word Power

Durrell speaks of building word power when he discusses the development of vocabulary.[1] He suggests by this term the need for students to be able to analyze words independently, to be shown how to add to their

---

[1] Donald D. Durrell, *Improving Reading Instruction* (New York: Harcourt, Brace, and World, Inc., 1956).

reading vocabulary without aid from teachers or fellow students. Only when a student has this power can reading be a pleasure; only then can reading be a major source for learning; only then will the content text be something more than a monument to frustration!

The purpose of this chapter is to present ways in which content teachers can help their students build word power, using the technical vocabulary of their own subject areas. The following major topics will be discussed: whether, when, and what vocabulary to teach; selection, teaching, and reinforcement of vocabulary; relationship of vocabulary reinforcement to levels of comprehension.

WHETHER, WHAT, AND WHEN

Many studies indicate the value of emphasizing the teaching of vocabulary in content areas.[2] As indicated above, ability to communicate in the language of a subject requires that one have facility with that language; hence, the need exists for emphasis on vocabulary development in each subject.

Many content teachers reject the teaching of vocabulary because they associate the process with teaching general vocabulary, a task they rightfully attribute to the English teacher. They say, "I'm a science (or history, or math) teacher, not an English teacher. My job is to teach science, not vocabulary." When shown a list of technical words for a unit of study in their subject and asked if students should know those words, the reply is, "Most certainly. That's the unit! But it's not vocabulary—it's my subject!"

"Vocabulary development" is a remote concept, associated with nebulous manipulation of words for the purpose of promoting general facility with language. When the content teacher understands that technical language (not unrelated, general vocabulary) is emphasized in vocabulary development in his subject, there is receptivity to the idea.

Words to be emphasized in vocabulary development by the content teacher rise out of what is being studied. There are several valid and useful sources from which teachers draw the words to be emphasized in their courses.

The most obvious is the textbook required in the course. Reading comprehension is aided when students are aware of those words which carry

---

[2] Peter Hasselriis, *Effects on Reading Skill and Social Studies Achievement from Three Modes of Presentation: Simultaneous Reading—Listening, and Reading,* Unpublished Doctoral Dissertation, Syracuse University, 1968; Mary Elizabeth Fowler, *Teaching Language, Composition, and Literature* (New York: McGraw-Hill Book Company, 1965); John J. DeBoer and Gertrude Whipple, "Reading Development in Other Curriculum Areas," *Development In and Through Reading* (Chicago: University of Chicago Press, 1961).

the meaning of the unit they are studying. When words emphasized by the teacher correspond to those which students encounter in their texts, greater understanding (and greater success) follows. As discussed in chapter 4, teachers analyze material to be read to identify potentially difficult vocabulary as well as concepts to be learned and reading skills to be employed.

Another source is the resource materials used by teachers as a basis for lectures and discussion with students. The teacher should screen the material being presented orally to make certain that the technical language is explained adequately. This will promote good listening comprehension.

Still another source is the curriculum guide which the teacher may follow as he develops the course. Such guides usually incorporate extensive lists of technical words for various units in the curriculum. The teacher must be selective in their use, however, and extract his own list according to ideas to be emphasized and the needs of his students. Arbitrary lists of words are no more appropriate to vocabulary development in a content area than are arbitrary lists of skills for reading improvement. Vocabulary development in a content area is functional. Specific vocabulary is studied for the purpose of improving communication and understanding of specific concepts. During the process of acquiring that vocabulary, certain skills can be emphasized which enhance a student's "word power." But vocabulary is not studied merely for the purpose of developing skills. The objective is to increase understanding of course content with the functional development of appropriate skills so students can improve and increase their vocabulary independently.

Furthermore, the teacher must consider more than the mere presence of words in the sources. He must also note the degree of reinforcement and aid provided in the sources used by the students.

Some texts provide no assistance—no word lists, no glossaries, no within-text clues to meaning. The assumption is that the readers already know the words and need no assistance in vocabulary development. Students are left on their own to discover meaning or skip over unknown words. If the material is filled with words that are unknown, comparatively little will be comprehended.

There are texts in which indirect help is given the student. While little aid is provided within the reading material itself, there are glossaries and word lists. These words may be carefully explicated and appear prior to the reading selection. The theory, obviously, is that students need to be exposed to the technical vocabulary prior to the reading. When students make use of these devices, their reading performance is much more satisfactory.

Other texts provide direct assistance in vocabulary development. In addition to word lists and glossaries, there are many within-text aids: italicized words, parenthetical definitions, contextual clues, marginal notations, footnotes, illustrations, and pronunciation keys. When students are taught how to use these devices, their comprehension of the material is greatly increased. The critical factor, however, is that *they are taught how to use these devices*. Merely having them available is no guarantee that they will be used well or at all. Students frequently ignore the devices as "filler," giving them less material to read when assigned "pages x to y." On the other hand, if students are shown how to make good use of those devices, teachers have less vocabulary to preteach, and there is less frustration on the part of both during recitation and discussion because the students have acquired more adequate understanding from their reading.

Selection for Emphasis

A vast number of words represent the language of a subject. Realistically and practically, not all of the important words in a unit can be taught; the extensive list must be narrowed to a relatively few words. The following criteria are suggested for the selection process.

KEY CONCEPTS   For each unit studied in a subject area, there are some very basic concepts that must be understood. The technical vocabulary representing those concepts forms the basic list of words to be taught. Even this list will be quite extensive.

When teaching inductively, a problem arises with this criterion, because the teacher wishes to evolve an understanding of certain concepts. *After* the concept has been developed, it is labeled and the words carefully taught. He cannot teach inductively if he tells students *beforehand* the meanings of specific words that represent the concepts to be evolved.

This objection is perfectly reasonable. However, there are many words which represent supporting ideas needed to evolve an understanding of the major concepts. (All major concepts to be developed have supportive concepts.) These words are used profitably for vocabulary development in a content area. The teacher first concentrates on the supportive vocabulary; then, after the students have developed the main concept inductively, he concentrates on the word or words representing that concept, in much the same manner that he taught the supportive words. Thus the teacher need not be fearful of "spoiling the lesson" by teaching ahead of time that which he wants the students to develop themselves.

Whether he teaches inductively or deductively, the teacher selects for emphasis only those words which represent or support the major concepts he wants his students to acquire. This makes it possible to reduce considerably the number of words to be used in the vocabulary development phase of the subject. The list is narrowed further by applying the two remaining criteria to it.

RELATIVE VALUE   The second criterion involves judging the importance of the unit being studied. If the unit is very important (among all of the units to be studied), many concepts must be emphasized and, as a consequence, more words taught. Because the unit is more important, more time will be given to it; therefore, more time is available for vocabulary development.

The "relative value" criterion is employed *within* units as well as *among* units. Of all of the key concepts related to this important unit (as the case may be), some have relatively greater value than others. These are the concepts to be emphasized through vocabulary development. Again, considering the factor of time, one has narrowed the list significantly.

STUDENT'S COMPETENCE   The final criterion focuses on the students who will encounter the vocabulary in their reading, discussion, and listening. What is their competence? That is, how able are they intellectually? What is their reading achievement level? What has been their experience in this subject, and, particularly, in the unit under consideration? Answers to these questions determine the final selection of words to be taught before the reading assignment is given.

Using these criteria, the teacher limits to realistic possibilities the total number of words to be taught. These words will develop understanding of the major concepts of the unit and will be appropriate to the needs and potential of the students. Students will learn the important language of the subject.

Some teachers become concerned about all of the words they do not select when applying the criteria. What happens to students who don't know the words that were not selected? They are in the sources to be read. Will they not be stumbling blocks for successful reading? Should they not be taught—or should we not find material on an easier level to be used with these students?

A person need not know every word in material he is reading in order to understand what is being said. If he has an understanding of the most important words, he can usually piece together a sufficient understanding of unknown words through context clues to keep him going. In addition, if grouping is used *within* content classes, there is opportunity for students to receive help from one another in reference to unknown words. For example, one teacher had students in a "slow learner" class in history divided into groups with each group being comprised of partners. If a given student encountered an "unknown" word, he asked his partner for its meaning. If the partner did not know, other members of the group were consulted. If no member of the group knew the answer, the teacher was consulted. Students learn well from one another and a system of this sort takes advantage of the fact.

There has been much discussion on the matter of using materials that are written "at the students' reading level." It is really an irrelevant argument when discussing the development of technical vocabulary. Certain language is needed to describe certain concepts. Merely because they are not at the students' reading level is not the issue. The fact remains that the students are studying the concept and, therefore, the vocabulary is essential. We cannot place a grade level value on this type of vocabulary, but only on the depth to which the concept is probed. The question to be raised regards the relevancy of the curriculum to the student, not the technical vocabulary to the curriculum.

There are those students who have so much difficulty in a subject that they understand very little through listening, let alone through reading. To substitute the lecture and an exhortation to take notes, is to avoid the real issue: the relevancy of the curriculum to such students. Many teachers who use the students' competence as an excuse for not teaching skills in general, and vocabulary skills in particular, will insist that students are responsible for the information given through lecture. This seems inconsistent. Difficulty of concept load is one thing; relevancy of the curriculum is quite another.

The Teaching of Vocabulary

Teaching of vocabulary should be practical for the teacher and effective for students. This desirable combination can be realized by considering a few basic factors related to the teaching of vocabulary.

TIME FACTOR   Having used the criteria to select words for pre-teaching, the content teacher may still have a lengthy list. His problem is reduced but not resolved.

From his final list, he chooses two or three words to teach carefully, emphasizing context, structure, or phonetic analysis, as appropriate. He makes this choice with students' need for skill development in mind.

He chooses the words for teaching because of the skill he can develop. This is consistent with the functional approach to teaching reading through content because he makes his choice from among several key words, all of which are important to students' understanding of the unit.

What does he do with the remaining words in his list? He merely pronounces the words for the students, calling attention to letter sequence and configuration. He may give a meaning, depending on the amount of aid provided in the text for that word. He may draw meanings from the class as part of his inductive development of concepts.

Many times the mere pronunciation of the words will trigger associations with listening and speaking vocabulary. When students see the words subsequently in their reading assignment, they have some basis for recognition and understanding, even though the words were not fully "taught."

PARTS OF VOCABULARY DEVELOPMENT   Vocabulary development can be divided into three parts: word analysis; word recognition; and word meaning. Though each of the parts serves a unique function, there is a relationship among them. All three function in an effective emphasis on the development of technical vocabulary in content areas.

Word analysis can be "structural analysis," utilizing the structure of a word to determine its meaning. Students examine a word to determine if there are clearly recognizable parts which reveal meaning: prefixes, roots, suffixes. Many technical words in various content areas do yield to structural analysis. Word parts not only give clues to meaning; they also give clues to pronunciation of unfamiliar words.

These words are taught inductively, in the following manner: "Look at this word. . . . Do you see anything in it that looks familiar to you? 'Pre?' Yes; what does that suggest? . . . What else do you see? 'ion?' Right. And what does that suggest? . . . Anything else? 'script?' Ok; which suggests. . . . Now, combine all of this; what might the word mean?"

Thus the teacher draws from students what they already know, functionally developing their awareness of the benefits of structural analysis and preparing them to use this competence independently. Word parts new to students are then explained, related to the word being taught. Problems with contemporary changes in meaning are explained so that students do not attribute "old" meanings of root words to "new" words. Problems with roots used as prefixes, and so on, are pointed out, as the words being taught dictate.[3]

Note that teachers do not teach a word part for its own sake, selecting a word to serve as the vehicle. Rather, they examine words from their lists to identify any that will yield to structural analysis, emphasizing those that clearly will be most valuable. This is far more effective than having students memorize lists of word parts.

Word analysis can take the form of "phonetic analysis" as well. Some words do not yield to structural analysis—there are no clearly identifiable parts to give clues to meaning or pronunciation. These words must be acquired as sight vocabulary. Knowledge of letter sounds is used to aid pronunciation. Definitions are associated with the sound of the word rather than its structure.

When the word is pronounced aloud, its sound may be familiar to the students, though its configuration is not. They are able to recall some meaning for the word. Through use of the dictionary, they are able to confirm both the pronunciation and the meaning.

When teaching words that require phonetic analysis, one has the opportunity (depending on the words being taught for a given lesson) to em-

---

[3] The reader is referred to the following text for a useful discussion of structural analysis and helpful lists of word parts: Lee C. Deighton, *Vocabulary Development in the Classroom* (New York: Columbia University Press, 1959).

phasize letter sounds, or combinations of letters that form single sounds, or peculiarities in spelling, syllabication, and so on.[4]

Word recognition is perceiving the configuration of a word. "Recognition" carries the implication that students have previously encountered the word in some form so that there is a degree of familiarity with the word.

One problem students face is the accurate recognition of words. Do they read what they see or what they think they see? Though some students have severe reading problems that cause them to read "was" for "saw" or "on" for "no," for example, many students misread words merely because they are inaccurate or careless in the recognition of words.

Practice exercises which require the speeded recognition of technical vocabulary in a content area seem to increase the accuracy of students' reading performance. Such exercises contribute to an increase in rate of reading comprehension.

These exercises are simple to construct and make use of the technical vocabulary of a unit of study.[5] The purpose is to place words with similar configuration in juxtaposition so students exercise accurate discrimination in selecting the target word. For example:

1. executive	executed	executive	exertion	executives
2. chief	cheer	church	chief	child
3. elected	electors	election	electorate	elected
. . . .				
25. term	team	term	torn	turn

Difficulty is controlled by the similarity of configuration between the target word and the distractors. For example, compare the preceding excerpt and the following:

1. libel	tax	wholesale	libel	alliances
2. income	pioneer	propaganda	coalition	income
3. labor	education	labor	press	custom
. . . .				
25. jury	jury	town	slavery	executive

Difficulty also is controlled by the manner in which students are to search out the target word among the distractors. In one case students

---

[4] The following texts have useful discussions of phonetic analysis and helpful suggestions related to tasks involved in phonics instruction: Arthur W. Heilman, *Principles and Practices of Teaching Reading* (Columbus: Charles E. Merrill Books, Inc., 1967); Nila Banton Smith, *Reading Instruction for Today's Children* (Englewood Cliffs: Prentice-Hall, Inc., 1963).

[5] These exercises are patterned after materials contained in: Harold L. Herber, *Success with Words* (New York: Scholastic Book Services, 1964).

look for a word the same as the first, as above. In another case, students look for two words that are the same:

1. financial	finance	financial	fiance	financing
2. collection	collectors	collects	collects	collect
3. maintenance	maintain	mainline	management	maintain
.	. . . .			
25. afford	afraid	affront	afford	after

Generally the exercises are organized in sets of 25 lines per exercise. The teacher can time students on the exercises to see how many seconds it takes to complete a set. Accuracy scores (number attempted divided into number correct) also can be computed. Progress charts can be made to record scores and show increase in time and accuracy. (For example see chart on next page.)

If one does not have a sufficient number of words in the technical vocabulary of a unit to make a set of 25, one can repeat lines as many times as necessary within the set until one has the 25 lines. The repeated practice is beneficial to the students.

One need not use exercise material of this type very frequently. Doing the exercises for a specific unit twice seems to be sufficient. The repeated practice on the vocabulary for each unit allows students to compare speed and accuracy and note their own progress. Each period of use of the exercises should consume no more than five minutes.

Teachers in science and math have used the same types of exercises for building accuracy in reading numerals and formulas. Increased accuracy in computation appears to be one of the direct benefits from the use of such exercise material. For example:

1.	2.	A	B	C	D
1. IRON	Fe	FE	fe	Fe	Fl
2. ZINC	Zn	zn	Zn	ZN	Zm
3. HYDROGEN	H	He	h	H	Hf
.	. . . .				
25. SULFATE	SO_4	S_4O	So_4	SO^4	SO_4

Word meaning. The last part of vocabulary development is word meaning: reinforcement and extension of meaning. Traditionally, vocabulary development takes the following form: students are given lists of words; students look up the meanings of words in the dictionary and use each word in a sentence; they memorize these meanings for a subsequent quiz; they are quizzed on the words periodically to determine whether or not they can recall and use meanings as they were memorized.

This is a rather meaningless ritual. The exposure to vocabulary has little apparent relevancy to the students' needs; the ritual does little to

PROGRESS CHART*

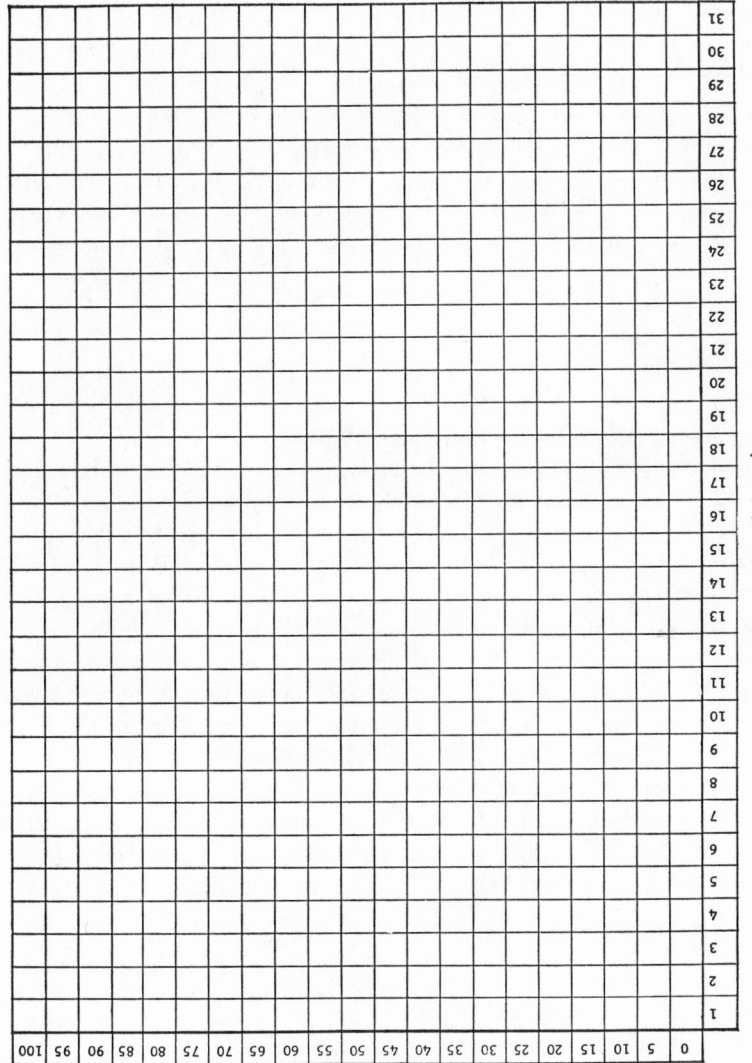

Exercise Number

Number of Seconds

* Place accuracy scores
in appropriate boxes

reinforce an understanding of the ideas represented by the words; the meanings selected and memorized by the students frequently are not the correct ones for the context in which the words are being studied.

There is evidence to indicate that words must be used many times in situations that have meaning before the words are sufficiently well assimilated into our vocabulary to be readily available for use.[6] Mere memorization of word meanings is not sufficient, nor is just having words written on the board and discussed with students before they read.[7] Students develop vocabulary when they use words in situations that have meaning, in conversations and animated discussion not only with the teacher but with fellow students. Thus words become part of the speaking vocabulary of the student as well as part of his listening and reading vocabularies. Experience and experimentation have shown that when students are provided meaningful contexts for the exploration and reinforcement of vocabulary, greater retention occurs.[8]

Sample exercises which provide this type of reinforcement are presented and discussed on pages 166–191. The Appendix contains additional illustrations. Variety is limited only by the imagination.

Now consider this very important point: If the words emphasized represent the major ideas teachers want students to acquire for a unit of study, then the reinforcement experience develops not only vocabulary skills but also an understanding of the subject content. This is the critical factor! Skills and concepts are developed simultaneously. Vocabulary skills need not be taught in isolation but only as they apply to words which represent basic concepts in the course. If we use the criteria suggested to select words for emphasis, then the experience supports an understanding of the content. The development of vocabulary skills meets the need for insuring independence in vocabulary development. Reinforcement of technical vocabulary insures understanding of course content. The language of the subject is learned, vocabulary development skills are learned, and the content of the course is learned. If this is done for each unit studied in a subject, greater success is the result: success in teaching and success in learning.

Tools for Independence

"Word power" is the ability to add to our vocabulary independently. As already pointed out, content teachers cannot teach students all of the words

---

[6] Fowler, *loc. cit.*

[7] E. Coston Frederick, *A Study of the Effects of Certain Readiness Activities on Concept Learning,* Unpublished Doctoral Dissertation, Syracuse University, 1968.

[8] Herber, *Success with Words;* also _____, *Teaching Reading Through Seventh Grade Science Content,* Unpublished Research sponsored by the Division of Research, New York State Department of Education, Central High School District No. 2, Franklin Square, New York, 1962.

they need to know in a subject but they can teach some in such a way that the students acquire skills needed to add to their vocabularies independently as they acquire an understanding of the concepts. The skills developed correspond to the parts of vocabulary discussed in the previous section: word analysis, word recognition, word meaning. The tools for independence incorporate the parts of vocabulary and build upon them: structure; context; dictionary.

STRUCTURE   As already discussed under "word analysis," knowledge of the structure of words aids the acquisition of their meaning. As teachers refer to the structure of words while teaching vocabulary, students develop a reservoir of knowledge about structure which they can apply independently when confronting unfamiliar terms in a content area.

Use of structure (as use of context and dictionary) assumes facility with *phonetic analysis*. Students need to have acquired relative independence in their ability to sound out words (to associate sound with symbol) before they can be expected to attain and demonstrate relative independence in the use of structural analysis.

Drawn from the teacher's example, students know that not all terms yield to structural analysis. Meanings for those terms may be secured independently through other tools.

CONTEXT   Use of context is another tool for securing the meanings of words. Again, independent use of context assumes skill in *phonetic analysis*. Once having acquired a meaning for a word through the use of context clues, students will want to be able to use the word orally in various reinforcing experiences. Phonetic analysis makes this possible.

Five types of clues are suggested [9] for deriving meanings of words from context:

1. The experience clue, which enables the students to draw on their own experience; e.g., their experience with crows enables them to define *raucously* in "A pair of crows called raucously."
2. The comparison or contrast clue, as in the example of *tractable* as in "The children were more tractable than she had anticipated; in fact, only Joel was at all stubborn."
3. The synonym clue, in which the sentence contains a near-synonym.
4. The summary clue: "He was completely *disheveled*. His hair was mussed, his shirttail was out . . ."
5. The association clue: "He was out of it in an instant with the *agility* of a pickpocket."
6. The reflection of a mood or situation clue, as with the word *melancholy* in the first sentence of "The Fall of the House of Usher."
7. The previous contact clue: students' knowledge of the Emancipation Proclamation should help them to understand *emancipate*.

[9] J. N. Hook, *The Teaching of High School English* (New York: The Ronald Press Company, 1965), p. 375.

Students must be taught how to use these context clues before they can be expected to use them independently. As one selects the technical vocabulary to be emphasized, he notes words with meanings potentially acquired by use of context clues. Rather than teaching these words by structural analysis (though possibly appropriate) he shows his students how to determine meaning from the context in which the words are found. He emphasizes the context clue appropriate to the word, never emphasizing a type of clue just for its own sake. This is consistent with the functional development of all skills when teaching reading through content.

DICTIONARY   The dictionary is one of the most obvious tools for acquiring vocabulary independently. Unfortunately, too often the student is exposed to the dictionary as a tool through series of rather meaningless drills which force him to work with words in isolation, words that have little currency or urgency or appropriateness.

The dictionary has more relevancy to students when it is used as a means to substantiate or refute meanings developed through use of context or structure. If the student applies structural analysis to a word but is uncertain if the meaning he attributes to the word is correct in that particular instance, he confirms his findings by referring to the dictionary. The same is true when using context clues to determine meaning. If he has a general idea of the meaning of a word through his use of context clues, he may wish to determine more precisely what the word means by consulting the dictionary.

Of course, it is possible that students will come upon words for which their skill in use of context and structure does them no good. In such cases, the dictionary is the obvious tool for them to use.

It is important for students to view the dictionary as such a tool and not as the means for series of torturous drills. Most skilled adults use the dictionary in a functional manner: using it to confirm hunches where there is uncertainty; using it to find meanings when no other tool provides the meaning. Recognizing the practicality of such a use of the dictionary, we should teach students how to use it in the same manner.

Rather than having isolated drill on the locational skills related to the dictionary (such as use of guide words or alphabetizing) point out these skills as one use of the dictionary to confirm hunches, to settle differences among students, and so on. Rather than having isolated drill on the use of the pronunciation key, make use of it when confirming hunches about pronunciation of words. Rather than isolated drill on reference to origins of words, make use of derivations when confirming hunches and analyses related to structure.

As in the case of the other tools for independent acquisition of vocabulary, the use of the dictionary is taught functionally, never just for its own sake.

As discussed briefly under "word meaning," it is necessary to provide opportunity for extensive reinforcement of the technical vocabulary deemed important for a unit. Merely referring to the words or having students memorize meanings is not sufficient. In many respects, the reinforcement of vocabulary is the most important part. Unless word meanings are reinforced and the words become part of a student's readily available vocabulary, useful for communicating in the language of the subject, then the word analysis and word recognition skills that are emphasized are rather futile gestures.

Because technical words do not have equal value, the same level of understanding is not required for all terms. Consequently, the reinforcement experience varies according to the degree of understanding desired. In this regard, it is useful to think of levels of comprehension discussed in chapter 5. We can apply similar levels of understanding when determining the extent of reinforcement desired for terms in specific units. The levels, you will recall, are: literal; interpretive; applied.

After the teacher determines the level of understanding he believes to be necessary for words emphasized in a particular unit, he can prepare reinforcement exercises at the appropriate level. In all cases the exercises should serve as a vehicle to promote discussion of the terms and, consequently, a discussion of the major concepts of the unit. (Recall again that the terms being used in the reinforcement material are those considered to be "key concepts" for the unit.)

Usually students work out their own answers first and then compare their responses in group discussions centering on the resolution of differences in answers. The teacher focuses his attention on the differences students are unable to resolve rather than going over all of the items in full-class discussion.

Understandings developed at the literal level are rapidly learned and rapidly forgotten. Learning words at the literal level tends to promote word naming rather than word meaning. Although it is needed for subsequent learning at higher levels, word naming should not be regarded as the goal of learning. Nevertheless, reinforcement exercises at the literal level are useful with some students whose current achievement is inadequate for handling the interpretive level. Until their achievement is increased, the teacher must give them the type of exercise material they are capable of handling. The following exercises are appropriate for this level. As you will note, they are taken from various subject areas and reproduced as teachers designed them.

EXERCISES ON LITERAL LEVEL

(1) Multiple Meanings: Social Studies

Directions: You will find that a word can have multiple meanings. Listed below are words and some of their meanings. Underline the correct meanings for each word.

Word	*Possible Meanings*
1. quarry	a. diamond-shaped pane of glass used in latticed-windows
	b. a mine
	c. excavations made by the removal of stone
	d. object of pursuit by bird of prey, hunter, etc.
2. gear	a. equipment
	b. combination of levers, wheels working on one another
	c. put machinery in action
	d. to laugh at someone
3. aboriginals	a. people who have no originality
	b. the first colonists
	c. indigenous peoples
	d. Indians
4. transhumance	a. across humid lands
	b. to move from one home to another
	c. seasonal moving of livestock to another pasture
	d. the manner in which the Swiss move their cattle at seasonal changes
5. sedentary	a. the film at the bottom of a bottle
	b. sitting position
	c. remaining in the same place because of occupation
	d. not migratory
6. combine	a. join together
	b. cooperate
	c. a farm owned by several farmers
	d. a reaping and threshing machine
7. subsistence	a. means of supporting life
	b. raising crops to support oneself
	c. sharing farmland with others
	d. a product

Note: No interpretive analysis is necessary, only the recall of meanings attributed to each word. Therefore, this is a literal-level exercise.

(2) Categorizing: Science

Directions: Below are a list of words. Each is to be placed under one or more of three categories. Be prepared to defend your decisions.

air	milk	neon
salt water	gasoline	blood
penny	chair	cold cream
ice	paraffin	cleaning fluid
alcohol	kerosene	iron
argon	natural gas	lead
helium	oxygen	coffee
carbon dioxide	glass	fuel oil
asphalt	paint	salt
tungsten		

SOLIDS   LIQUIDS   GASES

Note: This literal-level exercise has considerable versatility. Some students categorize words on the basis of general recall of the meaning. Others engage in higher level interpretation and place words under headings accordingly.

(3) Word Puzzle: Social Studies

Directions: To solve this puzzle, look at the definitions below. Think of a word which fits the definition, has the same number of letters as the number of spaces provided in the corresponding line, and has the given letter in the same position as indicated. Write the word on the line. The first one is done for you.

```
        I  N  D  E  P  E  N  D  E  N  C  E
1.      __ __ D  __ __ __ __ __ __ __ __ __
2.         __ E  __ __ __ __ __ __
3.         __ M  __ __ __ __
4.         __ O  __ __ __ __ __ __ __ __
5.      __ __ C  __ __ __ __ __
6.         __ R  __ __ __ __ __
7.         __ A  __ __ __ __
8.      __ __ __ C  __
9.         __ Y  __ __ __ __ __
```

DEFINITIONS:

1. state of being free from outside control
2. country where citizens rule through elected representatives
3. people and territory controlled by one power
4. ruling body in a particular area
5. one who has absolute authority over others
6. state or quality of being free
7. to agree or approve idea
8. public security under law
9. government with absolute power invested in a single ruler

Note: This literal-level exercise provides definitions, and the number of letters in each word along with a variation of clues provided by the placement of letters on the line to spell words, indicate similar letters in all words, and so forth. The crossword puzzle is similar in purpose.

(4) Word Analysis and Meaning: Social Studies

Follow these directions:

1. Give the two syllable word which *describes* the ground on a small hill.
   S ___ ___ ___ / ___ ___ ___
2. Give the two syllable word which describes what is left in the ground after grain is cut.
   S ___ ___ ___ / ___ ___ ___
3. Give the one syllable word which means "a container for storing liquid or solids."
   K ___ ___
4. Give the two syllable word which tells of the process when a community was organized or established.
   F ___ ___ ___ ___ / ___ ___ ___
5. Give the two syllable word which describes rich land, good for grain crops.
   F ___ ___ ___ / ___ ___ ___
6. Give the three syllable word which tells what people must be when they have different beliefs and yet must live together.
   T ___ ___ ___ / ___ ___ ___ / ___ ___ ___
7. Give the two syllable word which tells what people are doing when they interfere in other people's business.
   M ___ ___ / ___ ___ ___ ___ ___

Note: This is a literal-level exercise. It promotes recall of definitions of words. It also promotes some word analysis skills: letter sequence; syllabication.

(5) Word Building: [10] Science

Directions: Below are listed prefixes, suffixes, and root words and their meanings. You are to use these word parts and "assemble" science words. To assemble each word, place each word part and its meaning in the correct column, and the meaning of the assembled word in its column. Some word parts may be used more than once. One is done for you.

PREFIXES	ROOTS	SUFFIXES
alti-, height	atom, small particle	-ize, to make
anti-, against	meter, measure	-er, one who
centri-, center	biotics, pertaining to	-ation, the act of
chrono-, time	life	-or, the state of
con-, with, together with	toxin, living or dead	-con, the act of
ex-, from, out of	organisms producing	-y, to make
tele-, distance	poison	
micro-, very small	fuge, to flee	
	dense, thick, thickly set	
	plode, drive	
	graph, write	
	vision, see	
	scope, to see	

Prefix and Meaning	Root and Meaning	Suffix and Meaning	Assembled Word and Meaning
alti-, height	meter, measure		altimeter, to measure height

Note: Word building exercises are literal-level type. Students use definitions of word parts to call to mind words to which they have been exposed. This exercise enhances structural analysis skills as well.

(6) Following Directions: Mathematics

Directions: Under each blank line listed below, you will find several words listed. You are to identify the category to which these words belong and write its name on the blank provided.

---

[10] Harold L. Herber, *Success with Words* (New York: Scholastic Book Services, 1964).

To help identify the category, you may find all of the letters in the word by following simple directions. You will notice single numbers (15, for example) and/or double numbers (4-3, for example) under each set of words. To the left of each single or double number is a blank.

A single number refers to a letter in the alphabet (15, for example, refers to the letter "O"); a double number refers to the letter in the list (4-3, for example, refers to the fourth letter in the third word from the left). You are to find each letter so identified, then unscramble all the letters and spell the name of the category you are seeking.

1. _____

    algebra   arithmetic   geometry

_____ 1-1; _____ 3-2; _____ 10-2; _____ 8-2; _____ 5-2; _____ 4-3;

_____ 2-3; _____ 1-2; _____ 6-2; _____ 19.

2. _____

    isosceles   right   scalene

_____ 1-1; _____ 3-2; _____ 3-3; _____ 5-2; _____ 6-3; _____ 5-3;

_____ 7-1; _____ 1-2.

3. _____

    integer   denominate   cardinal   ordinal

_____ 21; _____ 7-1; _____ 5-2; _____ 2-2; _____ 2; _____ 19;

_____ 3-2.

4. _____

    diameter   radius   curve   circumference

_____ 12; _____ 1-2; _____ 12-4; _____ 2-4; _____ 5-1; _____ 1-3;

_____ 6-2.

5. _____

    coefficient   deviation   formula

_____ 2; _____ 5-2; _____ 3-1; _____ 7-3; _____ 3-3; _____ 6-3;

_____ 7.

Note: This is a transitional exercise, bridging literal and interpretive levels. By perceiving the relationship among the key words, students may generalize the name of the category (interpretive level). Or, they may follow the directions, unscramble the name of the category (literal level).

Interpretive level exercises require students to analyze relationships among terms with which they may have demonstrated facility at the literal level. Through group discussions prompted by exercises of the type listed below, students learn to think about the significance of ideas related to the unit under consideration.

EXERCISES ON INTERPRETIVE LEVEL

(7) Categorizing: Science

Directions: Listed below are several words from the unit under consideration. They would be grouped under three broad categories. Look for
relationships among the words and identify the three categories, listing them
below in the spaces provided.

air	milk	neon
salt water	gasoline	blood
penny	chair	cold cream
ice	paraffin	cleaning fluid
alcohol	kerosene	iron
argon	natural gas	lead
helium	oxygen	coffee
carbon dioxide	glass	fuel oil
asphalt	paint	salt
tungsten		

_____   _____   _____

Note: This is an interpretive-level exercise, a variation on exercise number 2 above. Students are to look for relationships among meanings of
words, requiring more than recall. Doing this exercise within groups provides profitable interaction among students.

(8) Categorizing: English

Directions: In each of the sets below, three of the words are related. Circle
the word that is unrelated. On the line at the top of the set, write the word
or phrase that explains the relationship existing among the remaining three
words.

_____   _____

1. formidable   3. container
   appalling   test
   tranquil   crucible
   hideous   trial

_____   _____

2. countenance   4. leech
   semblance   physician
   aberration   doctor
   likeness   psychiatrist

5. revered venerated scrupled adored	7. foretell portend partake sign
6. preternatural miraculous abnormal inexplicable	8. vague obscure archaic ancient

Note: This exercise requires students to interpret meanings of words in relation to meanings of other words. This generalizing activity is at the interpretive level.

(9) Categorizing: Science

Directions: Carefully read the terms in the following three columns. You will notice category headings below. Place the terms under the headings to which they belong. Some may belong to more than one category. Some may belong to none of them. Be prepared to defend your choices.

moment arm	pound foot	moment of force
force	FPS	centimeter dyne
resultant	torque	rotation
meter newton	second	sine

MASS   MAGNITUDE   GRAVITY   VECTOR

Note: This is an interpretive-level categorization. The terms are sufficiently abstract that one must have more than a literal understanding to determine whether to categorize them under one, several, or no category. Potential relationships among categories through specific terms stimulate interpretive-level responses.

(10) Understanding Relationships: Mathematics

Directions: Listed below are five words on each line. Draw lines under three in each row which have something in common. Under each row write the word (words) expressing the relationship. Is there one set in each row?

1. numeral   number   name   idea   symbol
    GROUP ONE: _____
    GROUP TWO: _____

2. prime   composite   finite   infinite   number
   GROUP ONE: _____
   GROUP TWO: _____

3. addition   sum   multiplication   product   subtraction
   GROUP ONE: _____
   GROUP TWO: _____

4. base   exponent   factor   number   product
   GROUP ONE: _____
   GROUP TWO: _____

5. universe   subset   intersection   union   null set
   GROUP ONE: _____
   GROUP TWO: _____

Note: This interpretive-level exercise has the same purpose as exercise number 8 above. Only the format differs, providing visual variety.

(11) Critical Thinking: English

Directions: Four sets of words appear below, with five words in each set. Circle two words in each set so that the remaining three will also have something in common other than not being selected. In the space provided, write the term which describes the relationship among or between words in each group.

Is there more than one set of combinations for each main set of words? If so, write them down.

1. host   guest   visitor   employer   company
   GROUP ONE: _____
   GROUP TWO: _____

2. game   quarry   prey   sport   chase
   GROUP ONE: _____
   GROUP TWO: _____

3. plot   author   play   theme   story
   GROUP ONE: _____
   GROUP TWO: _____

4. wealth   values   culture   ideals   education
   GROUP ONE: _____
   GROUP TWO: _____

Note: In this interpretive-level exercise, one looks for multiple relationships among meanings of the words listed. The words are sufficiently abstract that each has several meanings within it so the interaction of multiple meanings among words requires critical, sometimes creative, reasoning.

(12) Interpreting Relationships: Mathematics

Directions: Place an "X" on the blank to the left of each word in the third column which could form a valid relationship when used with the other two words in the section.

1. acute   adjacent   _____ complementary
                                        _____ supplementary
                                        _____ vertical
                                        _____ equal

2. obtuse   adjacent   _____ complementary
                                        _____ supplementary
                                        _____ equal
                                        _____ corresponding

3. interior   supplementary   _____ exterior
                                        _____ adjacent
                                        _____ right
                                        _____ triangle
                                        _____ alternate

4. vertical   central   _____ equal
                                        _____ obtuse
                                        _____ acute
                                        _____ supplementary
                                        _____ complementary

5. corresponding   complementary   _____ acute
                                        _____ obtuse
                                        _____ equal

Note: This exercise is a variation on numbers 10 and 11.

(13) Analysis: English

Directions: Examine the words listed below each phrase. Before those that are closely synonymous with the given personality trait put an "S." Before those characteristics that are likely to accompany the given one, put "+." If the characteristic *could* accompany the given one but probably would not, put "√." If the trait is definitely incongruous, put "—."

I.	II.	III.
a *straight-laced* person	a *sedate* person	a *volatile* person

_____ 1. tolerant	_____ 1. loquacious	_____ 1. steadfast
_____ 2. conservative	_____ 2. talkative	_____ 2. stolid
_____ 3. compliant	_____ 3. conservative	_____ 3. sensitive
_____ 4. sedate	_____ 4. cautious	_____ 4. constant
_____ 5. garrulous	_____ 5. cynical	_____ 5. cautious
_____ 6. indulgent	_____ 6. grave	_____ 6. phlegmatic
_____ 7. amorous	_____ 7. aggressive	_____ 7. emotional
_____ 8. fastidious	_____ 8. shrewish	_____ 8. consistent
_____ 9. reticent	_____ 9. fervid	_____ 9. listless
_____10. suave	_____10. persistent	_____10. garrulous
_____11. voluptuous	_____11. contentious	_____11. pertinacious
_____12. fluent	_____12. stubborn	_____12. flighty
_____13. frivolous	_____13. glib	_____13. aggressive
_____14. whimsical	_____14. fluent	_____14. colorless
_____15. melancholy	_____15. strait-laced	_____15. conventional

Note: This exercise promotes understanding on the interpretive level. Students are guided to consider complex and refined meanings of the words, gained from extensive reading in and thinking about the subject.

(14) Analogies: Social Stud

Directions: Complete the following analogies.

1. vindicate – censure : assent – _____
2. integrate – mix : ancestor – _____
3. legislature – mix : ancestor – _____
4. capitalism – competition : communism – _____
5. predecessor – progeny : ancestor – _____
6. chivalrous – progeny : ancestor – _____
7. longitude – Greenwich meridian : latitude – _____
8. economy – frugal : acquit – _____
9. terminal – depot : powerless – _____
10. foreign – exotic : increment – _____

Note: The analogies exercise is perhaps the most difficult of the interpretive-level type. It requires the student to perceive concepts in new, specific, and perhaps unusual relationships.

The interpretive-level exercises are the most exciting and useful. The teacher must be prepared, however, to allow divergent thinking among his students. Frequently students will perceive associations and relationships that he did not have in mind when constructing the exercise. This, of course, is exciting teaching and learning and the teacher should never fear declaring his pleasure to the students for having seen something that he himself did not see until told by the student. Similarly, he should not have an answer key for these exercises to which all students must conform. Certainly the teacher will have his own set of answers for the exercises, but he must allow sufficient latitude to provide for the flash of insight and resulting divergent application that will occur frequently when such thinking is promoted.

There are no "applied" level exercises. Reading the selection in which the words are found is the application.

How to Teach Vocabulary

How do we put together all that has been discussed in relation to vocabulary development? Consider what a science, a history, an English and a math teacher did to emphasize the technical vocabulary for a unit of study in their subjects. They applied the criteria to select the words for preteaching and emphasis; they determined whether to stress phonetic analysis, structural analysis, or context; they determined in what way the dictionary would be used; they decided whether or not students needed word recognition exercises for the units in question; they constructed a variety of word meaning exercises, some on the recall level, others on the interpretive level. The materials are reproduced just as they were designed. All could have benefited from "editorial polishing" had the teachers had the time, but, of course, this is not the major factor. Even without the polish, the materials were effective with students.

Science—Grade 8

Blanc, Fischler and Gardner, *Modern Science,* 2 (New York: Holt, Rinehart and Winston, 1964), Chaps. 4, 5, 6 ("Energy").

Word List

alloy	complementary	energy
audible	degrees	force
calorie	diffusion	fossil fuel
calorimeter	dispersion	fuel cell
cesium cell	eclipse	heat
chemical energy	electrical energy	illumination
coal	electromagnetic	infrared light
combustion	electron	kinetic

light	potential	thermodynamic
lumen	primary colors	thermometer
luminous	prism	translucent
lunar	radiant energy	transparent
mechanical energy	reflection	turbine
motion	refraction	ultraviolet
nichrome	resistance	umbra
nuclear	shadow	vibrate
opaque	solar furnace	work
pendulum	sound	wavelength
penumbra	spectrum	

I. Word Puzzle

Directions: The following is a puzzle of words which are defined below. Starting with number one, read the definition for one and think of a word that fits it, has as many letters as provided blanks, and has the letter "e" in same blank as provided on line. Do the rest the same way, but make sure they have "e's" in the same position as on line.

```
 1.        e _ _ _ _ _ _ _
 2.          _ e _ _
 3.        _ _ e _ _ _
 4.        _ _ e _   _ _ _ _
 5.        _ _ e _ _ _ _ _
 6.      _ _ _ e _ _ _ _ _
 7.      _ _ _ e   _ _ _ _ _ _
 8.      _ _ _ e _ _ _
 9. _ _ _ _ _ _ e
10. _ _ _ _ _ _ e
```

Definitions

1. atomic particle which can move around the nucleus and carry a negative charge
2. amount of it is due to speed molecules of a substance are moving at
3. the capacity or ability to do work
4. changes chemical energy directly into electricity
5. range of electromagnetic energies
6. energy stored in matter
7. distance from one crest to the next crest
8. energy of matter in motion
9. measurement of heat energy
10. sound vibrations between 20 and 20,000 times/sec., which humans can interpret

Directions: Below are ten rows of four words each. In each row there are three words which are related to one another in some way. In some of the examples there might be more than one relationship possible. Circle the word in each row that you feel is not related to the other three. Be ready to tell why you chose the word you did, and what the relationship between the other three words is.

1. energy   (kinetic)   (force)   motion
2. (light)   wave lengths   spectrum   (electron)
3. (nuclear)   mechanical   energy   (turbine)
4. sun   (turbine)   fossil fuel   solar furnace
5. light   radiant   energy   (work)
6. transparent   (luminous)   translucent   opaque
7. primary   (complementary)   yellow   red
8. (solar)   lunar   eclipse   moon
9. light   prism   (reflection)   dispersion
10. lumen   foot-pound   calorie   (force)

Directions: Below you will find sets of two words each. In the first set, the two words have a definite relationship. Following the two words is a single word and then a blank. Below the blank are three words, one of which you are to write on blank and have it relate to the single word as first two words do to each other.

1. motion:kinetic————rest:_____
   energy, work, potential

2. bend:refraction————return:_____
   bounce, vibrate, reflect

3. fuel:coal————electromagnetic:_____
   ultraviolet, thermodynamic, sound

4. work:foot-pound————heat:_____
   lumen, calorie, degree

5. dispersion:prism————refraction:_____
   lens, mirror, shadow

6. light:lumen————sound:_____
   amplitude, decible, pitch

7. water:sonar————air:_____
   audible, ultrasonic, radar

8. sound:vacuum————light:_____
   opaque, transparent, translucent

Directions: Each of the below scrambled words is followed by a definition that states the meaning of the word when put in its correct spelling. Read each of the definitions and then unscramble the word to mean a word corresponding to the given definition. Write the new word on blank given.

rkow	— produce of force times distance	_____
rgyene	— the capacity or ability to do work	_____
barmu	— the uniform dark area in a shadow	_____
nsle	— a polished, transparent substance with at least one surface curved and not parallel to the other surface	_____
fionsfuid	— scattering of light rays hitting an irregular surface	_____
qernueycf	— the number of wave vibrations per second	_____
oefrc	— an action which affects the state of rest or motion in matter	_____
munel	— unit used to measure the amount of illumination on a surface	_____
tbomcusoin	— a rapid chemical reaction of a fuel with oxygen in which heat and light energy are released	_____
arelnuc	— having to do with energy in an atom's nucleus	_____

Directions: Select from the answer column at the left the word which best answers each of the statements at the right. Put the number of the word in the proper space in the magic-square answer box. If your answers are correct, they will form a magic square. The total of numbers will be the same in each row across and down to form a magic number. Add up the rows across as you do them to check if you're coming out with the same number for each row. If not, better check your answers in the row that doesn't have the same number as the majority.

ANSWERS

1. energy
2. work
3. nichrome
4. infrared light
5. reflect
6. calorimeter
7. pendulum
8. coal
9. resistance
10. cesium cell
11. thermometer
12. combustion
13. mechanical energy
14. ultraviolet
15. kinetic
16. turbine
17. sound energy
18. alloy

A. Occurs when a force moves an object
B. Device where a weight is arranged so it swings back and forth
C. A compound made of two or more elements
D. Chemical reaction of a fuel with oxygen
E. A type of fossil fuel
F. A bouncing back or giving off of heat and/or light by a light surface
G. Device for measuring changes in temperature
H. Energy of matter in motion
I. Energy produced by a moving machine
J. Energy produced by vibration of matter
K. Device for measuring amount of heat produced by a substance
L. A wire of extremely high electrical resistance
M. Large water wheels to turn generators
N. Produces electricity by the Edison effect
O. Type of heat energy which has a short wavelength than visible light
P. The opposition to flow of electrons in a conductor

A	B	C	D
E	F	G	H
I	J	K	L
M	N	O	P

The Magic Number is ___39___

World Geography—Grade 9

Word List

CONTEXT
apex
elevation
altitude
relief
mountains
hills

STRUCTURE
topography
intensive
switch-back
piedmont

PHONETIC
butte
mesa

Word List

CONTEXT	STRUCTURE	PHONETIC
plateaus		
plains		
subsistence crop		
money crop		
density		
slope		
escarpment		
fissures		
erosion		
deposition		
continental shelf		
Fall Line		
delta		
alluvial fan		
native		

Matching

Directions: In Column B there are definitions for the words listed in Column A. Match each word and its definition. Place the letter of the definition on the line in front of the word it defines. If you are in doubt as to the definition of a term you may look in your text to determine its meaning. Next to each term you will find in parentheses three numbers which will locate the term in your text. The first number is the page, the second is the column, and the third is the paragraph.
EXAMPLE: (356;1;3) page 356, column 1, paragraph 3.

COLUMN A	COLUMN B
_____ 1. alluvial fan (221;1;2)	a. between 500 & 1000 feet relief with more sloping than flat land
_____ 2. deposition (216;2;2)	
_____ 3. delta (222;2;2)	b. long line of steep cliffs forming boundary between two plateaus
_____ 4. relief (192;2;0)	
_____ 5. escarpment (213;2;1)	c. dropping of broken rock and other materials by wind, water
_____ 6. erosion (216;2;2)	
_____ 7. Fall Line (218;1;0)	d. sloping edge of a continent between the shore and the ocean basin
_____ 8. hill (194;1;1)	
_____ 9. plateau (194;1;1)	e. relief under 500 feet; more flat than sloping land; cut by steep valleys
_____10. continental shelf (216;2;4)	
_____11. plain (194;1;1)	f. wearing down and smoothing out of land by wind, water
_____12. mountain (194;1;1)	g. point where rivers pass from hard

COLUMN A   COLUMN B

rocks of old land surfaces to soft rocks of coastal plains & in so doing creates rapids & falls

h. land surface at base of mountain created by deposition of sand, dirt

i. cracks in the surface of the earth

j. at least 1000 feet of relief with more sloping than flat land

k. mouth of river where sediment is deposited as it enters sea

l. difference in elevation of related land surfaces

m. relief under 500 feet; more flat than sloping land

Multiple Meaning Words

Directions: You will often find that a word can have different meanings depending on how it is used in a phrase, sentence or paragraph. Listed below are words and some of their possible meanings. Underline each possible meaning for each term. The first is done for you.

WORD	POSSIBLE MEANING
1. fissure	a. <u>a narrow opening</u>
	b. <u>a cleft</u>
	c. interlocking
2. escarpment	a. cliff-like ridge of land
	b. steep sloping land
	c. line of steep cliffs
3. dense	a. stupid
	b. sparse
	c. thick
	d. concentrated
4. intensive	a. increased emphasis or force
	b. a more thorough tillage
	c. concentrated
5. relief	a. help or assistance given to remove distress
	b. difference in elevation
	c. comfort
	d. let go

WORD	POSSIBLE MEANING
6. subsistence	a. continuance
	b. the providing of support
	c. lack of surplus
	d. producing just enough to get along
7. native	a. natural to
	b. indigenous
	c. original inhabitant
	d. occurring in nature pure or uncombined
8. plain	a. evident; obvious
	b. simple
	c. homely
	d. smooth out
9. elevation	a. loftiness; dignity
	b. disclosure
	c. height

Categorizing

Directions: Following the list of words below there are four categories. Place each word under the category to which it belongs. If you believe a word properly belongs under more than one category, you may list it more than once. One is done for you.

altitude	Fall Line	alluvial fan
escarpment	switch-back	mesa
fissures	butte	slope
erosion	continental shelf	relief
deposition	delta	piedmont

MOUNTAINS	HILLS	PLATEAUS	PLAINS
slope	slope		

Word Puzzle

Directions: To solve the following puzzle, look at the definitions below. Think of a word which fits a definition and has the same number of letters as the number of spaces provided in the corresponding line. Write the word on the line. Do this for each definition. After you have completed the exercise, look at the first letter of each word. You will find that as you read down the letters spell one of your vocabulary words. The first one is done for you.

1. e l e v a t i o n
2. _ _ _ _ _
3. _ _ _ _ _ _ _ _ _ _ _
4. _ _ _ _
5. _ _ _ _ _ _
6. _ _ _ _ _ _ _ _ _
7. _ _ _ _
8. _ _ _ _ _ _ _ _
9. _ _ _ _ _ _
10. _ _ _ _ _ _ _ _ _ _

1. distance above sea level
2. the angle or amount of slant
3. the sloping edge of a continent between the shore line and the ocean basin is called the _____ shelf.
4. narrow point; tip
5. difference in elevation between high and low points of a given area.
6. a plain formed at the foot of a mountain on the surface of an alluvial fan
7. a lone, steep-sided, flat-topped hill
8. wearing away of land by wind, water, glacier
9. occurring naturally in a particular area
10. description of the earth's surface.

Word Association

Directions: In each set of words given below, you will find the following: two words that have a definite relationship, as employer:employee. Following these two words is a single word followed by a blank. Below the blank are three words. You are to choose the word that is related to the word preceding the blank in the same way as the first two words are related, and insert it in the blank.

    EXAMPLE:

        employer:employee—management:_____
                    trade, *labor,* employment

1. elevation:altitude—butte:_____
        plain, mesa, escarpment
2. subsistence crop:money crop—erosion:_____
        destruction, ice built plains, deposition
3. mountains:rough lands—plateaus:_____
        flat lands, dry lands, rough lands

4. plains:money crops—mountains:_____
   surplus crops, subsistence crops, sturdy crops
5. plains:straight roads—hills:_____
   switch-back roads, curved roads, veined roads
6. mining:mountains—farming:_____
   mesas, deltas, plains
7. lowlands:plains—highlands:_____
   hills, alluvial fans, plateaus
8. dense:sparse—apex:_____
   summit, piedmont, acme
9. rivers:mountains—lava flows:_____
   plains, fissures, deltas
10 hills:valleys—plains:_____
   rivers, continental shelf, fall line
11. mountain:topography—alluvial fan:_____
    river plain, river, deposition
12. density:thickness—elevation:_____
    relief, altitude, dizziness
13. snow line:mountains—fall line:_____
    hills, plains, mountains

Following Directions

Directions: Under each blank line below, you will find several words listed.
You are to identify the category to which each of these words belongs and
write its name on the line provided.

To help identify the name of the category, you may find all of the letters
in the name by following simple directions. You will notice single numbers
(15, for example) and/or double numbers (4-3, for example) under each
set of words. To the left of each single or double number is a blank.

A single number refers to a letter in the alphabet (15, for example, refers
to the letter o); a double number refers to the letter in a word in a list (4-3,
for example, refers to the fourth letter in the third word from the left in the
list). You are to find each letter so identified and write it on the line provided. Then unscramble all of the letters and spell the name of the category
you are seeking. The first one is done for you.

1. **TOPOGRAPHY**
   mountains, hill, plateaus, plains
   y̲ 25 h̲ 1-2 p̲ 16 t̲ 4-3 o̲ 15 p̲ 1-4 g̲ 7 a̲ 6-1 r̲ 18 o̲ 2-1
2. _____ _____ (two words)
   piedmont, flood, delta
   __22 __18 __2-1 __2-4 __18 | __19 __7-1 __3-4 __2-1 __16 __3-4

3. _____
   deep rivers, steep valleys, flat land surface
   __2-7 __12 __3-5 __2-6 __4-2 __2-3 __4-1
4. _____ _____ (two words)
   ice scoured, ice built, loess
   __2-1 __13 __4-4 __1 __1-5 __1 __7 | __1-2 __14 __1 __16
                                        __1-1 __12
5. _____ _____ (two words)
   cotton, wheat, jute
   __6-1 __3-2 __26 __2-1 __13 | __5-1 __18 __16 __1-1

English—Grade 9

Word List

1. disguise
2. pretense
3. disheveled
4. erratic
5. sullen
6. vindicate
7. neurotic
8. ornate
9. promenade
10. incredulity
11. malicious
12. amiable
13. ludicrous
14. ominous
15. elude
16. pantomime
17. assimilation
18. grudgingly
19. vicious
20. sulky
21. quizzically

Context
* assimilation
  disguise
  sullen
  grudgingly
  vicious
  quizzically

Phonics
* disheveled
  amiable
  ornate
  ominous
  elude

Structure
* indictment (same family)
* vindicate
  incredulity
  erratic
  neurotic
  malicious

Teach by giving interesting history
* sulky
  pantomime
  ludicrous

The following words appear in the play *A Raisin in the Sun* by Lorraine Hansberry. Note the definitions.

(This column will
be filled in later
for Exercise B.)

disguise —	to change the dress or appearance of _____ in order to conceal one's identity or counterfeit another's.
pretense —	an excuse or subterfuge _____
disheveled —	ruffled, unkempt, mussed up _____
erratic —	wandering, eccentric, deviating from _____ a wise or common course
sullen —	ill-humoredly unsociable, gloomy _____
vindicate —	to sustain or justify; to maintain as _____ true or correct against denial, censure or objections
neurotic —	nervous, high-strung _____
ornate —	adorned excessively _____
promenade —	noun: a walk in a public place for _____ pleasure, display, or exercise verb: to walk
incredulity —	unbelief, skepticism _____
amiable —	friendly, agreeable, sociable _____
indictment —	official charging of person of an offense _____

A. Without looking at the definitions above, insert the correct words in the spaces below.
1. Because she did not wear a hat even though the wind was blowing, her hair was completely _____.
2. Since her tastes were simple, the _____ furniture did not appeal to her.
3. The wife's _____ at seeing her husband alive after he had been missing for five years was understandable.
4. In an attempt to throw the police off his track, the expert safe-cracker planned to _____ himself.
5. Using the _____ that her skin was allergic to soap, the clever girl was not required to wash the dishes at the evening meal.
7. Because he would break off in the middle of a conversation and begin talking about something completely unrelated, the students in the classroom realized that the professor's thinking was

_____.
8. The actress was proudly _____ her saucy French poodle through the crowded airport.
9. The young boy swore that he would _____ his father's good

name even if everyone else believed the incriminating stories published in the newspapers.

10. He was chosen president of his class because he was _____ with everyone.

11. His manner was insulting and _____, for he had been denied the use of the car by his father.

B. Now cover up the words to the left of the definitions. Looking at just the definitions, write the correct vocabulary words on the lines at the right corresponding with the definitions.

C. Look at the definitions below the puzzle. Think of a word from the vocabulary list which fits the definitions and place it in the corresponding line. Do this for each definition.

If you complete the puzzle correctly, the name of the author of the play *A Raisin in the Sun* will appear in one of the columns. The first letter of her name is inserted and capitalized on the first line. You supply on this line the rest of the word which means "ruffled or untidy."

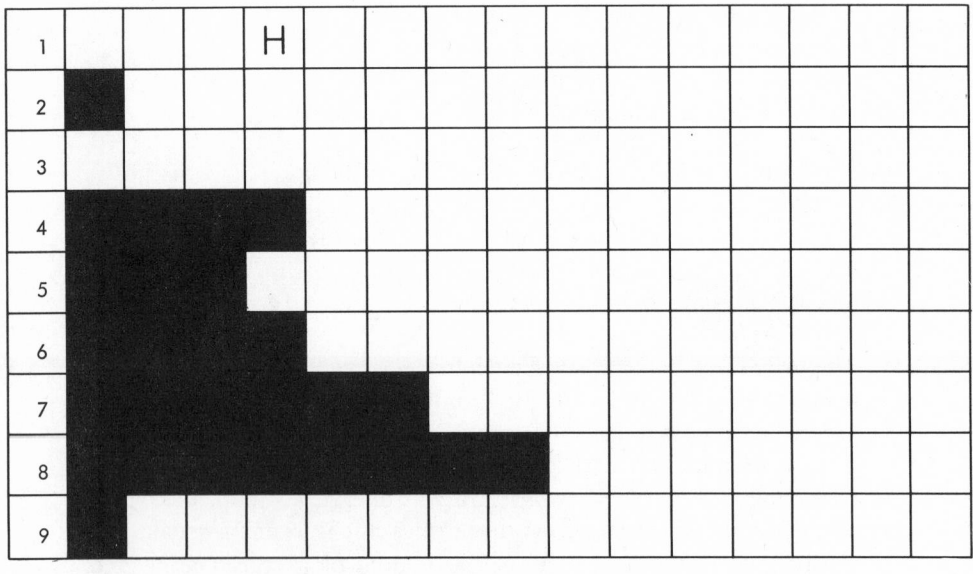

1. ruffled, untidy
2. overdone, decorated excessively
3. excuse
4. to change or hide one's identity
5. friendly, sociable
6. sulky, gloomy
7. nervous, high-strung
8. wandering, eccentric
9. unbelief

D. In each set of words given below, you will find two words that have a definite relationship. Choose from this vocabulary list one of the words that fits the single word in the same way as the paired word. Insert this word in the blank where the *?* appears.

Ex. $\dfrac{\text{Editor}}{\text{newspaper}} = \dfrac{\text{producer}}{?}$ answer is *play*

1. $\dfrac{\text{disheveled}}{\text{tidy}} = \dfrac{\text{amiable}}{?}$

2. $\dfrac{\text{erratic}}{\text{incredulity}} = \dfrac{\text{consistent}}{?}$

3. $\dfrac{\text{vindicate}}{?} = \dfrac{\text{pretense}}{\text{excuse}}$

4. $\dfrac{\text{sullen}}{\text{sulky}} = \dfrac{?}{\text{neurotic}}$

5. $\dfrac{\text{walk}}{?} = \dfrac{\text{disguise}}{\text{conceal}}$

Mathematics—Junior High

Muskopf, M. F., R. L. Morton, J. R. Hooten, and H. Stiomer, *Modern Mathematics for Junior High School* (Morristown, N.J.: Silver Burdett Company, 1961), pp. 110, 111, 112, 113.

Word List

1. arc	20. plane ***
2. cone	21. horizontal ***
3. ray	22. perpendicular ***
4. angle	23. vertical ***
5. number	24. point ***
6. square (abbr.)	25. oblique ***
7. pi	26. line ***
8. area	27. set ***
9. foot (abbr.)	28. diagram ***
10. inch (abbr.)	29. unlimited ***
11. discount	30. oblique parallel ***
12. meter	31. betweenness ***
13. precision	32. skew lines ***
14. error	33. Geometry ***
15. per cent	34. measure
16. commission	35. line segment ***
17. interest	36. intersect ***
18. ratio	37. common ***
19. decimal equivalent	38. indefinitely ***

(*** Words to be pretaught or examined in context.)

Eliminate the word that does not belong to the group and place the number of the group in the *correct column* below.

(1.)	(2.)	(3.)	(4.)
plane	line	meter	interest
horizontal	point	foot	ratio
angle	oblique	precision	commission
perpendicular	set	error	decimal equivalent

(5.)   Correct category is as follows:

diagram   GEOMETRY   MEASURE   PER CENT
unlimited
oblique parallel   _____   _____   _____
betweenness
                          _____   _____   _____

                          _____   _____   _____

The words that you will be using in the crossword puzzle below are words that we are now using in the chapter or words found in the previous chapters. They all have mathematical meaning. Read the selections carefully and then decide which word you should use.

CROSSWORD PUZZLE

ACROSS

1. The branch of math that deals with space
2. A set of points that has no beginning or end
3. From right to left
4. From north to south
5. The abbr. for number
6. A smooth flat surface that has length and width, but no depth
7. A quadrilateral that has square corners and equal sides
8. Anything without bound or limit
9. To continue without end

DOWN

1. Collection of objects
2. Part of a circle
3. A line that is slanted
4. The ratio of the circumference of a circle to its diameter
5. The set of points which describe the interval from one fixed point to another
6. A solid that has a circular base and whose sides taper into a single vertex
7. A line that has a starting point and runs in only one direction
8. Any line drawing such as a geometrical figure, sketch, or plan
9. The figure formed by two lines meeting at a single point
10. The abbr. for square
11. Set of points enclosed by straight lines
12. Abbr. for foot
13. Abbr. for inch

Vocabulary Reinforcement Material

Matching Exercise

1. Geometry
2. Unlimited
3. Indefinitely
4. Plane
5. Diagram
6. Horizontal
7. Vertical
8. Oblique
9. Point
10. Line
11. Set
12. Intersect
13. Betweenness
14. Common
15. Parallel
16. Perpendicular
17. Line segment
18. Oblique Parallel
19. Skew lines
20. Analyzing

For the following definitions place the number of a word to be found above on the line before the definition which would best fit the word.

(A)   11   a well defined collection having some quality in common, as the group of points or like elements

(B)   10   that which best describes the edge of a book or paper

(C)   12   what is said about two lines that cross

(D)   1   that branch of mathematics dealing with space and its relations; the study of form

(E)   7   lines that go straight up or down

(F)   16   two lines that intersect to form right angles

(G)   4   a geometric surface with length, width, but no depth

(H)   14   similarity, likeness, sameness

(I)   6   lines that extend to the right or left in the same manner as the horizon

(J)   17   a piece of a line is called by this name

(K)   3   anything which is boundless or not restricted

(L)   20   if we state the appearance of something such as the description of a toy, we are said to be

(M)   9   an indication of a place or position which has no length, width, or depth

(N)   19   two lines which are not in the same plane and neither intersect nor are parallel

(O)   15   two lines in the same plane which do not meet are said to be

(P)   5   any line drawing such as a geometrical figure, sketch or plan

(Q)   13   set of points which describe the interval from one fixed point to another

(R)   2   having no fixed limit or amount

(S)   18   two lines which are both slanting and parallel are called

Inclusion of these materials is not to suggest that *every* unit in each subject area be treated in this manner. This would become dreadfully boring for the students and the teacher. However, early in the year such emphasis is needed. After students are looking for the structure of words, making good use of context clues, thinking of words on the interpretive level, the teacher can reduce the intensity to a maintenance emphasis, focusing on parts of the whole program rather than the whole. He should never completely abandon emphasis on vocabulary since that would be assumptive teaching again. However, since his purpose is to develop independence in the use of vocabulary skills, he needs to program into his year the opportunity for students to exercise independence at the level of sophistication he demands of them.

At the beginning of the following year, however, one starts again with his new students, even though there is a well-established, all-school program for teaching reading in content areas. As said before, each new grade and/or subject requires new levels of sophistication and understanding. Because the previous teacher has done an excellent job is no excuse for us not to do the very same at the new level of sophistication required for the course and grade level—and to teach students how to function independently at this new level.

This is the challenge of teaching reading through content: helping each student to attain a degree of independence appropriate to his needs at each successive grade level in each of his subjects.

PRACTICE

To practice (and have a basis for comparison with your colleagues) on the various phases of vocabulary development, the following word list is provided. Examine the list and determine which words you would use to teach structural and phonetic analysis. Words for contextual emphasis already are noted.

Design word meaning exercises at the literal and interpretive levels. Compare them with your colleagues' and those given at the end of the chapter. These exercises were designed by a classroom teacher and are reproduced as they were designed and used.

Word list **

* element	* proton	* mixture
* properties	* electron	* compound
* atom	* neutron	* molecule
* metal	* orbit	* inert
electrolysis	combination	physical
nonmetal	sub-atomic	nucleus
luster	definite	chemicals

* Meanings to be derived from context clues.
** Words from *Modern Science,* 2 (New York: Holt, Rinehart, and Winston, 1964), Chap. 2 ("Behavior of Matter").

SUMMARY

The language of a subject is its technical vocabulary. Until a student has facility with that language he cannot communicate ideas essential to the subject.

Functional development of the technical vocabulary has several advantages: word analysis, word recognition, and word meaning are developed in a context that has relevance to a teacher's desires and his students' needs; students develop understanding of and competence with skills that enable them to add to their vocabulary independently; as skills are developed, so is an understanding of basic concepts represented by the words to which the skills are applied.

Vocabulary development can be a continuation of the principle of teaching skills and course content simultaneously.

REACTION GUIDE

CATEGORIZING

Directions: Below is a list of words and phrases. According to the meaning you give each item, place it under one or more of the categories which follow. Discuss your responses with colleagues to compare and resolve differences. (Some items in the list may not relate to any of the categories.)

textual aids	speaking vocabulary	writing vocabulary
listening vocabulary	relative value	students' competence
reading vocabulary	analysis of text	structure
context	dictionary	word lists
word power	language development	interpretive
key concepts	technical vocabulary	literal
multiple exposure	structure of lessons	decoding
categorizing	matching	analysis
vocabulary load	concept density	
	teacher preparation	

SELECTION	TEACHING	REINFORCEMENT
_____	_____	_____
_____	_____	_____

GENERALIZATIONS

Directions: Place a check before each of the following generalizations you can accept, having responded to this chapter and examined your own point of view. Discuss your responses with your colleagues.

_____ 1. A student should not be allowed in a course unless he has an understanding of the basic vocabulary of the subject.

_____ 2. Language development is the responsibility of all teachers.

_____ 3. Words selected determine skills to be taught by a content teacher.

_____ 4. Skills selected determine words to be taught by a content teacher.

_____ 5. Subject area word lists are as valid as subject area skills list.

_____ 6. Independence in vocabulary improvement is quite relative: to students' competence; sophistication of material; grade level; etc.

_____ 7. One can teach content and not teach the technical vocabulary but not the reverse.

_____ 8. Word analysis is unrelated to word meaning.

_____ 9. Students use both visual and auditory clues to derive meanings.

_____10. More words are caught than taught, usually, in content area classrooms.

Examples for "Practice" (see page 193)

Chapter 2 (pp. 40–62)—"Behavior of Matter"

CRITICAL THINKING

Seven rows of five words each are listed below. You are to cross out one word in each row and be prepared to tell how the other four relate to one another. The relationships differ and you might be able to work out several relationships. If so indicate them by stars.

1. physical change   chemical change   mixture   compound   water

2. atomic weight   molecule   atomic number   element   neutron

3. litmus   phenolphthalein   pH   salt   indicator

4. orbits   electrons   stable   inert   protons

5. base   metal   salt   acid   neutral

6. matter   elements   volume   mass   weight

7. symbol   equation   formula   proportion   mixture

Chapter 2 (pp. 40–62)—"Behavior of Matter"

WORD ASSOCIATION

Below you will find two sets of two words each. In the first set, the two words have a definite relationship. Following the two words is a single word and then a blank. Below the blank are three words, one of which you are to write on the blank and have it relate to the single word as the two words that come first do to each other.

1. acid:base————mixture: _____
      element, compound, matter
2. molecule:atom————kilogram: _____
      liter, meter, gram
3. compound:mixture————chemical change: _____
      property change, physical change, combination
4. nucelus:neutron————orbit: _____
      proton, molecule, electron
5. neon:inert————sodium: _____
      inactive, active, stable
6. weight:gravity————mass: _____
      matter, molecules, electrons
7. form:state————shell: _____
      electrons, element, orbit

Chapter 2 (pp. 40–62)—"Behavior of Matter"

FOLLOWING DIRECTIONS

Under each blank line listed below, you will find several words listed. You are to identify the category to which these words belong and write its name in the blank provided.

To help identify the name of the category, you may find all of the letters in the word by following simple directions. You will notice single numbers (1, for example) and/or double numbers (3–7, for example) under each set of words. To the left of each single or double number is a blank.

A single number refers to a letter in the alphabet (1, refers to a); a double number refers to the letter in a word from the list (3–7, refers to the third word and its seventh letter). You are to find each letter so identified and write it on the line provided. Then unscramble the letters and spell the name of the category you are seeking.

1. _____

      nucleus   proton   electron
   ___3–7 ___2–4 ___1 ___13

2. _____

    metal   nonmetal   inert

    __3–5 __2–4 __5 __12 __1–2 __2–3 __1–2

3. _____

    formula   iron oxide   proportion

    __3–1 __15 __2–5 __1–4 __3 __2–3 __1–5 __3–10

4. _____

    litmus   bitter   hydroxide

    __1–6 __3–9 __1 __2–1

5. _____

    salt   acid   base

    __14 __2–1 __1–4 __25 __3–4 __2–3 __14

    __1–3 __21 __18 __9 __20 __2–3 __15

Chapter 2 (pp. 40–62)—"Behavior of Matter"

MODIFIED NOUNS

In Section I are six words which have been used as adjectives in our study of chapter 2. In Section II are ten words which have been used as nouns related to our study of science. Take the words from Section I and combine them with the words of Section II so as to construct correct science terms. Words from each section may be used more than once if necessary.

SECTION I

atomic	physical
molecular	chemical
periodic	inert

SECTION II

change	weight
number	nucleus
element	property
formula	equation
table	symbol

Chapter 2 (pp. 40–62)—"Behavior of Matter"

SCRAMBLED WORDS

Each of the scrambled words below is followed by a definition that states the meaning of the word when put in its correct spelling. Read each of the definitions and then unscramble the word to mean a word corresponding to the given definition. Write the new word on the blank given.

  1. dpmnucoo-   a substance consisting of two or more
                    elements in a chemical combination   _____

2. esptiprroe-   the characteristics that distinguish one substance from another   _____

3. ntuerno-   atomic particle found in the nucleus of an atom and does not have a charge   _____

4. xutreim-   two or more substances physically combined so that properties of each are not changed   _____

5. mnleete-   the simplest form of matter that cannot be broken down into other substances by ordinary means   _____

6. ucslenu-   the dense part of an atom composed of protons and neutrons   _____

7. oamt-   the smallest particle of an element that has all the properties of the element   _____

8. lleeucom-   the smallest part of an element or compound and has all the properties of the substance   _____

9. aemlst-   elements that have a luster, can be hammered, stretched and can conduct heat and electricity   _____

10. enloercts-   atomic particles which move around the nucleus of an atom and have a negative charge   _____

9

INDIVIDUALIZATION, GROUPING, AND EVALUATION

Two new terms have particular significance in this chapter:
— work groups
— training groups
Another term, previously introduced, is analyzed further:
— functional analysis

IDEA DIRECTION

This chapter summarizes and extends two topics that have been implicit in the previous eight chapters: individualizing instruction; grouping for instruction. You should reflect on the consistency of the third topic, evaluation, with the other two.

READING DIRECTION

Topics in this chapter embody emotional issues. Read with objectivity and look for consistency as you relate the explication of these topics to the preceding portions of the text.

Individualizing instruction in content areas is extremely difficult, if not impossible. Yet a generally accepted principle in education is that a teacher should determine the ability and achievement levels of his students and instruct them in such a way that each progresses as fast and as far as his own capabilities will allow. This is individualizing instruction.

It is a rare teacher who can completely individualize instruction for his students. Whether on the elementary or secondary level, enormous time and energy are required to prepare for such instruction. Generally elementary level teachers have fewer students than secondary, but they work with those students for all subjects. Secondary teachers have fewer subjects to teach but they have a greater total number of students enrolled in all of their courses. At both levels, therefore, teachers have approximately the same load to consider if they individualize instruction.

The alternative to individualizing instruction, however, is not full class, lockstep, instruction with all students receiving the same fare whether they need it or not. Certainly this is more convenient for the teacher, but it is hardly valuable for the students. There is a more practical alternative: grouping with differentiated assignments for the groups, combined with total class instruction where practical.

The emphasis given in this book has been on ways to accommodate various achievement levels by differentiating assignments through lesson materials. The use of such materials by students grouped according to relative levels of achievement approximates individualized instruction. When students work together in groups, guided by these materials, the teacher is free to move among the groups, to identify students who need individual assistance, and to help them on the spot.

Grouping students for instruction *within* one's class is of critical importance. Such organizational structure makes possible the kind of instruction advocated in this text. It helps to accommodate both teacher and student needs described in chapter 1. It does not make complete individualization of instruction possible; but it does allow us to come as close to it as practicable, much closer than we observe in most content area classes.

GROUPING FOR INSTRUCTION

Organizing a total school population into grades and classes within grades is a gross kind of grouping. This section is devoted to intraclass grouping, but grouping of a more refined nature in that we are dealing only with the population of a given classroom rather than an entire grade or school.

Purposes for intraclass grouping are twofold. One, maximizing the individualization of instruction, is discussed above. The second, maximizing students' active involvement in learning, is discussed in chapters 1 and 2. Both purposes are crucial and speak to the needs that teachers are anxious to serve through practicable means.

TYPES OF GROUPS   Groups can be classified into two broad categories: training groups; work groups.[1] Training groups are formed when students with comparable needs or strengths are to be instructed in an activity or concept. Work groups are formed when students with comparable strengths and interests have a specific task to perform that requires them to utilize skills they already possess.

A teacher can become quite frustrated if he does not keep these distinctions clearly in mind. He can form a training group and expect students to develop some product. Since the group's purpose is to learn a specific skill or develop understanding of a specific concept, it is not realistic to expect it to develop a product using that skill or concept. Or he can give students a work task to perform and be frustrated because they have not developed new skills in the process. This is assumptive teaching, assuming that merely by giving students a task they will automatically develop new skills. If skills development is the desired product, the teacher should form a training group, not a work group.

COMPOSITION OF GROUPS   Most training groups should be homogeneous in composition, students having been grouped according to some specific need. It is quite likely that work groups would be heterogeneous in composition. That is, groups would be organized according to the task to be accomplished with students being assigned to groups according to the strengths that they can bring to the task to be performed. Hopefully there would always be homogeneity in work groups in terms of interest in the task to be performed, though that is not always possible for all students. Heterogeneous work groups offer students the opportunity to work with others of differing talents and capabilities, learning how to accept the strengths and weakness of others when working cooperatively on a task, learning how to appreciate the contributions of others as well as one's own. This is an extremely valuable by-product of group work.

Flexibility, of course, is the hallmark of grouping. The fact that we should distinguish between the two types of groups makes the point. If we are to use grouping to its fullest potential, we must be flexible. We should not consign students to a group forever, but rather, for the moment, to serve specific needs and purposes. There should be a somewhat loose state

[1] Matthew B. Miles, *Learning to Work in Groups* (New York: Teachers College Press, 1967), p. 35.

of organization, with students shifting according to their needs and the instructional purposes. If we do otherwise we defeat the purposes of grouping, and might just as well engage in lockstep instruction with all students doing the same thing at the same time in the same situation.

Styles of Leadership

What leadership options are open to teachers with reference to the style or attitude they display while exercising their leadership role? Miles presents several options. Though these suggestions are related to the role of a leader within a group, they are equally appropriate in a discussion of the role of the teacher during the organization and functioning of various groups within the class.

AUTOCRATIC: where the leader dictates the task, assigns workers to subtasks, and determines when the tasks have been completed satisfactorily.

BARGAINING: where a horse-trading approach involving rewards and punishments is central. The focus tends to be on the leader's agreeing to meet members' personal needs if they in turn will work on the official group task.

PATERNALISM: where the leader supplies nearly all the functions— benevolently—and does not permit members to perform leadership acts.

LAISSEZ-FAIRE
INACTION: where the leader supplies no functions, and does nothing to help members supply them.

COOPERATIVE
PROBLEM-
SOLVING: where the demands of the problems and the needs of persons are both central, and anyone who sees a missing function is expected to supply it.[2]

Obviously we must function with groups in the manner and style that is natural for us. Equally obvious is the fact that the COOPERATIVE PROBLEM-SOLVING style is most consistent with the emphasis of this text. Laissez-faire inaction style is assumptive. Paternalistic style does not allow students to develop independence. Bargaining seems unnecessary.

[2] Miles, *Learning to Work in Groups,* pp. 18–19.

Leadership Functions

What roles are open to the teacher within these styles? Again one can turn to Miles for a delineation.

INITIATING: keeping the group action moving, or getting it going. (for example—suggesting action steps; pointing out goals; proposing procedures, clarifying)

REGULATING: influencing the direction and tempo of the group's work. (for example—summarizing, pointing out time limits, restating goals)

INFORMING: bringing information or opinion to the group.

SUPPORTIVE: creating emotional climates which hold the group together, making it easy for members to contribute to work on the task. (for example—harmonizing, relieving tension, voicing group feelings, encouraging)

EVALUATING: helping group to evaluate its decisions, goals, or procedures. (for example—testing for consensus, noting group processes) [3]

Specific Suggestions for Intraclass Grouping [4]

As stated above, grouping within the classroom (accompanied by adequate materials designed for such use) makes it possible for a teacher to serve a range of individual differences with a minimum of effort. Some specific suggestions basic to intraclass grouping are discussed below.

ORGANIZATION OF GROUPS   Pairing is the easiest form of grouping. If you have never grouped your students for instruction, you would be wise to begin on this level. Ask students across the aisle from each other to form pairs.

Pairing students and combining pairs into "pairs of pairs" requires no movement of chairs or students. It is ideal for rooms with fixed furniture. It is excellent for a teacher's first attempts at grouping because it minimizes reorganization and movement of students and equipment, yet has the advantage of allowing exchange of information and point of view, expression of opinion, approval of peers, and opportunities for success. However,

[3] Miles, *Learning to Work in Groups,* p. 20.
[4] Harold L. Herber, *Learning Your Language,* Teacher's Guide (Chicago: Follett Publishing Company, 1967), pp. 21–24.

it does not provide for students of comparable ability and achievement levels to work together unless students are paired with that in mind. If "ability pairing" is done, it necessitates the movement of some students to insure this compatability.

If a teacher has had experience in grouping and feels at home with the procedure, he may have students work together in threes or fives. Having an odd number facilitates decision making where the majority opinion is to be determined. The teacher assigns students to groups according to his estimate of their homogeneity in ability and reading achievement.

BASIS FOR FORMING GROUPS   Grouping need not be based on an elaborate analysis of students' abilities or achievement. It is possible, early in the year, to organize your groups initially more on intuition than on any other criteria; unless, of course, you have access to standardized test scores, are able to interpret them accurately for this intraclass grouping, and have time for the process.

Initial grouping may be arbitrary. But this is no problem as long as you are not rigid and are not, in effect, consigning the student to a specific group for the entire year. The crucial factor in grouping is the functional diagnosis that is possible (see pages 208–209). By carefully observing students' performances in the groups, you can easily determine whether they are properly placed. During subsequent lessons, you may change the composition of the groups to better serve the needs of the students, according to your observation. Trust your judgment. You know your students better than anyone else does. But remain flexible. Composition of groups should change—as should the instructional activity—as frequently as the functional analysis indicates it can.

OPERATION OF THE GROUPS   Organize students into groups before they begin work on a reading guide, if they are to work on it in class: pairs, pairs of pairs, threes, fives, and so on, depending on the organizational pattern you have selected. Then, as students finish their work, they can begin discussion of their responses immediately. If the reading guide has been assigned as homework, students should be organized into groups when they come to class so they can discuss their responses to the material.

If you have arranged groups homogeneously, have the students exchange seats so that members of each group sit close together. Then have them move their chairs so they form a circle. Although the process will be confusing at first, students soon will become used to it and it will take only a few minutes to form the groups.

If you have fixed furniture, you can have the students work in pairs or pairs of pairs, as suggested above, moving them prior to their reading into combinations you have judged to be most effective and compatible.

When poorer readers are working together in groups, have them read the material silently first. They may ask an adjacent member of the group for help on any word or phrase causing them difficulty. After finishing the reading, they will do their work on the guide. On one occasion they may work together; on another they may work separately and then compare answers after they have completed the work. A representative of the group or pair may present their consensus in the full class discussion, the group or pair having resolved its differences in answers to questions. (This process, by the way, is an excellent opportunity to emphasize the necessity for and process of arriving at group opinion and the importance of presenting a united front on an issue even though all points advocated are not entirely compatible with one's own opinion.)

It is important to remember that a student can benefit from the lessons even though he does not answer every question on an exercise. The discussion on "levels of comprehension" makes this point clear. He can learn from other members of the class, too, and grouping enlarges this possibility.

TEACHER'S ROLE IN GROUPING   You do not remain idle during the group work. This period of time provides an excellent opportunity to observe your students' strengths and weaknesses as part of the functional diagnosis. (See page 208.) You should be ready to step in and help a group resolve a problem. If the entire group is following an erroneous line of reasoning, a quick question on your part will direct them. If one group is doing the work only superficially, a question from you will show them the superficiality. If a group is spending too much time on each step, a word from you will urge them on. If two or three individuals, or an entire group, are having particular difficulty with any combination of the skills, you can realistically devote time to these students as the remainder of the class is engaged in purposeful activity.

PROBLEMS IN GROUPING   Sometimes one student will not be finished reading the material when others begin their work on the exercise; or he may not be finished with his exercises when others are ready to discuss their answers. The group should not wait for him; he can begin the exercises with them, using the knowledge he has, contributing as much as he can and learning from the other members of the group in the areas he has not completed in his work. On subsequent lessons you may wish to move this student to another group. To move him during a lesson would be humiliating to him.

Occasionally one group will finish considerably later than the other groups in the class. What should be done in this case? There is an easy solution. Have this group do only the portion of the guide that you consider the most essential. When the entire class discusses answers and points of difference, let this slower group contribute on the parts they have completed. Then have them listen carefully to the other groups and record the findings on the others' answers. Do not, however, have this group give all their answers first and then just listen for the remainder of the time.

They should be called on to contribute their findings on each section covered, as the section is discussed. Do nothing to make their slowness conspicuous (though it is not hidden from anyone; students know as well as teachers who are the best, average, and slowest in the class).

BENEFITS FROM GROUPING   Grouping provides for what Durrell calls "multiple recitation." [5] When a teacher works with his class as a single group, each student has an opportunity to participate in the discussion only as often as the teacher calls on him. On the average it would be unusual for a student to recite more than twice in a given class period. However, when a student is a part of a small group, he has many more opportunities to participate in discussion. This allows each student to consider ideas and pursue questions in depth. His peers' reaction to his ideas, and his defense of them, cause him to learn more thoroughly. He participates actively, not passively, in the learning experience. He has more frequent opportunity to succeed than in the traditional class format.

Grouping within a class makes it possible to serve individual differences adequately. Group members are given a reasonable task; they have an opportunity to contribute and to receive peer approval; their achievement is recognized; they learn from others in the class; the more able students are not held up to wait for the slower group; the slow group is not frustrated by an unrealistic pace. It is better in every way.

EVALUATION IN CONTENT AREAS

Evaluation is inevitable in any content area. The degree to which it has a grip on the various curricula needs to be challenged, however. Also, there are several implications related to evaluation, growing out of the prescriptions in this text, which should be explored. Three specific questions, then, are discussed in the remainder of this chapter: 1) to what extent is evaluation necessary in content area classes; 2) if instruction is individualized (through grouping), how is achievement to be tested; 3) if instruction is individualized, how is achievement to be graded?

The discussion of these questions assumes two central purposes for testing in a content classroom. The first purpose is to enhance and crystallize learning. If properly instructed so they develop skills and concepts simultaneously, students are in a position, periodically, to marshal these skills and concepts to demonstrate their knowledge of both. If tests are properly constructed, they will reflect both the purpose of and procedures used in teaching the unit over which the test is constructed. This being true, then

[5] Donald D. Durrell, *Improving Reading Instruction* (New York: Harcourt, Brace, & World, Inc.), 1956.

the examination should be only an extension of the learning experience. Frequently students' "failure" on teacher-made tests is not a reflection of their lack of knowledge and skill but an indication that the test does not measure what was taught nor reflect the way it was taught. We recall our own experiences in college or university courses when we were certain we had the professor "psyched out." We knew, from the analysis of the professor and the course, how to prepare for the final exam—but discovered, to our dismay, that the examination reflected neither the professor nor the course! Too often teachers fail to measure what was taught and neglect to incorporate in the test design the methods used for instruction. The latter point is overlooked more than the former.

If, for example, we provide reading guides of the type that includes considerable assistance and numerous clues, we must design a test that will assess the students' competence at the same level of independence. To instruct this way and then to test with an instrument that demands complete recall and a high level of independent thinking is unrealistic. Students certainly will fail. How, then, can one test to reflect such methods?

Designing tests to measure content objectives is not difficult though it does require careful thought. The English teacher who has stressed composition during the marking period and then designs an objective test which measures students' knowledge of parts of speech is not measuring content objectives. Nor is the history teacher who stresses the effect of the Cold War on current deficits in the balance of payments and then designs an objective test that requires students to know names and places and dates related to the Cold War since World War II.

However, when properly designed to reflect content and procedure, tests (evaluation procedures) are profitable extensions of the learning process.

The second purpose for testing, assumed during this discussion, is to identify areas of strength and weakness. Strengths then can be built upon; areas of weakness can be overcome. The purpose of testing is *not* to provide a set of grades that can be averaged and entered in the grade book. Many content teachers, when discussing candidly their testing procedures and their reasons for giving relatively frequent tests (some are very proud over giving one, even two, tests or "quizzes" each week, and take great pride in a "full" grade book), say they are required by the administration to have a certain number of marks recorded in their grade book each marking period. So—they test!

When asked about the validity of such claims, administrators say their only protection against parents of children who fail the course or do poorly is a grade book with the student's marks recorded and averaged, showing the derivation of the grade recorded on the report card. We might ask, "Of what value is the professional judgment of teachers and administrators? Must we test in order to keep parents from questioning our judgment?"

To What Extent Is Evaluation Necessary?

Too much time is spent on formal testing in our schools. There is a common concern among teachers that they do not have enough time to prepare lessons and to give the kind of instruction that would be more profitable for their students. Yet these same teachers spend countless hours preparing and correcting tests, and too many class periods administering exams. If only half the time now devoted to testing were used for preparing those "better lessons," (and also better examinations, reflecting the first assumed purpose for testing), our instruction would be much better.

One way to solve the problem is to change the type of analysis that is commonly emphasized. There are really three types of analysis: functional, informal, and standardized. The latter two dominate education; the former has not yet had its day.

Functional analysis involves continual analysis of students' needs by observing how they respond to differentiated instruction. A teacher needs to account for achievement levels among his students. He observes how students respond to instruction which serves these levels, noting whether they experience success at their expected levels of achievement. In subsequent lessons, the students' activities are adjusted according to their responses during the previous lesson. The analysis, therefore, is functional in nature, occurring as part of the instruction and not as a separate operation. No formal data are collected; no scores are computed. Subjective judgment is the criterion, and this is effective.

Intuition, or subjective judgment, of the teacher is an important factor in functional analysis. A teacher who has a "feeling for" his students can estimate their levels of achievement on a given activity with considerable accuracy. If he accounts for those levels by differentiating assignments, he is beginning the process of functional analysis. The next step is to observe response and to adjust, intuitively, again, subsequent assignments according to that response. If the assignment was too difficult, involve the student in an easier type; if too easy, adjust upward; if just right, continue at that level to reinforce for a period of time.

Given a sensitivity to students' needs and a willingness to be flexible in teaching, one can engage in functional analysis while using lessons and materials described in this text. He will know more about his students' needs than if he relied on either informal or standardized analysis.

As already mentioned, analysis is misused if information is sought for its own sake and not used to aid the student. By its very nature, functional analysis obviates this danger. Both informal and standardized testing, however, are subject to the danger, since they focus principally on skills and concepts for their own sake, rather than on their use and value and the student's application of them.

Tests providing informal analysis are usually teacher made. They are designed to analyze achievement on specific skills and understandings, often related to the subject area taught by the teacher making the analysis. The teacher identifies selections from material used in the subject and the types of skills and ideas they embody. He designs questions which require use of these predetermined skills in order to obtain the answers. He determines students' levels of achievement according to their responses on the informal test. Subsequent instruction is planned to meet their needs.

Informal analysis is much like functional except that informal diagnosis makes the analysis a separate step, to gather information on which subsequent instruction is based. When the instruction meets students' needs, the information becomes obsolete because students' needs have changed. Hence, reanalysis is necessary. It is much more efficient to omit the collection of data from the informal analysis and concentrate on functional.

Standardized diagnosis, on the other hand, should be considered basic to any program designed to build skills as well as concepts. Standardized tests have been validated on large samplings of the populations which they were designed to analyze. The reliability of such tests is well determined; we are relatively certain that a given test really diagnoses the kind of achievement it purports to measure.

Standardized tests indicate a general index of achievement for an individual in comparison with other students of his age/grade level. One should examine the tests used to identify the subskills which contribute to the total test score. This gives meaning to the total score and to an analysis of the performance of an individual.

Assuming such examination, the standardized test score does serve as a point of comparison. Scattergrams can be made to plot the correlation between reading achievement and ability for each student. Entering scores on the scattergram reveals groups of students with comparable achievement. This information can serve to identify levels on which initial attempts for individualized (group) instruction might be based.

Engaging in functional analysis, using the time saved to prepare tests that enhance learning, relying more on teachers' judgment, resisting outside and uninformed pressures—all these factors put evaluation in the content classroom in proper perspective. With such perspective, evaluation consumes a share of instructional time more appropriate to its value.

How Is Individualized Instruction To Be Evaluated?

To be fair and to have completely valid instruments, if we completely individualize instruction, we should design a separate test for each individual. Given the present organizational structure of our schools, this would be impossible. This, of course, says nothing about the fact that few, if any, teachers would have either time or energy to prepare an examination for each of their students.

However, if we individualize instruction to the extent of having work and/or training groups functioning within the structure of lessons, using guides designed to accommodate levels of achievement in the class, then we should design examinations that reflect such instruction. And this *is* quite possible. We need only to use the same principle involved in the construction of reading guides for the three levels of comprehension as the basis for constructing multilevel examinations. We can also use the same format. The purpose is to have the measuring instrument evaluate the student's performance at the same level of independence required of him when he was instructed.

One can understand the point more clearly perhaps by examining excerpts from a test designed for a course organized by the author, based on the concepts contained in this text. In one particular class, among the 51 students, there was a considerable range of ability, experience, and achievement. The class, therefore, was organized into six groups which stayed together as both work and training groups most of the time. Periodically during class periods the students were regrouped to form other training groups.

Differentiated assignments were given to the groups, reflecting the levels of independence and background represented in each. Separate seminars were held with the most advanced students. Discussion sessions were held with other groups and individuals to meet their specific needs in reference to the assignments. Various degrees of guidance were provided, reflecting the groups' needs and the independence they had attained.

What kind of evaluation instrument, then, is valid for such a class? The following excerpt suggests an answer: design a test that reflects levels of comprehension. Each student was responsible for all of the content of the course. Depending on the group to which he belonged, a student would have responded to the content at the literal, interpretive, or applied levels of comprehension. Also, within the levels, individual students would have responded at different levels of sophistication. Therefore, the test allows some response at the factual level. Some items on the test reflect understandings at the interpretive level; still others, at the applied level. In all cases, there is sufficient guidance provided to accommodate the various levels of independence attained by the students in this course.

Similar examinations can be constructed for any content area, with any class, at any ability and achievement level. Note that this is not a complete test; that sections within it are illustrative.

Illustrative Segment of Evaluation

Part One

A. Check the statements, from those listed, which represent viewpoints presented by the instructor and/or material designed for the course.

_____ 1. Teachers spend an excessive amount of time testing.

_____ 2. Differentiation in instruction depends more on teachers' methods applied to materials than on the materials themselves.

_____ 3. "Comprehension" can be viewed as having three "levels."

_____ 4. Five specific criteria can be applied to material to select vocabulary for "pre-teaching."

_____ 5. The DRA and IF are identical in organization and purpose.

_____ 6. Transfer of skills is equivalent to transformation of skills.

_____ 7. "Structure of" lessons is not the same as "structure within" lessons.

_____ 8. Every teacher is a teacher of reading.

_____ 9. Etc.

B. Review the items you did *not* check in Section A of Part One. In the space provided below, rewrite the statements so they could be as "acceptable" as the ones you checked.

(Provide adequate space)

Part Two

A. Listed below are several details touched on during the course. When considered in various sets, they provide the basis for interpretations of the content of the course. Read over the list and then proceed to Section B.

a. Each subject has a technical vocabulary.

b. Students should be actively involved in the learning process.

c. There are three levels of comprehension.

d. Students in any class reflect a range of ability and achievement.

e. Lessons should be well structured.

f. Content teachers frequently engage in assumptive teaching.

g. Any expository material can be read at various levels of understanding.

h. Any skills can be applied at many levels of sophistication.

i. A student needs to use a word several times before he develops understanding of the concept it represents.

j. Concept development is not the same as information acquisition.

k. Word attack skills can be taught when technical vocabulary is taught.

l. Group work is profitable for most students.

B. On the line before each statement you believe represents a correct interpretation of the content of the course, write letters of the details you would interrelate to produce the statement.

_____ 1. Basic text material can be used to teach content-related skills as well as basic ideas in the curriculum.

_____ 2. Differentiated instruction can be provided profitably in any content classroom.

_____ 3. Learning needs among students of varying abilities differ in degree rather than kind.

_____ 4. The essence of good teaching is to show a person how to do what is required of him.

_____ 5. Students working in groups can accomplish tasks suited to their abilities, interests, and/or needs.

_____ 6. "Knowing" is not the same as "understanding."

_____ 7. Etc.

C. In the space below, write out any other statements that you believe represent the important content of the course suggested by the details in Section A. On a line before the statements you write, note the letters of the details you are relating to develop your statement.

(Provide adequate space)

Part Three

A. Listed below are names of several authors referred to during this course. Please read over the list.

1. Karlin
2. Strang
3. Marksheffel
4. Bruner
5. Bamman
6. Niles
7. Courtney
8. Raths
9. Russell
10. Durrell
11. Etc.

B. Listed below are several statements, each preceded by a line, each followed by space for written response. Write the author(s') number before statements which could represent a combination of the author(s) thinking and the content of the course. In the space below the statements, give your reasons for identifying the particular author(s) you select. Draw on your readings and class discussions.

_____ 1. Observation of response to differentiated instruction produces reliable evidence of students' learning needs.
(Space)

_____ 2. Students' needs are met by how—not what— they are taught.
(Space)

_____ 3. Children think at many levels of sophistication.
(Space)

_____ 4. Students should do more than to "sit behind their eyes."
(Space)

_____ 5. Models—or patterns—enhance rather than restrict learning.
(Space)

_____ 6. Etc.

How Is Individualized Instruction To Be Graded?

A science teacher once quit a program for low achievers because the students were doing too well! Principles expounded in this text were being used and several of her students were achieving at levels higher than students in the "regular" class. However, because they were in the so-called "low-achiever" class, they were not allowed to receive higher than a "C" on their report cards for any marking period. This teacher had to give examinations she knew would be too difficult for the students in order to bring down their average to the acceptable limit! Believing this to be immoral and terribly poor education, she quit in protest.

One deplores such situations—yet, they are widespread. In many systems, students consigned to "low achiever" classes are, by school policy, unable to attain more than a minimum passing mark, regardless of how well they do in the course.

Several arguments are given in favor of such a system. One is that we must have "standards" for the grades that are given and an "A" should represent outstanding achievement. But according to what criteria? Is not the very best achievement of the least able student as outstanding as the very best achievement of the most able? Why should his accomplishment go unrecognized?

The answer, then, is to give an effort mark, a number that reflects the effort one has expended in attaining the mark given. Who among us, one needs to ask, would be content with F^1 during his educational career? This says to the student, "You are failing but we know you are doing your best!" There is some saying about being kicked while down . . .

But, then we hear, "This is life as it really is—the competitive world. In real life everyone doesn't get A. Given A's during their schooling, such students will be in for a shock when they get out and compete with people much more able than they." To the contrary: life is such that one gravitates into association with people of like capabilities, like interests, enthusiasms, skills, accomplishment. Certainly within that homogeneity there are ranges, but rarely are they so clear as we are led to believe. Why cannot there be "A's" within groups at those various levels? There are, if we know life as it really is.

But then we hear the argument that these students from less able ranks will think they are college material and want a scholarship to Harvard because of all of their A's. Let them try, if they really do follow through. How many currently successful professionals would never have accomplished anything in life if they had been held to what appeared to be their "potential for success" while in elementary or secondary school? More than we can imagine. Moreover, we should not worry about this problem. Students know what's going on in the world. They measure themselves against students who "really have it" and know they are not college material. They know that even though they are getting good marks in the courses they are taking, they could not "cut it" if required to do the work in the "college prep" courses.

But then comes the big objection: what will the parents say? When Mrs. Jones shows George's "A" to Mrs. Smith, what will Mrs. Smith do when her Agnes has a "B" and everyone knows that George is rather slow and in the "dumb class" and Agnes is in the honors class and is "smart as a whip." What's the answer? Let them complain! Should we engage in improper practice just to avoid bruising the sentitive ego of some parent? Of course we shouldn't, and yet, it is being done constantly.

A major objection to grading students according to the success of their response to the differentiated instruction given to them, is potential complaints of the parents. Any number of systems, such as the following, can avoid this problem: numbers to indicate the track so that an F^1 indicates failure in the honors class rather than failure in spite of one's best efforts; colored report cards with the red, white, blue, and black designating various tracks; and so on.

Then, the final objection: a student from the slow class will quite likely be the valedictorian! Perhaps there *should* be one for each of the tracks— would there be anything wrong with that? For valedictorian of the entire population of a given grade, we can multiply into the averages a factor for the track in which the student took his courses—enter the factor of 5 for the honors, 4 for academic, 3 for . . . and so on. Thus the overall valedictorian would be representative of intertrack competition, avoiding inaccurate grading of students in lower tracks in relationship to what they are really doing. Perhaps the best action would be to abolish the practice of identifying a valedictorian.

Students in the graduate course described above (particularly those in the three groups whose members had limited teaching experience and background in disciplines related to the course) were asked if they preferred to be graded in the manner commonly used or in the manner advocated in the course. They believed that a grade reflecting their response to the demands placed on them, and the degree of independence they achieved according to those demands, was much more representative of their achievement than their being measured against the Ph.D. candidate who was an experienced classroom teacher of a content area, an experienced reading teacher, or an experienced school administrator. I agreed with them and graded accordingly. Many in all six groups received A's. Was this wrong? I think not.

Why cannot this same procedure and principle be applied in content classes in elementary and secondary schools?

SUMMARY

Teachers' problems are compounded when they attempt to individualize instruction. Complete individualization is next to impossible, so we settle for the practicable compromise—grouping.

Differentiated assignments must be prepared. These are made possible by using reading and reasoning guides. Evaluation is difficult if the teacher reflects both process and content in the examination. However, we can prepare fewer examinations of better quality and depend more on functional analysis for gathering information on students' achievement than on formal testing.

Grading becomes a problem because poor students do well on what is required of them and should receive a grade that properly reflects this achievement. The teacher must resist ego-based pressures from parents to grade according to arbitrary and invalid criteria.

Of course, we can teach, evaluate, and grade in a lockstep manner. But isn't it about time for a change?

REACTION GUIDE

Directions: Several pertinent statements from this chapter are listed below. They warrant analysis and discussion. Reflect on and discuss them with your colleagues. If you do accept them, what are you doing about it? If not, what are your alternatives?

1. It is the rare teacher who can completely individualize instruction for his students.
2. The alternative to completely individualizing instruction is *not* full class, lockstep, instruction with all students receiving the same fare whether they need it or not.
3. Flexibility, of course, is the hallmark of grouping.
4. Grouping within the classroom makes it possible for a teacher to serve a range of individual differences with a minimum of effort.
5. Composition of groups should change, as should the instructional activity, as frequently as the functional analysis indicates it can.
6. Testing should enhance and crystallize learning.
7. The purpose of testing is *not* to provide a set of grades that can be averaged and entered in the grade book.
8. Too much time is spent on formal testing in our schools.
9. In many systems students consigned to the "lower achievers" classes are, by school policy, unable to attain more than a minimum passing mark, regardless of how well they do in the course.
10. Is not the very best achievement of a less able student as outstanding as the very best achievement of the most able? Why should his accomplishment go unrecognized?
11. How many currently successful professionals would never have accomplished anything in life if they had been held to what appeared to be their "potential for success" while in elementary or secondary school?
12. Of course one can teach, evaluate, and grade in a lockstep manner. But isn't it about time for a change?

APPENDIX

USING THE READING AND REASONING GUIDES

On the following pages are representative reading and reasoning guides written by students and teachers with whom I have associated over the past few years. Each of these guides has been used in regular classrooms at the grade levels designated. When used in these classes, they were prefaced with appropriate activities from the Instructional Framework.

All of the guides presume (and were used with) intraclass grouping. Grouping varied depending on students' needs: sometimes occuring while the guide was being completed by the students; sometimes following the completion of the guide, for the purpose of resolving differences in students' responses.

Formats and purposes vary in these guides, as do grade levels, since they are representative. You will note that some emphasize organizational patterns and others levels of comprehension. Some are idea guides while others combine types. This is appropriate since they represent teachers' ability to adapt the ideas developed in this text to their own purposes and their students' needs.

You will find it useful to study these guides. You will gather many ideas for the construction of your own Reading and Reasoning Guides. Sections A, B, C, and D present guides from English, social studies, mathematics, and science respectively.

I appreciate the contributions to this section by Jeanne Clark, Joan Hendress, Betty James, Amy Rouy, Richard Baggett, Peter Sanders, Ruth Simmons, Tish King, Donald Elwell, Sr. Teresa Miriam, Edward Quinn, and Karen McKee.

READING AND REASONING GUIDES: ENGLISH

THE TIME MACHINE, H.G. WELLS   GRADE LEVEL: 9

I. APPLICATION OF CONCEPTS

Directions

Below in section A are some quotations from *The Time Machine* which express the Time Traveler's viewpoint on humanity. In B are some attitudes which contribute to these viewpoints. Place the correct number of the viewpoints in A in the spaces provided next to their counterparts in B.

A

1. "Even today there is a tendency to utilize underground space for less ornamental purposes of society."
2. "Above ground were the "haves," pursuing pleasure and comfort and beauty. Below were the have-nots, getting used to the conditions of their labor."
3. "Strength is the outcome of need. Security sets a premium on weakness."
4. "What is the cause of human intelligence and vigor? Hardship and freedom; conditions under which the strong and clever survive and the weaker fall."
5. "With perfect comfort and security, that restless energy that within us is strength would become weakness."

B

_____ 1. Why don't you take the subway to work this morning?
_____ 2. If I don't pass the final, I'll be grounded for the rest of the year.
_____ 3. Oh, I don't have to worry about a date this weekend. Dad will give me the car and some cash.
_____ 4. Why should I bother studying? Dad promised me a job as vice-president of his bank.
_____ 5. Why should I have to pay to keep someone else's family on welfare?
_____ 6. I wish I didn't have to work such long hours in school. I can't even come home in time to see the 2:00 Bugs Bunny show.
_____ 7. Oh, we have our basement fixed up nicer than our house.
_____ 8. What do we need labor unions for?
_____ 9. I think all (Italians, Jews, Negroes, Irish, German, Spanish, French, Chinese, Russian, etc.) people are inferior to us.
_____10. Look, if we don't stick together as a team, we'll blow the whole tournament!

II. PLANS AND PROBLEMS

Directions

The Time Traveler developed five plans to solve his problems in *The Time Machine*. Identify the plans by which the problems listed below might be solved. Write the letter of the plan on the line before the statement of the problem which it solves. More than one problem may be solved by a plan.

Plans

1. Secure a safe place of refuge and make himself arms of metal or stone.
2. Saving Weena from drowning.
3. Finding sulfur in the Palace of Green Porcelain.
4. Descending into the wells.
5. Breaking open the bronze doors under the white sphinx.
6. Travel on in future time.

Problems

_____a. Fighting off the Morlocks.
_____b. Curious to know how the Morlocks lived.
_____c. Be accepted by the Eloi.
_____d. Finding the Time Machine.
_____e. Learning the language of the Eloi.
_____f. Getting a description of the Morlocks.
_____g. Finding a companion.
_____h. Making an escape from the future.
_____i. Making a torch.
_____j. Finding out how mankind would finally end.

III. APPLICATION OF CONCEPTS TO SOCIETY

Directions

In the future world of the Time Machine, mankind had split into two species, one working and laboring underground and one pursuing pleasure and beauty above. Some practices and inventions today might contribute to this future state of affairs if carried to extremes. In the exercise below, circle the numbers beside those practices which might lead to the kind of society the Time Traveler saw. Be ready to defend your answers.

1. subways
2. basement restaurants
3. construction work
4. racial discrimination
5. Midtown Plaza parking
6. television
7. invention of the jet
8. coal mining
9. leisure time
10. sewer systems

IV. DRAWING CONCLUSIONS FROM EVIDENCE

Directions

In the blank spaces provided, supply the conclusion the Time Traveler drew from the evidence.

1. The flickering pillars and cupola-covered wells dotted the landscape.

2. The Eloi slept together in droves and seemed afraid of the dark.

3. The Morlocks only came out at night.

4. The Eloi wore beautiful garments and fancy sandals, but there was no sign of labor on the Earth.

5. The Eloi were weak, fragile people with the intelligence of five year old children.

LITTLE YELLOW DOG, STRINGFELLOW BARR

Below are some of the little yellow dog's quotes and actions:

A. "It is not so much a question of what my master must be like, as of what he must not."
B. "There are no men that I have seen in Poitiers or Tours that I could follow."
C. "I have hunted ever since I knew what my ideal was like."
D. "One aches to follow him and serve him."
E. "We are indeed restless, but how we crave someone to come back to from our strayings."
F. "I have never seen him."
G. "If I had once found him, you may be sure I would not have lost him again."
H. "Every morning at dawn I want my master to lead me off."
I. "I know what you are thinking. You are thinking that better dogs than I find masters in these places."
J. He seemed, by his gentle manner, used to this treatment.

Directions

1. Consider the following thoughts expressed in the slogans, song titles, statements, etc. below. Do you think the dog, *if he were consistent to his character as presented in the story*, would have approved of them? In Column A, answer *yes* or *no*.
2. In Column B write the letter indicating the quotation(s) of the dog which you considered in deciding your answer.
3. For number 17, write an original slogan, song title, etc. which would be appropriate for G.

A	B		
_____	_____	1.	Anything goes
_____	_____	2.	I've got to be in the "in" group
_____	_____	3.	I've gotta go where you are
_____	_____	4.	I'd rather fight than switch
_____	_____	5.	Seeing is believing
_____	_____	6.	Pride goeth before a fall
_____	_____	7.	True to you only
_____	_____	8.	You'd be so nice to come home to
_____	_____	9.	Nothing but the best
_____	_____	10.	The best is none too good for me
_____	_____	11.	Aim high
_____	_____	12.	Someday he'll come along
_____	_____	13.	Should a gentleman offer a Tiparillo to a lady?
_____	_____	14.	Never count the cost
_____	_____	15.	Blondes have more fun
_____	_____	16.	Night and day
yes	G	17.	

1. Write the name of your textbook.
2. Rewrite it as one word with no capitals.
3. If the article "If I Were Seventeen Again" is on p. 135, cross out all the a's.
   If not, cross out the n's.
4. If Sidney Lanier wrote "The Battle of the Kegs", change the r's to s's.
   If Francis Hopkinson wrote it, every time 2 or 3 consonants appear together, cross them out.
5. Consult the biographical introduction to Four New England Poets. Did
   Longfellow teach French and Spanish at Bowdoin College? If so, change the
   i to *o*.
   Did Lowell write the Bigelow papers? If so, drop the last two letters and
   any double letters.
   Consult the glossary. If the word *encroach* means to *drive out*. . . change
   every *e* to *o*.
   If it means to intrude. . . change the first *r* to *c*.
6. Consult the General Index.
   Is there an account of Stephen Crane's life on p. 608? If so, change the *si* to
   tt.
   On p. 806? If so, change the *si* to *ll*.
7. Consult the index of Art Reproductions in the Text. What is the first
   portrait by Charles Willson Peale?
   If it is one of John Adams, drop the last 2 letters.
   If it is one of Washington, change the first 2 letters to *re*.
8. If we are going to begin our work on p. 410, change the *r* to an *n*.
   If we are going to begin on p. 7, change the *t* to an *s*.
9. Does the poem "The Marshes of Glynn" have marginal notes?
   If it does, change the *u* to *x* and you will find that your answer to "following
   directions" is_____.

THE AMBITIOUS GUEST, HAWTHORNE
DISCOVERING CONTRAST

There are many examples of contrast in this story. List some details showing different kinds of contrast. The page, column, and paragraph are given to identify the location of your answer.

		Situation	Contrast
*	A.	Peace and quiet inside the house (550,1,1)	Disturbance outside (details)
**	B.	The family's remote situation. (550,1,3)	Their communication with the world. (details)
*	C.	The appearance and manner of the stranger when he arrived at the house. (550,20,2)	His manner after he entered the house. (details)
**	D.	The host's comment that the family had a sure place of refuge in time of danger. (551,1,4)	What is the contrast?
***	E.	The solitary life of the stranger. (551,1,4)	The unity of the family. (details)
*	F.	The stranger's ambition in life. (551,2,1)	In death? — (details)
***	G.	The actual location of the house and the father's occupation. (552,2,1)	What is the contrast?
***	H.	The little boy's wish. (552,2,5)	What would have happened if they had followed the boy's plan?
**	I.	What the family thought would happen when the slide started. (554,2,2)	What did happen?
***	J.	The stranger's ambition.	What is the contrast?

IDEA GUIDE

Directions

As you work together in groups, try to answer the following questions about this poem and attempt to resolve your differences as best you can. Always draw your support from the poem itself—not from what you wish the poem had said; not from what you want the poem to say.

From time to time, you may feel that the choices given are not adequate—especially near the end where the questions are more abstract; if you desire to add to the choice or formulate your own (or group) response, feel free to do so.

next to of course god
by e.e. cummings

'next to of course god america i
love you land of the pilgrims and so forth oh
say can you see by the dawn's early my
country 'tis of centuries come and go
and are no more what of it we should worry
in every language even deaf and dumb
thy sons acclaim your glorious name by gorry
by jingo by gee by gosh by gum
why talk of beauty what could be more beautiful than those heroic happy dead
who rushed like lions to the roaring slaughter
they did not stop to think they died instead
then shall the voice of liberty be mute?'

He spoke. And drank rapidly a glass of water

I. THE SPEECH

A. Cummings has presented us with a speech that is
  1. well developed
  2. impressionistic
  3. an outline
B. The speech is essentially
  1. patriotic
  2. religious
  3. historical
C. There is no punctuation used in the speech because
  1. the speaker is stupid
  2. cummings is stupid
  3. speeches should not be punctuated

D. The speaker obviously uses slang. Cite an example.

E. What assumption has the speaker made about his audience? What is your evidence?

1. They are just plain folks.
2. They are politically well-informed.
3. They are generally well educated.

F. The purpose of the speech is to get the audience to

1. support a war.
2. declare a truce
3. celebrate a victory.

What is your evidence?

II. THE CHARACTER OF THE SPEAKER

Directions

Beside each statement below place (an) a *S* for *speaker,* *C* for *cummings,* or *SC* for both if you think either or both would agree with the assertion:

1. The ends justify the means.
2. Don't let anything about communism be taught in school.
3. Most people can be lead by the nose.
4. The Pilgrims believed in religious freedom.
5. Mothers are wonderful people.
6. Dogs are man's best friend.

III. THEME

1. According to the speaker, what is "most beautiful"?
2. Is this also beautiful to you?
3. Do you think it is "beautiful" for cummings?
4. What characterized those "heroic happy dead"?
5. Does that characterize you?

IV. FORM AND FEELING

As you have learned, a poem is essentially *a pattern of feeling*—the dynamics of feeling being accounted for by the form of the poem.

1. What feeling has cummings accounted for?

A. Joy
B. Acceptance
C. Indignation
D. Melancholy
E. Regret
F. Other . . .

2. How has he done this?

A. By having the speaker use transparent patriotic cliches which, in their cumulative effect, ironically produce a feeling they might not otherwise create . . .
B. By using fragments of phrases and ignoring the rules of punctuation, which insult the intelligence of the reader . . .
C. By dividing the poem into two sections plus using slang and an informal approach, which achieve a mixed pattern of feelings . . .
D. Other . . .

DARKNESS AT NOON, ARTHUR KOESTLER   LEVEL: 12TH GRADE HONORS ENGLISH

I. Below is a list of communist maxims as stated at various points in *Darkness at Noon*. Following these maxims is a list of events which occur in the novel. In the blank space to the left of each event write the number of the maxim or maxims which, according to the communist philosophy as stated in the book, justify the actions referred to.

Maxims

1. the ultimate truth is penultimately always a falsehood
2. a revolution conducted according to the rules of cricket is an absurdity
3. the principle that the end justifies the means is and remains the only rule of political ethics.
4. our sole guiding principle is that of consequent logic
5. we are sailing without ballast; therefore each touch on the helm is a matter of life or death
6. for us, the question of subjective good faith is of no interest
7. we know that virtue does not matter to history and that crimes remain unpunished
8. finally we have to recur to faith—axiomatic faith in one's own reasoning
9. god is an anachronism
10. history is *a priori* amoral; it has no conscience

Events

_____ a. the execution of Bogrov
_____ b. the imprisonment of Rip Van Winkle
_____ c. the accusation of Arlova
_____ d. the trial of Rubashov
_____ e. the arrest of Ivanov

II. Rubashov's philosophic position undergoes considerable change as the story progresses. Listed below are several statements which he makes at various points in the book. Indicate in the blank to the left of each statement whether that statement would be acceptable to Ivanov (I), to Gletkin (G), to Bogrov (B) or to none of these men (N). You may want to place more than one letter in a single blank.

_____ 1. "If the Party embodied the will of history, then history itself was defective."
_____ 2. "It is that alone that matters; who is objectively in the right."
_____ 3. "The Party can never be mistaken."
_____ 4. ". . .in those days we made history, now you make politics."
_____ 5. "Honor is to be useful without vanity."

_____ 6. "...it is just such a generation of [consequential] brutes that we need now."

_____ 7. "History has taught us that often lies serve her better than the truth."

_____ 8. "The definition of the individual was: a multitude of one million divided by one million."

_____ 9. "Obviously, [suffering was justified] if one spoke in the abstract of 'mankind'; but, applied to 'man' in the singular, to the cipher 2-4, the real human being of bone and flesh and blood and skin, the principle led to absuridty."

_____ 10. "Death is an abstraction, especially one's own."

III. At the beginning of the Third Hearing Rubashov uses two analogies to explain the logic which enables him finally to confess (see pp. 143-147). Examine each of the statements below and determine whether they are true (T) or false (F) according to the analogies. You may conclude that the analogies provide insufficient information (I) for you to make a determination. Place the appropriate letter in the blank to the left of each statement.

_____ 1. Conflict between people and their government is to be expected as a natural occurrence of history.

_____ 2. The differences between communism and capitalism are differences in the maturity of the masses involved and not in the degree of advancement of the two social orders.

_____ 3. The political maturity of the civilized countries of the 20th century is greater than that of an Australian aborigine tribe.

_____ 4. Utopias can never be realized.

_____ 5. A single phenomenon cannot be explained by both analogies.

IV. The quotation below appears opposite the title page of *Darkness at Noon* and thus helps to set the stage or tone for our reading. Examine the statements which follow the quotation. Which of these reflects an accurate interpretation of the quotation as you think Koestler intended it? Indicate your choice(s) by placing a check mark in the appropriate blank(s).

"Man, man, one cannot live quite without pity."

–Dostoevsky:
Crime and Punishment

_____ 1. A commentary on the events of the book and on the apparent futility of man's efforts to reach a utopia.

_____ 2. A commentary on the communist philosophy, pointing out its shortcomings.

_____ 3. A "summary" of the lesson Rubashov finally learns.

_____ 4. A commentary on Rubashov as the author (and perhaps the reader) sees him.

_____ 5. Other_____

READING AND REASONING GUIDES: SOCIAL STUDIES

MAKING A LIVING IN NEW ENGLAND IN COLONIAL TIMES AND TODAY
GRADE LEVEL: 5

Directions

Find the answers to the questions listed below. The page, paragraph, and sentence clue will help you. Write your answers beneath the questions. Work with others in your group.

1. What products grew well in Maine? (p. 125-0-1)

2. Where did the Colonists get most of their furs? (p. 125-1-2)

3. What was most New England land like when the Pilgrims came? (p.125-3-1)

4. Who was the first man to discover the fishing grounds off the coast? (p.126-1-1)

5. Where did the Colonists sell much of their fish? (p.126-2-2)

6. Where is whaling done today? (p. 127-4)

7. What is the meaning of trading? (p.129-4)

8. What kind of ship did the early traders use? (p.129-3-2)

9. Name three articles that are made using "mass production". (p.132-6-1&2)

CAUSE AND EFFECT

Directions

Read the statement. Read the page in your book to find the *cause* for each *effect*. Select the best cause from those listed at the bottom of the page. Write it on the line after the page number.

1. Cause: (p.125)_____
   Effect: The Pilgrims cut down trees.
2. Cause: (p.125)_____
   Effect: The colonists brought boatbuilders from England.
3. Cause: (p.125)_____
   Effect: Some farmers grow cranberries.
4. Cause: (p.127)_____
   Effect: The fishing banks make good fishing grounds.

5. Cause: (p.128)_____
   Effect: The whaling industry came to an end.
6. Cause: (p.129)_____
   Effect: New England ship owners became rich.
7. Cause: (p.132)_____
   Effect: All of Eli Whitney's guns were alike.

Causes to Choose From

People used kerosene in lamps.
Large fish gather there to eat smaller fish.
They needed land for crops.
Some of the land is swampy.
They wanted to travel and fish.

CAUSE AND EFFECT

Directions

When certain situations are true (cause), other situations result (effect). Below are listed causes and effects. Match them to show a cause-effect relationship. Prepare to defend your decisions. Jot down page numbers so you can refer to them when we get into groups.

Cause

a. Most settlers had been fishermen.
b. The fishing banks were not far off.
c. They could not get enough meat.

Effect

1. New England became noted for fishing.
   Cause:

a. Wooden houses were best in winter
b. They brought excellent carpenters.
c. Wood was plentiful.

2. Most N.E. houses were made of wood.
   Cause:

a. Diesel trawlers were used.
b. The whaler's life was too dangerous.
c. Kerosene was better and cheaper.

3. The whaling industry died out.
   Cause:

Now the *cause* is given. Find the *effect.*

4. Boston ships traded all over the world
   Effect:

a. Clipper ships sailed to China.
b. Boston became an important city.
c. Exports are goods shipped out.

5. There are so many people in N.E.
   Effect:

a. N.W. farmers cannot grow food enough to feed N.E.
b. Special crops are grown.
c. The whaling industry died out.

Now find the *causes* yourself.

6. Cause: 6. Shopowners took in apprentices.

7. Cause: 7. Handmade shoes cost more than factory-made shoes.

Directions

Read each item. Decide in which of the four categories each belongs. Put the number of the item on the line beside the heading you decide upon. You may use an item in more than one category.

1. Make a living from the soil. (p.124)
2. Raise all the food they need. (p.124)
3. Fur trading an important industry. (p.125)
4. Skilled shipbuilders build boats. (p.125)
5. Wood pulp made from wood. (p.125)
6. Fishing a good business. (p.125)
7. Whaling done near South Pole. (p.127)
8. Buying and selling in harbors all over the world. (p.129)
9. Freighters come from all over the world. (p.129)
10. Barrels made for shipping fish. (p.130)
11. New England streams furnish power. (p.132)
12. More cloth made in New England than any other place. (p.131)
13. One third of shoes produced in this country made in New England. (p.132)

Categories

A. True in *Colonial* times but *not now.* _____
B. True *now* but *not in Colonial times.* _____
C. True in *Colonial* times AND true *now.* _____
D. *Not true* in *Colonial* times or now. _____

Look at the items that were "True in Colonial times and are true now," (C). Be ready to discuss each item with your group telling what marks the difference between Colonial times and now. Using the other side of your paper, write the number of the item and a few words to remind you of what you will say about each.

GROUP I

Directions

In Column I are listed some early American patriots. In Column II you will find what they did listed. Match them, by inserting the number next to the patriot beside the statement under Column II which will correctly identify the patriot. Your attention is directed to the specific pages in the text listed next to the names.

	Column I	*Column II*
(193)	1. Patrick Henry	_____Boston lawyer who was a loyal patriot, helped write the Declaration of Independence, and became our second president.
(192)	2. John Hancock	
(192)	3. Paul Revere and 4. William Dawes	_____Boston patriot, leader of Minutemen, first to sign Declaration of Independence.
(193)	5. John Adams	
(193)	6. Dr. Benjamin Franklin	_____Commander-in-Chief of the Revolutionary Army; our first president.
(192)	7. Samuel Adams	_____Virginia representative to House of Burgesses, remembered for his passionate words: "give me Liberty or give me Death!"
(193, 205)	8. Thomas Jefferson	
(199)	9. John Paul Jones	_____Did much for our struggling young navy and won important sea battle.
(184, 204)	10. George Washington	_____A man whose flaming pen fired Boston patriots into open rebellion. Organizer of the Minutemen.

_____Chief author of the Declaration of Independence; 3rd president.

_____Great statesman, writer, patriot, inventor; helped write both Declaration of Independence and Constitution.

_____Men who rode from Boston to Lexington to warn Minutemen the British were coming.

GROUP II

Directions

Below are 12 statements dealing with George Washington's life. They are not in the correct order of sequence. Read them over carefully. You are to put them in the order in which they happened by numbering 1-12 next to each statement. You may consult your textbook, pages 183-93. The first has been done for you.

_____ a. Lord Fairfax of Virginia hired George Washington to do survey work for him in that colony.

_____ b. Washington became a major in the Virginia army.

__1__ c. George had only a few years of schooling after his father died, but he learned the 3 R's.

_____ d. At the end of the French and Indian War, at age 26, he married Mrs. Martha Custis, a wealthy widow.

_____ e. The Second Continental Congress decided to raise an army to defend the colonies and chose George Washington to be Commander-in-Chief.

_____ f. Washington studied and experimented with scientific farming at Mt. Vernon.

_____ g. He was a representative to the House of Burgesses.

_____ h. Governor Dinwiddie of Virginia sent Washington on a mission through the wilderness to the French Fort, "le Boeuf," near Lake Erie.

_____ i. General Braddock, leader of the British Army, and accompanied by a young officer named Washington, was killed in battle with the French and Indians.

_____ j. St. Pierre told Washington that he refused to leave the lands around Lake Erie, Ohio River and Mississippi River, "French have first claim!"

_____ k. Washington always accepted the responsibility entrusted to him, used good judgement, did his job, and did it well.

_____ l. He learned how to take care of himself in the wilderness.

GROUP III

Directions

Below are listed some causes and some effects which, because of their interaction upon each other, finally resulted in the start of the Revolutionary War. Read them over carefully. Match the cause with its effect by putting its number in the blank next to the effect. You will notice that in turn, some effects lead to events listed under causes. Put its number in the space provided for it. Use your textbook.

Causes	Effects
_____1. News of the battles at Lexington and Concord spread through all the colonies.	_____1. Colonists refuse to follow trade laws or pay stamp tax.
_____2. New Trade laws and new taxes made for colonies by England.	_____2. Stamp Tax repealed.
_____3. British keep soldiers in the colonies after French and Indian War.	_____3. New taxes, including tax on sugar, levied on colonies to help pay for King's Army in America
_____4. Colonists become very angry over stamp tax, crowds burn tax offices and feelings run high against England.	_____4. General Gage closed Port of Boston and his soldiers took over Boston.
_____5. The Boston "Tea Party."	_____5. Patriots throughout the colonies began preparing for war.
_____6. Trading stopped in Boston by order of the King.	_____6. Patriots in other colonies send supplies and food to Boston.
_____7. Feeling throughout colonies runs high and they decide they must band together to present their case to the King.	_____7. Minutemen line up on Lexington Green.
_____8. Paul Revere and William Dawes had a mission: A "Ride."	_____8. A war had begun with "the shot heard 'round the world," on April 19, 1775.
_____9. At Lexington, British and the Minutemen exchange shots.	_____9. First Continental Congress meets in Philadelphia, 1774, with representatives from all colonies except Georgia.

GROUP IV

Directions

Washington's army met many difficulties during the long years of the War. Listed below, in sections, are some problems which had to be dealt with, names and places that can be associated with these problems, and possible solutions to these problems.

For each problem in Section I, you are to select from Section II, any names which can be associated with that problem. Put the letter next to it beside the problem. From Section III, you are to select the appropriate solution to each problem, and place its letter beside the problem. You may find more than one from each section.

Remember: Some of these problems were never solved and therefore you will have no answer. You may use this textbook and any other resource book.

Section I: Problems and Difficulties

_____1. Uniting the Continental Army under a common purpose, namely, independence, rather than just the rights of the colonists.

_____2. Not enough guns, cannons, or ammunition to fortify Boston.

_____3. No uniforms, gun, or ammunition that were standard for all the soldiers.

_____4. Long winter spent in cold without heat, sufficient food.

_____5. Congress quarreled among themselves and could not agree how much each state should pay for the Army's supplies of food and clothing.

_____6. Not enough money or experienced officers in the colonies to finance the long war, or lead it expertly.

_____7. No Navy.

Section II: Names and Places

A. Philadelphia
D. Ethan Allen
G. Lafayette
J. The French
L. John Paul Jones

B. Valley Forge
E. Trenton
H. John Adams
K. privateers

C. Thomas Jefferson
F. Benjamin Franklin
I. Second Continental Congress

Section III: Solutions to Difficulties and Problems

M. Battle of Fort Ticonderoga; capture of British cannon which was dragged by oxen over the mountains and wilderness to Boston.

N. Washington used his own money to clothe and feed his soldiers.

O. Capture of British guns, ammunition, and food supplies at Trenton.

P. Second Continental Congress voted to declare independence in June, 1776.

Q. Congress voted money for soldiers' uniforms.

R. Privateers, or sea raiders, raided British ships, captured men, supplies, and ships.

S. Declaration of Independence, publicly announced, Liberty Bell in Philadelphia pealed out its excitement.

5TH GRADE SOCIAL STUDIES, UNIT 6

GROUP I

Directions

Below are some statements about these men. Circle the statements that are true for all of them.

1. They all lived in Boston, Massachusetts.
2. They had courage; they tried to help their young country by doing what they honestly felt to be right for her. In some instances, this devotion to their country cost them their fortunes, endangered their lives; some lost theirs.
3. The new country paid these men well for their services.
4. They suffered hardships and worked long hours.
5. They were more loyal to their own particular state than to the United States.
6. They were all rich and had either servants or slaves.
7. They loved England and her King better than the idea of becoming independent and having their own country.
8. They never argued among themselves about what was good for the new country.
9. They were able to put together the principles contained in the Declaration of Independence and the Constitution with hardly any disagreement among themselves.
10.

For #10, write a statement telling the reasons you know of, that caused the Revolution to start in the Boston area. Bring in the following points:

1) How people in Boston earned their living.
2) What men like Samuel Adams did and how it affected the citizens of Boston and those in nearby towns.

GROUP II

Final Question for Group II

As one studies the life of George Washington, one begins to realize the qualities of leadership this man had, and how his earlier experiences helped him to develop these qualities. What were some of these qualities? What were the experiences that helped develop them?

Qualities that Make for Leadership

A. patience	B. loyalty	C. self-reliance
D. capacity for work	E. resourcefulness	F. intelligence
G. skill	H. endurance	I. compassion
J. courage	K. integrity	L. purpose

Directions

Read the following statements carefully. You may use your text or other

sources to check them. Circle those statements which are true. In the space before each statement, put the letter(s) of the qualities that the experience helped
to develop.

Statements

_____ 1. As a surveyor, Washington spent months alone in the wilderness.

_____ 2. He was often very ill, and as a result, there was nothing about his
appearance to command respect.

_____ 3. On his return trip to Virginia from the French Fort, Le Boeuf, he
experienced many hardships, including falling off a raft into an icy
stream, and spending the night in frozen clothing.

_____ 4. While at Fort Le Boeuf, Washington carefully observed the fort,
number of guns, people in it, the Indians who were armed, even the
number of canoes along the creek.

_____ 5. At all times, Washington showed great concern for the men under
his command, he was concerned about their food, their comfort,
their supplies, or lack of them.

_____ 6. The Congress of the United States, during the War, gave Washington
all the supplies and money he needed for his armies.

_____ 7. As an officer in the Virginia Militia, Washington learned how to
battle the Indians successfully.

_____ 8. Washington was the unanimous choice of the Continental Congress
to be Commander-in-Chief of the new army.

_____ 9. He set his own slaves free, and wanted to see slavery end in the
south.

_____10. All the work on his farm at Mt. Vernon was done by others, for
Washington, as a military man, had little knowledge of farming.

_____11. In his conduct of the Revolution, Washington earned the name,
"fox" and "foxy" from the British.

GROUP III

Final Question for Group III

Directions

In examining the causes and events that led to the Revolutionary War, we
find the following to be true. Circle any of the following statements which are
true. (You may use your textbooks or any other source material.)

1. Separation from a parent country by an ocean (6-8 weeks in time)
helped to make it difficult for England to understand her colonies and
vice-versa.

2. All of the colonists felt that England's trade laws and new taxes were
wrong; as a result, they all agreed that they would be better off independent of England.

3. It was difficult to be prosperous in the English colonies and most
colonists found themselves so highly taxed that they were left with little
or no money for necessities.

4. The English Parliament was made up of people who were unanimous in

their dislike of the colonists and could never see their side in the argument about "rights of colonists."
5. Almost all of the patriots were what we call "good" people, whereas the loyalists were almost always "bad" people.
6. It is probable that the war would not have started had it not been for men like Samuel Adams, Patrick Henry, and Paul Revere, who did their best to excite people against the British, who used newspapers and letters of the committees to keep citizens aroused at a fever pitch; thus were the colonists kept in a state of rebellion.
7. Most of the open rebellious acts of the colonists took place in Boston.
8.

For #8, write a true statement declaring the reasons that caused the Revolution to start in the Boston area. Bring in the following points:
1) How people in Boston earned their living.
2) What men like Samuel Adams and Paul Revere did and how it affected the citizens of Boston and those in nearby towns.

GROUP IV

Final Question for Group IV

You have seen some of the problems with which Washington and the young country had to deal; the problems were so great that you may well wonder how the Revolutionary War was ever won by the Americans instead of the British. You may use your text or any other source.

Directions

Circle any of the following statements which may be true.

Statements

1. The British had a superior navy and a superior army.
2. Both the army and the navy on the British side were well supplied.
3. British officers and generals were very patriotic and eager to win the war for their King.
4. British officers, such as Howe and Cornwallis, were brilliant soldiers and fought a well-planned war.
5. Washington took advantage of any situation he found: Christmas morning he struck at an unsuspecting and sleeping British Army at Trenton; at Yorktown, he trapped Cornwallis.
6. Washington's armies were ill fed, ill clothed, and poorly armed.
7. The young country required very short enlistments of 3-6 months for its soldiers; as a result, there was a great turnover of men, and Washington could not depend upon the size or strength of his army.
8. There were so many deserters in Washington's army, as well as soldiers who left because their enlistments had expired, that in a few months time at the beginning of the war, his army was reduced in size by almost 4,000.
9. Congress voted enough money to make the Continental Army the best equipped and best fed in the world.

10. The patriots who remained in Washington's ragged army became well trained and well-drilled that terrible winter at Valley Forge and became loyal followers of their determined General, George Washington.
11. The British officers and generals made so many errors in fighting the war, that they were considered "bus missers" and in general, seemed to "just miss" winning the war many times over.
12. It was probable that the direction of the British side of the war being 3,000 miles away in London, caused many mistakes on the part of the British officers.
13.

For #13, write what you consider to be the biggest reason for the Americans' winning the war.

EXERCISE I

Where there are areas of conflict, and a final resolution of that conflict, history would seem to imply that one philosophy was superior to another, that the one philosophy must succumb to the logic of the other. The following exercise represents such a conflict as discussed in unit 7.

Directions

The answers to the following six questions are found in Section B. Section B contains 8 possible short answers, and 6 possible longer answers.
1. Identify immediately the conflict under discussion.
2. When a justification is asked for, determine which answer in Section B is a justification and write it in the corresponding blank.
3. Do the same for principle, conditions, and conflict.

Section A

1. _____ plus _____ = conflict?
2. Justification plus principle = Case of the loser? _____
   plus _____ = _____ .
3. Justification plus principle = Case of the victor? _____
   plus _____ = _____ plus
   _____ = successful solution.
4. Underlying conditions of this conflict _____ ,
   _____ , _____ , _____
   _____ .
5. Present day conflict = _____ v. _____

Section B

1. compromise
2. reason
3. legislation
4. force & greater numbers
5. small business v. big business
6. Indian v. whiteman
7. cattleman v. farmer
8. Communism v. capitalism
9. The race had seemingly lacked initiative, imagination, and energy in developing the continent.
10. A way of life was threatened by people who had conditioned him to its honesty and kindness, but who in the end had betrayed him.
11. Inherent racial need for permanency of status, resistance to change, inflexible as to outlook.
12. Practical recognition of problems and their solutions, love of change, challenge, progress.
13. Treaties can be broken under certain extenuating circumstances, progress must advance at any cost.
14. Complacent regard for a way of life based on ignorance, superstition, and signs of nature.

EXERCISE III

This guide attempts to point out the seriousness involved in creating the proper policy toward underdeveloped peoples by the United States Government.

Directions

Examine the policies listed below. Examine the "Results of Policies" also listed below, and examine the various "Lands or Peoples Involved." Then determine and list which peoples are subjected to which government policy, and what the result of that policy was as far as the particular people were concerned.

Policies

1. Paternalistic
2. Cooperative-aid
3. Presumptive (imposing our ideas on people)

Results of Policies

a. bitterness, silent rebelliousness, hate that saps the mind of creative powers, and will of energy.
b. lethargy, loss of self-respect.
c. independence, self-help.

Lands or Peoples Involved

America's island possessions
American Indian
Underdeveloped countries such as Africa

Land or Peoples	Policy	Result

EXERCISE VIII

This guide is concerned with the problems, solutions to the problems, and the ideas or philosophy attendent to the phenomenal growth of American Industry.

Directions

1. The first four questions may be answered by using words only from the "Solutions" column.
2. The next four questions may be answered by using words form both columns (or numbers, as the case may be).

Solutions	*Ideas—Philosophy*
transportation	1. rigid class system
laissez-faire	2. humanity improves in an environment of freedom & opportunity
patent system	
corporation	3. a mass-market underwrites business success
daring individuals	
foreign investments	4. an alliance between the government establishment & the higher classes
governments subsidy	
foreign labor supply	5. a market limited by the prohibitive costs of goods
communication devices	
	6. an expanded market due to a decent wage
	7. non-rigid class system

1. _____ plus _____ overcame the problem of factory construction and operating cost.
2. _____ plus _____ prohibitive costs of building a railroad in the West.
3. _____ plus _____ individual inertia and fear of control by the government.
4. _____ plus _____ limited markets.
5. Number_____ of the ideas ensured an almost unending business growth.
6. Numbers_____ best characterize the democratic philosophy.
7. No. 6 under ideas, came about only when _____ under solutions, was altered a bit.
8. Upon what democratic philosophy did the idea of No. 3 depend? No._____?

EXERCISE I

This guide has as its purpose a comparison of "Developing America," which is included in unit 8, and "Contemporary America," which is the America of today. These two America's are very different particularly in their demands upon the individual. Despite this fact, many of the old ideas and ideals are still applied, and perhaps it is because of this reason that we have serious psychological problems today.

Directions

1. Identify the items in list A which describe "Current America" and "Developing America." On the line at the left place CA or DA.
2. Decide whether list B should be entitled Solutions or Problems.
3. Decide whether list C should be Solutions or Problems, and place the proper title in the space provided.
4. Match the solution to the problem, place the number or letter in the space provided.

List A

_____ A. Physical action, energy, stamina, tough mindedness.
_____ B. Mental production has replaced physical production.
_____ C. Success determined by long hours of work and hard labor.
_____ D. Era of specialty-restricting the man of energy.
_____ E. Success determined and measured by creative mental energy.

List B

_____ 1. Leisure time sports and do-it-yourself projects.
_____ 2. Creation of neighborhood centers where small children from age 1-5 can have a pre-school environment, such things as stories, picture books, fieldtrips, etc.
_____ 3. Apprentice system.

List C

_____ a.)   Designing the kind of education suitable to physical type people in a mental type environment.
_____ b.)   Tensions developing from limited outlets for energy.
_____ c.)   Training and nurturing of human beings who will be geared to a mental type environment.

EXERCISE V

As students we are aware of all the virtues that our nation possesses as a democratic political system, and the opportunity for self-development through education. But unit 8 suggests that we must continue to be concerned about people and problems that have not been completely solved. This guide will refer to these problems as "defects"; some of them have been solved while some are in the process of being solved.

Directions

In the case of "The Defects of the United States" vs. "The People of the United States," carefully read the twelve statements. Then decide where they are to be placed on the chart, whether in the "People's Defense" category, or in the "Modern Approach" category.

1. The law of the "survival of the fittest" makes it inevitable that a few will do well, and the ill-equipped for the race must lead a degraded existence.
2. By exercising voting rights, deprived citizens can use their voting power to elect people who are sympathetic to their cause thus helping to enact measures helpful to themselves and the country.
3. The key to releasing the chains of poverty and degradation lies in EDUCATION. This lengthy process can sharpen the mind so that the learner is inspired to pull himslef up by the bootstraps; to overcome an apathetic slumber of passive acceptance of his heritage; to acquire a self-identification as opposed to a nothing.
4. Certain peoples, must, by the nature of things, accept their secondary position as citizens and make the best of it.
5. Basic mental attributes of the genders is essentially the same, so that when accorded rights based upon the law of the land, behavior resulting from the exercise of these rights will be prudent and thoughtful.
6. Drinking is a question of morality, hence can be controlled by law; evil can be forbidden!
7. Concepts of "compassion for the poor" and "we are our brother's keeper" inspire local fund drives that ask all to provide for those in want.
8. The inability of the human organism to adjust satisfactorily to certain difficult social demands, often reveals this weakness in the form of a need for a superimposed oblivion. The weakness is what must be treated psychologically.
9. Ghettos and unpleasant living conditions are created by those who do not have pride; those nurtured in a low standard of living. This merely indicates the imbedded lack of desire to improve.
10. Structural defects, such as the lack of physical strength, deserve an inferior legal status.
11. The adjustment of the human organism, simultaneously to a new language, customs, rules, regulations, may create emotional tensions and disharmonies that reveal themselves as peculiarities and idiosyncrasies.
12. Foreigners display biologically inferior manners, which render them as undesirable new Americans.

THE CASE OF THE DEFECTS OF THE UNITED STATES VS. THE PEOPLE OF THE UNITED STATES

PLANTIFF	PEOPLE'S DEFENSE	MODERN APPROACH
		The inability of the human organism to adjust satisfactorily to certain difficult social demands, often reveal this weakness in the form of a need for a superimposed oblivion. The weakness has to be treated psychologically.
	Foreigners display biologically inferior mannerisms, which render them as undesirable new Americans.	
		The key to releasing the chains of poverty and degradation lies in EDUCATION. This process can sharpen the mind so that the learner is inspired to pull himself up by the bootstraps; to overcome an apathetic slumber of passive acceptance of his heritage; to acquire a self-identification as opposed to a nothingness.

EXERCISE VIII

This guide attempts to penetrate the mysteries of the process known as "Maturation." Human beings often mature at a more rapid rate when confronted unexpectedly with an unusual responsibility. Perhaps this is true also of nations, for our own country seemingly evidenced maturity for the first time after the turn of the century.

Directions

1. On chart will be found a list of situations that evoked an American response.
2. Immediately below are the American responses to the listed situations.
3. Place the response next to the most appropriate situation.
4. Measure each response against given criteria of maturity.
5. Check each response as to "Mature" or "Immature," which will be your personal judgement after applying the criteria.

Responses

a. Refusal to join other countries in an alliance for the preservation of peace.
b. Declaration of war against Spain, 1898.
c. Development of the islands freed from Spain; industry, health, education, governmental institutions.
d. Declaration of neutrality during World War I.
e. Encouragement of the Panama Revolt.
f. United States supports the Hague.
g. Operation Bootstrap.
h. United States intervenes in 1916 Mexican Revolution.

Criteria of Maturity

1. Emotional detachment.
2. Thoughtful rather than impulsive.
3. Faith in the present and the future.
4. The ability to accept change.
5. Personal responsibility for actions.
6. Care for the consequences of one's personal actions, either in terms of one's self or others.
7. Conduct realistically motivated.
8. Capacity to act regardless of personal gain or glory.
9. Acceptance of "self" and respect for the self.
10. Unselfish in actions.
11. Ability to accept criticism.
12. A realistic recogniton and acceptance of situations that cannot be changed.
13. A cheerful attitude toward mistakes as something involving learning.

Situation Evoking Response	Responses to Certain Situations	Mature	Immature
1. Explosion of the "Maine."			
2. Washington's Advice, "To stay clear of European differences."			
3. Ratification question of the Versailles Treaty and the League of Nations.			
4. Columbia's refusal to agree to America's terms in the Hay-Herran Treaty for construction of a canal in her land.			
5. Peace of Paris, 1898.			
6. Puerto Rico's Domestic-Economic Problem.			
7. Plan for Keeping International Peace, 1899.			
8. Property, business interests, and lives had to be protected.			

249

EXERCISE IX

Perhaps history can have more meaning and interest for students if American actions in the past represent something other than a date to remember. Let us examine the courses of action below, and from the vantage point of time, determine what principles of human behavior can be said to explain the action.

Directions

1. Place the letter of the Principle that explains the action on the line at the left of the action.
2. Answer the questions following "Principles" by placing the correct letters on the line at the left.

Actions in History: American and others

_____1. President Wilson involved the United States in World War I, so as "To save the world for Democracy."

_____2. The attitude of aloofness by the political parties between 1865-1900.

_____3. Split of the Republican Party in 1912.

_____4. The decisions of the Supreme Court around 1900 tended to reinforce the sanctity of property and the interest of business, as opposed to the well-being of the average American.

_____5. Much goodwill was built up as a result of President Roosevelt's interest in the Treaty of Portsmouth, but it was largely destroyed by the race-riots against the Japanese in California and the threatened exclusion laws.

_____6. Theodore Roosevelt was regarded as a worthy candidate for the Presidency, more because of his leadership of the "Rough Riders" in Cuba, than because of his experiences in public service.

_____7. Germany's reaction to the Versailles Treaty and to the Allied nations who wrote the treaty, was one of revenge.

_____8. China demonstrated ill-will toward the Western countries that had exploited and partitioned, and seized part of that country, and toward the United States, a nation that had not done these things.

Principles of Human Behavior

A. The people of the United States, or perhaps of any nation, respond more to a person because he is a hero, than because of his proven ability and experience in public service.

B. Whenever logic is missing as a reason for our actions, we often feel compelled to justify them on the grounds of moral principles.

C. Resistence to change, either because of personal bias or fear of the unknown, can often be found motivating the most august of men, as well as those of lesser stature.

D. To exclude, to isolate, is to brand as inferior, and is as much a physical wound as a spiritual one, never to be forgotten by the victim.

E. Conservative views and progressive political views stem from two opposed temperaments, and can never really be reconciled.

F. To look backward to past glories, to refuse to meet the problems of the "How", is much easier than confronting current problems.

G. Those who have been hurt, tend to cast blame upon those known to be associated with the wrongdoer, as well as upon the wrongdoer himself.

H. It is human nature to seek revenge against those who have pronounced "judgment of guilt upon us, and then leveled a pound of flesh as punishment."

Questions

_____ 1. To insure the selection of the most qualified of leadership, what principle of human behavior should the American people seek to overcome?

_____ 2. To survive as a world leader, what principles should America constantly bear in mind?

_____ 3. One principle, indulged in by Americans for many years, has seemingly been overcome as far as one issue is concerned at least, so that we are held in higher esteem today than in many previous years, regarding that particular issue?

_____ 4. The political arena has, in many instances, acted contrary to one of the above principles during the past few years, so that one might say the principle no longer is true. What principle?

_____ 5. What principle is America currently acting upon because there seems to be no alternative to act upon?

EXERCISE X

Important among the many objectives of an education is learning to recognize, immediately, the heart of a problem within the maze of an author's verbiage (words).

Directions

1. Read the list of long and short statements.
2. Decide which of these are not important of and by themselves, but together help to develop ideas. Place them under "Details" on the chart that follows.
3. Decide which statements really present to the reader something to think about. Place them under "Ideas."
4. Decide which statements get at the heart of the argument, and reveal the author's point of view. Place it or them under "Generalization."
5. From the list of possible titles, select the one most appropriate to the meaning of the essence of the argument, and place it under "Title."

Statements

1. The open-door was designed to insure equal trade for Americans.
2. For one hundred years after our government was set up, Americans were occupied with the job of pushing boundries westward, conquering a wilderness, and peopling a continent.
3. The United States improved conditions in the islands in five ways, health, education, government, farms, trade.
4. America's efforts toward geographical and economic development, were put forth with such energy that a serious interest in matters pertaining to the world before the turn of the century was not possible, however once the oceans became our frontiers, and our food and factory products ex-

ceeded demand at home, our interest in other nations was aroused commensurate with their ability.

5.   Toward 1890 American farms and factories were producing more than enough for its people.

6.   The Monroe Doctrine forbade European nations to interfere in the Western hemisphere.

7.   Despite our initial feeling of parental responsibility toward the newly freed island possessions, such altruism did not usually provide the only guide for our excursions into the new sphere of "foreign relations," for markets to absorb our surplus, trade, security, and independence constituted the goals of our major foreign policies such as the Monroe Doctrine, open-door, and even today's "containment of Communism" policy.

8.   When Spain left the islands in 1898, chaos and confusion prevailed because there was no leadership.

9.   Other than our very mature approach toward our island possessions gained from Spain, which took the form of a serious attempt to change a primitive way of life into a civilized one, our relations toward foreign countries came to be primarily based upon a foreign policy designed to insure our security, economic interest trade and independence.

10.   Some country had to replace Spain and assume some responsibility for these uneducated people who had no leadership.

TITLES

1. The United States enters World War I.
2. The way the United States handles the problems of colonies freed from Spain.
3. America's foreign relations.
4. The United States designs the Monroe Doctrine and the open door.
5. United States gains possessions.

Title	DETAILS	CONCEPTS	GENERALIZATIONS
	Toward 1890 American farms and factories were producing more than enough for its people		

EXERCISE VI

This guide is designed to attempt to show that History does not necessarily repeat itself; that similar sets of conditions may be subject to factors that vary from period to period.

Directions
1. Place the items below in the proper spaces on the next page. Three have already been done for you.
2. Concentrate first on finding the differences between the conditions.
3. Concentrate next on finding the Circumstances that followed Condition number 1. The Predictions will be those items remaining.

Circumstances—Differences—Predictions
1. Continued association with the U.S. as one of the 50 states.
2. Cooperative effort will be of little value in a war involving the masters of the hydrogen bomb.
3. Great Depression.
4. More legislation to help the needy and create the "Great Society."
5. Political instability—dictatorship.
6. People not treated as conquered slaves.
7. Countries belonging to the many alliances would again be drawn into serious disagreements between several members.
8. Semi-wartime defense spending might serve to sustain good times.
9. World War I.
10. A recession or depression—an inevitability in the Business Cycle Theory.
11. New Deal measures designed.
12. Collapse of the economy during the depression rendered many, many people poor. Today the "poor" constitute those who are culturally deprived, educationally untrained, or who possess structural defect.

Sets of similar conditions	Circumstances following first conditions	Differences between the sets of similar conditions	Predictions based on the more recent set of conditions
1. Agreements made by European States prior to World War I. 2. Post War II alliances such as NATO, SEATO.		Cooperative effort will be of little value in a war involving the masters of the H–bomb.	
1. Prosperity in the 1920's 2. Prosperity in the 1960's		New Deal measures designed	
1. Poverty in the 1930's 2. Poverty in the 1960's			
1. Mixture of races in Latin-America 2. Mixture of races in Hawaiian Islands			Continued association with the U.S. as one of the 50 states.

254

EXERCISE VIII

The conflicts in the world today, and the conflicts in the world prior to World War I appear to be quite different. Those in the past concerned themselves with concrete issues; as an example, one nation had something that another nation did not have, and a simple conflict arose. Today our sources of conflict very often lie within ideas. Rather than the tensions becoming less severe, they are seemingly becoming more fraught with danger for the human race. This guide attempts to reinforce and clarify this concept.

Directions

1. In column A write the letter of the conflict which in your judgment represents an "abstract" idea or theoretical idea.
2. In column B write the letter of the conflict which in your judgment represents a "concrete" issue.
3. On chart, place the letters of the sources of conflict under the War with which each is associated.

Column A	Column B
	A

Revolutionary War	World War I	Civil War	World War II	Cold War
	A			

(EXERCISE VIII—Cont'd.)

Sources of Conflict

A. Desire for more power.
B. Dignity and worth of the individual.
C. The question of the ability of governments, dedicated to democracy and freedom, to solve modern tough economic problems.
D. Desire for more territory.
E. The question of the relative power of the federal government and the state government.
F. The question, whether governmental and economic problems can adequately be solved by means of the "will of the people," as revealed through votes and representatives, or by the arbitrary "will of the state."
G. Search for markets and raw materials.
H. Imposition of political and economic ideas on weaker neighbors by means of terror.
 I. The question of "taxation without representation."
J. The question of the relationship of the individual to the state, and the state to the individual.
K. The question of the importance of "human rights" within a nation.

I. ANALYSIS OF PROPAGANDA USED IN THE AMERICAN REVOLUTION

Many writers produced pieces of literature to help promote independence from Britain. This exercise may help to (1) identify ideas in three important documents, (2) infer the purpose of the authors in using the ideas, and (3) apply the ideas to today's world.

For purposes of this exercise we are considering that the three documents selected are "propaganda" in the sense that they were intended to (1) change beliefs of the readers, (2) change attitudes of the readers, or (3) cause readers to take a particular action.

Directions

For each of the documents listed in column I, indicate the ideas found in each document by placing the letter representing each idea on an appropriate line in column II. (An "idea" may be used more than once. Make your selection from the second page of this exercise.)

In column III indicate the inferred purpose for which the author used each idea by placing the number representing the appropriate purpose. (More than one purpose may exist for each idea. (Make your selection from the second page of this exercise.)

In Column IV indicate what man today might be expected to use each of the ideas. (Use the letter representing each man; more than one man may be used for the same idea. Make your selection from the second page of this exercise.)

I. Document	II. Ideas Expressed in each Document	III. Purpose of each Idea	IV. Who Might Use the Idea
Letters from a Farmer in Pennsylvania, by John Dickinson, 1767-68 (p. 41)			
Common Sense, by Tom Paine, 1776 (p. 51)			
The Declaration of Independence, by Thomas Jefferson, 1776 (p. 54-58)			

II. IDEAS EXPRESSED IN THE DOCUMENTS

A. Hereditary kingship was based on superstition.

B. All men are created equal, with certain God-given rights.

C. American colonies were basically members of one larger body, united by common interests.

D. If a government becomes destructive of the natural rights of people, the people have the right to alter or abolish the government.

E. America should be free from British rule.

F. No man should pay a tax unless he wants to.

G. Americans have done everything possible to preserve peace.

H. The American colonies were, and ought to be, independent from Britain.

I. King George III was a poor king.

J. Governments are created to serve the people.

III. PURPOSES OF IDEAS EXPRESSED IN THE DOCUMENTS

1. To change beliefs of the readers.
2. To change attitudes of the readers.
3. To cause readers to take a particular action.

IV. WHO, SINCE 1960, MIGHT USE THE IDEA?

a. Brezhnev

b. Eldridge Cleaver

c. Martin Luther King

d. Norman Thomas, long-time Socialist candidate for President

e. Governor Wallace

f. President Nixon

g. Not applicable since 1960

I. INFERRED POSITION OF SOCIAL CLASSES IN THE AMERICAN REVOLUTION

We sometimes think of the American Revolution as a patriotic fight for political liberty, of a struggle against the tyranny of King George III. In the following exercise we look at it from a different point of view, concentrating on the differences in viewpoints of the various social classes in America.

For each of the statements of action during the Revolutionary Period, place in the appropriate blank the letter representing the kind or kinds of people who probably would have participated in it. (Some items may be irrelevant or false. Do not feel too frustrated if you cannot be sure of the answer.) (p. 65-66.) Each action may require more than one letter.

H = Hudson Valley farmer of substantial wealth.
C = Church of England clergyman.
P = Plantation owner from the Tidewater.
M = Merchant.
F = Farmer of Scottish origin from a small backwoods farm.
S = Slave.

_____ 1. Carried on guerilla warfare in Rockland County on the side of Britain.

_____ 2. Fled to Canada.

_____ 3. Tried to get the slaves to rebel against their Patriot masters.

_____ 4. Voted in the Virginia legislature against freeing the slaves.

_____ 5. Voted against the Bill for Religious Freedom in the Virginia legislature.

_____ 6. Favored having a strong state governor with a long term in office and veto power.

_____ 7. Tried to avoid trouble and stay out of the war.

_____ 8. Joined a mob to tar and feather Loyalists.

_____ 9. Purchased a small farm carved out of land confiscated from Loyalists.

_____10. Voted in the Virginia legislature to abolish primogeniture and entail.

_____11. Introduced a bill to the Virginia legislature that would give all slaves in Virginia their freedom.

_____12. Voted for the Bill for Religious Freedom in the Virginia legislature.

_____13. Gained the right to vote for the first time.

_____14. Hoped through the Revolution that soon all men would have the right to vote.

_____15. Joined the Patriot Army.

_____16. When the war broke out, he was in debt to Englishmen; never paid the debt.

_____17. After six months in the army he moved to Kentucky, west of the Appalachians.

II. Check the conclusion that you think is most accurate, based on the preceding exercise.

_____A. Most Americans fervently supported the Revolution.

_____B. The occupation of a man determined which side he chose to support.

_____C. Many of those who supported the Revolution against Britain also supported democratic reforms within America.

_____D. There was probably no relationship between a man's occupation or social class and his actions in the Revolution.

BRAGDON AND MCCUTCHEN: CHAPS. III, IV, VI; "THE AMERICAN REVOLUTION," "ONE STATE OR THIRTEEN," "THE CONSTITUTION OF THE UNITED STATES"

Comparison of principles of the Revolution, the Articles of Confederation, and the Constitution

This exercise may help one to see (1) to what extent the Articles of Confederation (ratified during the Revolution) embodied the principles held by Patriots at that time, and (2) what changes were made in writing the Constitution less than a decade later.

Directions

For each of the provisions listed in column I, indicate by appropriate letter(s) in column II the principle(s) of the Revolution that the provision may illustrate or reflect. If no principle is involved, write "not applicable."

In column III briefly state any major change to each provision listed in column I. If the Constitution continued the provision, write "no change."

I. Provisions included in the Articles of Confederation (p. 82)	II. Principles of the Revolution (ch. 3) that may be reflected in each provision of the Articles of Confederation	III. How each provision of the Articles was changed by the Constitution (ch. 6)
1. Congress consisted of representatives of the states, sitting in one house.		
2. Only Congress could declare war or peace.		
3. Congress could raise armies and navies.		
4. Congress could borrow money.		
5. Congress could establish a postal system.		
6. Congress could manage with the Indians.		
7. Congress could coin its own money, and so could states.		

8. Congress had no control over commerce, domestic or foreign.		
9. Congress had no power of taxation.		
10. States were to "give full faith and credit to the public acts of other states."		
11. Escaped criminals and slaves were to be returned across state lines.		
12. There was no separate executive department.		
13. There was no federal court system.		

II. Principles of the Revolution (ch. 3) that may be reflected in each provision of the Articles of Confederation. (This list is to be used in completing column II of the chart above.)

A. All men are created equal, with certain God-given rights.

B. People have a right to change their form of government.

C. Taxation without representation is tyranny.

D. People should be relatively free from governmental control.

E. Government should do those necessary things that the people cannot do for themselves.

F. Hereditary kingship is undesirable.

MAIN IDEA: Without referring back to the text, write a short paragraph summarizing the kinds of changes that were made in our government by the adoption of the Constitution and the basic reasons for these changes.

IV. Division of powers (enumerated and implied powers, reserved powers, powers denied to government)

In our federal system the important governmental powers are divided between the federal government and the state governments; and other powers are denied to any government.

A. Begin this exercise by defining the following words (p. 115):
   1. Enumerated powers:
   2. Implied powers:
   3. Concurrent powers:
   4. Reserved powers:

B. Listed are issues about which one might wish to consult or influence the proper level of government. Place the number representing each issue in the proper place on the diagram to indicate which level of government to consult. (pp. 112-118)

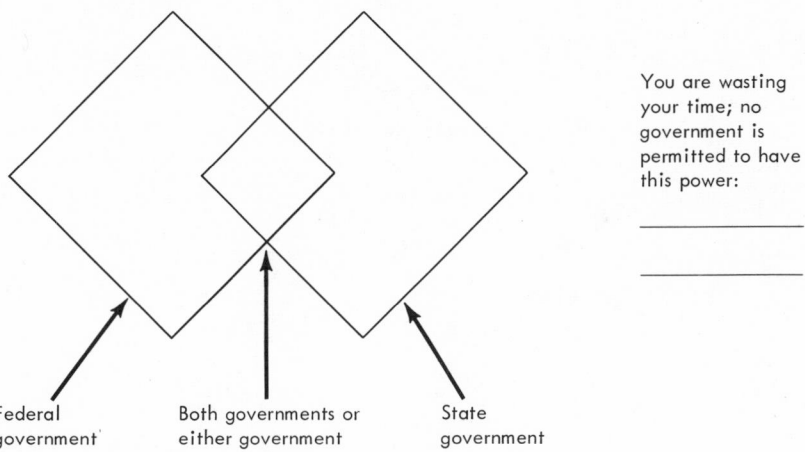

You are wasting your time; no government is permitted to have this power:

_____

_____

Federal government

Both governments or either government

State government

1.   You want to write a letter urging a nuclear test ban treaty.
2.   You want to make it easier for people to obtain a divorce.
3.   You want a post office established in New Square.
4.   You want to have the compulsory education laws abolished.
5.   You want to prevent the selling of alcoholic beverages to people over twenty-five years of age.
6.   You want the maximum speed limit for all passenger cars set at thirty-five miles per hour.
7.   You want the export tax on American cigarettes raised to discourage foreigners from smoking.

8. You want to impose a fine on all men who purchased dangerous weapons last year.
9. You want to have coins minted in a thirty-five cent denomination for use in school lunch vending machines.
10. You want New York to lower the voting age to eighteen.
11. You want to have all people who are suspected of liking Red China locked up in jail and kept there with no judicial hearing.
12. You want to stop the sale of furniture made by segregated labor in the South from being sold in New York.
13. You want to have laws passed to prevent law enforcement officers from using "police brutality."
14. You want to have the legislature convict Jimmy Hoffa and put him behind bars.
15. You hope to become a baron in recognition of your distinguished service on the track team.
16. You want to make twelve year old children eligible to obtain driving licenses.

READING AND REASONING GUIDES: MATHEMATICS

Directions

Relate the diagrams to the vocabulary by putting the number from Column I before the diagram related to it in Column II

	Column I		Column II	
*	1. Perpendicular line	____a.	A B C D	not parallel not intersecting not in same plane
*	2. Intersecting lines	____b.	//	
*	3. Parallel lines	____c.	X	
*	4. Line segment	____d.	•——→	
*	5. Oblique line	____e.	⊥	
**	6. Ray	____f.	/	
**	7. Cone	____g.	⌒	
**	8. Arc	____h.	∠	
**	9. Angle	____i.	△	
***	10. Oblique parallel	____j.	↑↓	
***	11. Skew lines	____k.	•—A—•—B—•	

Directions

Many times the use of geometric lines and diagrams generates other geometric figures or diagrams. Match the causes in Column II to the effects in Column I.

	Column I	Column II
*	____ 1. Line	a. right angles are formed
**	____ 2. Perpendicular line	b. edge of a book or paper
***	____ 3. Parallel lines	c. two rays that start at the same
*	____ 4. Intersecting lines	point but run in different direc-
***	____ 5. Skew line	tions

***   _____ 6.   Cube

***   _____ 7.   Triangle

**   _____ 8.   Angles

**   _____ 9.   Simple closed figure

*   _____10.   Plane figure

d. top and bottom edges of chalk board

e. one strut crossing another

f. figure having length and width only

g. lines on different planes

h. thru lines intersecting to form one inside region and one outside region

i. an area bound by lines so that there is a single inside region and a single outside region

j. six squares placed in a specific manner

Directions

Check the definition which best suits the italicized word in each set.

1. *   *Point*
   1. a scratch on the wall
   2. a period at the end of a sentence or a pencil dot
   3. a ray of sunshine

2. **   *(Line) Point*
   1. two lines going in the same direction
   2. a model of a dot
   3. part of a line

3. ***   *Point*
   1. an idea of a place having no length, depth or width
   2. vertex of an angle
   3. corner of a square

1. *   *Line*
   1. from one place to another
   2. the marker which is found in the center of a highway
   3. place where two things meet

2. **   *Line*
   1. set of points that lie in the same path
   2. set of points included in a plane figure
   3. set of points in a cone

3. ***   *Line*
   1. set of points included in the circumference of a circle
   2. set of points from A to B
   3. set of points unlimited in extent which run in opposite directions

Directions

There are several important details in this section of Chapter 5. As you read, answer the questions assigned to you. Sometimes the page, column and paragraph are given to help you identify the place of the answer.

***	1.	Is a carpenter's straight line the same as a geometric straight line?
**	2.	How should a line be correctly labeled? (p. 111)
*	3.	What are parallel lines? (p. 112 #5)
****	4.	What are oblique perpendicular lines?
**	5.	Why is a chalk board considered a plane surface? (p. 114)
*	6.	Name 3 plane figures. (p. 117, col. II)
***	7.	How many planes can be drawn through a line?
**	8.	Which of the figures below are simple closed figures? (p. 129)

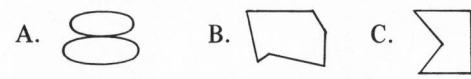

*	9.	Name 3 polygons. (p. 117 col. II)
*	10.	What is another name for five, six, or eight sided figures? (p. 117, col. II)
***	11.	What are adjacent vertices?
**	12.	Are ∠ AED and ∠ BEC vertical? Why? (p. 120)
*	13.	Name 3 parts of a circle. (p. 126 #3)
**	14.	A cube has how many faces, vertices, and edges? (p. 138)
***	15.	A cone and a cylinder have the same height and the same base diameter. What is the ratio of the Volume of the cone to the V of the cylinder?

Directions

For the statements listed below do the work assigned your group.

*   Tell whether the statement is True or False.

**   If the statement is false, write it correctly.

***   If a statement is false, give the reason why you think it is so.

a. When we tell the features of anything such as size, shape, or color we are analyzing.

b. The edge of a book or paper is best described by the word plane.

c. If we do not know how many things belong in a group or their likeness, we say this is a set.

d. A part of a circle is called a segment.

e. Two lines that cross are said to intersect.

f. If we say that two lines cross we say they are parallel.

g. We call a geometric surface with length, width but no depth a plane.

h. Two lines which are not in the same plane but will intersect or are parallel are skew lines.

i. Lines which have no fixed limit or amount are said to be infinite or un-limited.

j. Lines which run parallel to the equator are said to be horizontal.

READING AND REASONING GUIDES: SCIENCE

CIRCULATORY SYSTEM

Answer the questions you have been assigned. Work together in your groups. You have only a few minutes to do this work.

Health for All, 6; Going on Ten

*   1. List the different kinds of blood vessels.

*   2. What direction does the blood move from one kind of blood vessel to another?

Your health

**   3. List the parts of the heart.

**   4. What direction does the blood move from one part to another?

Health for All, 5

***   5. Name the parts of the blood.

***   6. What does each part do to insure life?

Now read those statements you have been assigned. They have to do with the circulatory system. Check those statements you think are correct. After you have checked your own statements, then discuss them with other members of your group. See if you can come to some agreement on the answers.

Everyone should check unstarred items. Check only those starred items which have been assigned to your group.

      _____1. Systems in the human body are made up of parts that work together perfectly.

      _____2. Systems in the body are independent of one another.

      _____3. There are three parts to the circulatory system: the material that moves through the system; the "canals" that form the system; the machine that moves the material through the system.

*   _____4. Both healthy and harmful things can be found in the blood.

**   _____5. The flow of blood is reversed once in a while to clean the blood vessels.

***   _____6. If blood vessels lose their *elasticity*, the heart is overworked.

*   _____7. The heart is the only organ in the body that never rests.

** _____8. The heart will work only if it has blood to pump. It will not work by itself.

*** _____9. Blood not carried in blood vessels moves through the body without control.

Directions

Below are five principles and nine statements. In front of each statement, write the number of the principle or principles which apply to that statement.

PRINCIPLES

1. Warm air holds more moisture than cold air.
2. Altitude affects temperature.
3. Humidity affects man's comfort.
4. Warm air is lighter than cold air, and is often forced upward by cooler air.
5. It takes much longer for a large body of water to become warmed by the sun than it does for the land.

STATEMENTS

_____ A. In the winter, moisture often appears on the inside of the windows of the classroom.

_____ B. It is usual on a hot summer day for clouds to form some distance above the earth's surface.

_____ C. A 90° temperature in the desert would be more comfortable than a 90° temperature in the Mohawk Valley.

_____ D. If the air in a room is perfectly still, the smoke from a cigarette will usually rise.

_____ E. On a hot humid June evening, air from over the land moves over the ocean. A fog occurs.

_____ F. You come into a warm room from outside on a cold winter's day, and moisture condenses on your glasses.

_____ G. In the winter months, moist air from the Pacific is carried over the mountain ranges of the Northwest coast. These winds are deflected upward. Clouds form and rains are frequent.

_____ H. Thunderclouds are likely to form on hot humid summer afternoons. They may grow upward and become thousands of feet high. Hail, as well as rain, often falls from these clouds.

_____ I. You can see your breath when you exhale on a cold winter day.

"BEHAVIOR OF MATTER"

Directions

According to the group you belong in, answer the below questions that pertain to that group. The first number in the parentheses after questions refer to the page number, the second number to the paragraph, and third is for the sentence in that paragraph.

*   1.   What is an element? (40, 2, 3)

*   2.   What two groups can elements be broken down into? (40, 4, 1, 2; 41, 1, 1)

**   3.   Describe the properties of metals and nonmetals. (40, 4)

***   4.   Why will aluminum always have the same properties no matter where it is found? (41)

*   5.   What is an atom? (41, 4, 2)

**   6.   What have scientists discovered about atoms? (42, 0)

*   7.   What are the two main parts of an atom? (42, 1, 2)

*   8.   Find the charge and location of a proton and neutron in the atom. (42, 1, 3)

**   9.   Describe the characteristics of an electron. (43, 1)

***   10.   Explain what makes atoms different from each other. (43)

***   11.   What statement can you make about all the particles in an atom? (43)

**   12.   Why does the author say electrons are like bees around a hive? (43, 2)

***   13.   Explain why even dense elements like iron and lead have a lot of space in their structure. (44)

*   14.   Define a mixture. (43, 6, 2)

**   15.   Why may salt and flour be called a mixture? (44, 0)

***   16.   How is a compound different from a mixture? (44)

**   17.   What is true of a chemical combination that is not true of a physical combination? (45, 1)

***   18.   If water has two atoms of hydrogen and one of oxygen, why would a substance having one atom of hydrogen and one atom of oxygen not be called water? (45)

**   19.   What is the Law of Definite Proportions? (45, 2)

*   20.   What is a molecule? (46, 0, 2)

**   21.   How can a molecule be separated into its atoms? (46, 1)

***   22.   Explain the difference between inert elements and metals and nonmetals. (47)

Directions

In reading science material, it is necessary to be able to select important facts to be remembered from the unimportant ones. This can be accomplished by using the chapter title and the subtitles in reading. In reading, you should try to relate the facts that you read to these ideas and discard those that don't relate.

Below are listed several subtitles from your reading and facts that are included under each. Check those details you feel are important to the reading.

Chapter Title—"Behavior of Matter"

I.   "All matter is made up of elements."

_____a. Not all metallic substances are elements.

_____b. By 1962 scientists had produced 11 elements.

_____c. Elements are the simplest form of matter.

_____d. Elements are divided into two main groups—metals and nonmetals.

_____e. Most metals can be hammered into thin sheets and stretched into fine wire.

_____ f. . . .metal mercury in its ordinary state is a liquid.

II.   "All elements are made up of atoms."

_____a. An atom is the smallest particle of an element.

b. Experimentation has led to the conclusion that hydrogen atoms are the lightest and uranium atoms are the heaviest.

_____c. Scientists have discovered that the atoms of one element are all the same size and the same weight.

III.   "Atoms are composed of different particles."

_____a. An atom consists of two main parts, the nucleus and the electron cloud.

_____b. The nucleus is made up of particles called protons . . . and neutrons.

_____c . A proton is 1836 times as heavy as an electron . . .

_____d. . . . and a neutron is 1837 times as heavy as an electron.

_____e . The electron cloud is made up of particles called electrons.

With details drawn from reading we are able to incorporate them into large ideas called "concepts". Below are some concepts. Check those you feel could be selected from the details selected above.

_____1. Elements are the simplest form that matter can take.

_____2. Grouping of elements cannot be done.

_____3. Elements are composed of atoms which are always alike in the same element.

_____4. The nucleus of an atom is made up of protons and electrons.

_____5. An atom consists of protons, neutrons and electrons.

Directions

Turn to page 42 in your textbook and look at fig. 2-2.

I.   Before we can use a graph, we must be able to determine its purpose. Check the statement below which correctly states the purpose of the graph.

_____a. To show all the elements the earth is made up of.

_____b. To show the rarest elements that make up the earth's crust.

_____c. To show only those elements that are most common in the earth.

II.   Interpreting graphic data:

1. The unit of measurement that this graph uses is a) pounds b) fractions c) percentages_____

2. To read this graph to get the most common to the least common elements of

the earth, we should read: a) top to bottom b) bottom to top c) graph doesn't give this _____
3. The longer the bar lines, the a) more abundant b) less abundant c) doesn't indicate anything about the elements _____
4. Iron makes up a)1.4% b) 219% c) 46.4% d) 5.1% of the earth _____
5. The most abundant element on the earth would be a) silicon b) oxygen c) potassium d) magnesium _____
6. The least abundant element on the earth is a) aluminum b) magnesium c) iron d) graph doesn't state _____

III. Applying graphic data:

1. If I were to go into mining, which element would you suggest I choose to mine?
2. The earth has been described as a mat of two elements with all the others scattered between them. What two elements would be the main ones making up this mat?

I. Read the directions to Student Activity on page 44, once through quickly. Before any experiment is performed, you should have a good idea what the main purpose is to be.
Choose from the below statements the one which best expresses this purpose. (Put number on the blank)
The purpose is to:

1. Show how to make a compound.
2. Determine how a mixture is formed.
3. Break a compound down into its parts.
4. Take apart a mixture by ordinary means.   _____

II. To do any experiment, it is always important to realize what steps are to be followed. Read the activity once more, now for sequence of steps to follow. After you have done this, put the mixed up steps listed below in the order that you would do them in lab. Indicate their order by numbering the first step "1" and so forth.

_____ fill a beaker half full of water
_____ pour the water from beaker into the funnel
_____ take out a sheet of paper
_____ record taste
_____ mix a teaspoon of sugar and sand on a sheet of paper
_____ taste the liquid that comes through
_____ examine the mixing results of sand and sugar with a magnifying glass
_____ record their descriptions
_____ put a little of the sand and sugar in the beaker and stir

Do the lab following these steps

An important part of any experiment is being able to interpret the data gained from it. Below are listed some interpretations that might be stated from this experiment. Check those that you feel can be made from the data you collected.
_____ a . When sand and salt are mixed, you cannot see single grains of each alone.

_____b. Because the grains still look the same as before mixing, the physical properties have not changed.

_____c. When the sugar, sand, water combination was poured into the funnel everything went through.

_____d. The putting of sand and sugar together by mixing must have made a mixture, not a compound.

_____e. To make a compound some outside source of energy is needed.

_____f. Mixtures can be broken down by easy, ordinary means and when separated from each other, the properties have not changed.

BIBLIOGRAPHY

I. JOURNALS AND OTHER SOURCES

1. ENGLISH

Benson, J.T., "Developing Competence in the Interpretation of the Materials of Literature," *Conference on Reading*, University of Pittsburgh Report, 1959, pp. 93-99.

Cooper, David, "Implications from Semantics for the Teaching of Mature Reading Skills in Secondary School English Classes." Unpublished dissertation, Stanford University, 1963.

Engelsman, Alan D., "Encouraging Students to Read in Depth," *English Journal*, 54 (Oct. 1965), 613-15.

Flanigan, Michael C., "Semantics and Critical Reading," *English Journal*, 55 (Sept. 1966), 714-19.

Gallup, B.H., "Creativity in the Basic Skills Class," *English Journal*, 52 (Nov. 1963), 622-24.

Ireland, Virginia, "A Method of Vocabulary Study," *English Journal*, 55 (Sept. 1966), 763-65.

Irvine, E., "Organizing a Reading Program in Literature," *Conference on Reading*, University of Pittsburgh Report, 1959, pp. 65-81.

Mullen, William B., "Teaching Contextual Definition," *English Journal*, 54 (May 1965), 419-24.

Olsen, James, "Some Suggestions for Writing and Adapting Materials for the Disadvantaged," *English Journal*, 55 (Dec. 1966), 1207-9.

Peltzie, Bernard E., "Teaching Meaning Through Structure in the Short Story," *English Journal*, 55 (Sept. 1966), 703-9.

Simmons, John S., "Teaching Levels of Literary Understanding," *English Journal*, 54 (Feb. 1965), 101-7, 129.

Smiley, Marjorie B., "Gateway English: Teaching English to Disadvantaged Students," *English Journal*, 54 (April 1965), 265-74.

Strang, Ruth and Charlotte Rogers, "How Do Students Read a Short Story," *English Journal*, 54 (Dec. 1965), 819-23.

2. SOCIAL STUDIES

Carpenter, N.M. and N.V. Gaver, "Making History Live Through Reading," *National Council of Social Studies Yearbook*, 1961, 398-414.

Duffy, Robert V., "Helping the Less Able Reader," *Social Education*, 25 (April 1961), 182-84.

Fredericks, Allen H., "Teachers, History, and Slow Learning Adolescents," *Social Studies*, 58 (April 1967), 168-70.

Gill, Clark C., "How Eighth-graders Interpret Indefinite Quantitative Concepts," *Social Education*, 25 (Nov. 1961), 344-46.

Goldmark, Bernice, "Critical Thinking, Deliberate Method," *Social Education*, 30 (May 1966), 329-34.

Hain, John H., "Selecting and Generalizing in the Social Studies," *Social Studies*, 58 (Jan. 1967), 29-30.

Luciano, V.D., "Reading Skills Approach in Social Studies General Classes," *High Points*, 46 (Jan. 1964), 64-67.

McAulay, J.D., "Social Studies Dependent on Reading," *Education*, 82 (Oct. 1961), 87-89.

O'Conner, John R., "Reading Skills in the Social Studies," *Social Education*, 31 (Feb. 1967), 104-7.

Park, Frances Hauser, "Teaching Social Studies to Poor Readers," *Social Education*, 20 (Nov. 1956), 327-29.

Preston, Ralph C., J. Wesley Schneyer, and Franc J. Thyng, *Guiding the Social Studies Reading of High School Students*, National Council for the Social Studies Bulletin 34, 1963.

Sister Josephina, "Comparing Study Skills of Gifted and Average Pupils," *Social Education*, 24 (Dec. 1960), 367-68.

Travel, David Z., "The Textbook and Skill Development," *Social Education*, 25 (Dec. 1961), 403-6.

Witt, Mary, "Developing Reading Skills and Critical Thinking," *Social Education*, 25 (May 1961), 239-41.

3. SCIENCE

Adler, Leona K., "Do They Mean What You Say?" *Science Teacher*, 32 (Feb. 1965), 23-25.

Beldon, Bernard R. and Wayne D. Lee, "Textbook Readability and the Reading Ability of Science Students," *Science Teacher*, 29 (April 1962), 20-23.

Blue, Larry Lamar, "A Study of the Influence of Certain Factors in Science Materials on the Reading Comprehension of Seventh Grade Pupils." Unpublished dissertation, Indiana University, 1964.

Carpenter, Finley, "The Effect of Different Learning Methods on Concept Formation," *Science Education*, 40 (Oct. 1956), 282-85.

Ediger, M., "Reading in the Elementary School Science Program," *Science Education*, 49 (Oct. 1965), 389-90.

George, Kenneth D., "A Comparison of Critical Thinking Abilities of Science and Non-Science Majors," *Science Education*, 51 (Feb. 1967), 11-17.

Haney, Richard C., "Concept Measurements," *Science Teacher*, 29 (Nov. 1962), 47-49.

Jacobson, Milton Durwood, "Reading Difficulties of Physics and Chemistry Textbooks in Use in Minnesota." Unpublished dissertation, University of Minnesota, 1961.

Lembesis, A.C., "Reaching the Remedial Reader Through Science," *Education*, 85 (Jan. 1965), 288-93.

Lener, Walter, "How to Succeed in Biology by Really Trying," *Science Teacher*, 32 (Dec. 1965), 29-30.

Mallinson, G.G., "Methods and Materials for Teaching Reading in Science," *Conference on Reading*, University of Chicago, 1960, 145-49.

_____ , "Reading and Teaching of Science," *School Science and Mathematics*, 64 (Feb. 1964), 148-53.

Mattila, R.H., "Accent on Thinking Through Reading at the Intermediate and Upper Grade Levels," *Science Education*, 46 (March 1962), 174-76.

Padendorf, I., "Accent on Thinking in Science for Children in the 60's in the Classroom Through Reading and Research." *Science Education*, 40 (March 1962), 184-85.

Parker, D.H., "Reading in Science: Training or Education?" *Science Teacher*, 30 (Feb. 1963), 43-46.

Pella, Milton O., "Concept Learning in Science," *Science Teacher*, 33 (Dec. 1966), 31-34.

Rickert, Russell K.,"Developing Critical Thinking," *Science Education*,51 (Feb. 1967), 24-27.

Romans, M.J., "Reading and Science: A Symbiotic Relationship," *Education*, 81 (Jan. 1961), 273-76.

Schiavone, J., "Science Teacher's Contribution to the Improvement of Reading," *Science Education*, 44 (Dec. 1960), 400-1.

Severson, E.E., "The Teaching of Reading Study Skills in Biology," *American Biology Teacher*, 25 (March 1963), 203-4.

Shores, J. Harlan, "Reading of Science for Two Separate Purposes as Perceived by Sixth Grade Students and Able Adult Readers," *Elementary English*, 37 (Nov. 1960), 461-68.

————, "Reading Science Materials for Two Distinct Purposes," *Elementary English*, 37 (Dec. 1960), 546-53.

Smith, Herbert A., "The Teaching of a Concept: An Elusive Objective," *Science Teacher*, 33 (March 1966), 103-12.

Smith, Paul M., "Critical Thinking and the Science Intangibles," *Science Education*, 47 (Oct. 1963), 405-8.

Weaver, E.K. and E. Black, "The Relationship of Science Fiction Reading to Reasoning Abilities," *Science Education*, 49 (1965), 293-96.

4. MATH

Balow, I.H., "Reading and Computation Ability as Determinants of Problem Solving," *Arithmetic Teacher*, 11 (Jan. 1964), 18-22.

Brune, Irvin H., "Symbols and Functions," *Mathematics Teacher*, 51 (April 1958), 232-33.

Call, R.J. and N.A. Wiggin, "Reading and Mathematics," *Mathematics Teacher*, 59 (Feb. 1966), 147-49.

Cleland, Donald L. and Isabella H. Toussaint, "The Interrelationships of Reading, Listening, Arithmetic Computation and Intelligence," *Reading Teacher*, 15 (Jan. 1962), 228.

Forseth, W.J., "Does the Study of Geometry Help Improve Reading Ability?" *Mathematics Teacher*, 54 (Jan. 1961), 12-13.

Hartung, M.L., "Methods and Materials for Teaching Reading in Mathematics," *Conference on Reading*, University of Chicago, 1960, 140-44.

Olander, H., "Developing Competence in the Reading of Arithmetic and Mathematics Material," *Conference on Reading*, University of Pittsburgh Report, 1959, 107-16.

Randall, Karl, "Improving Study Habits in Mathematics," *Mathematics Teacher*, 55 (Nov. 1962), 553-55.

Scott, Carrie M., "The Relationships between Intelligence Quotients and Gain in Reading Achievement with Arithmetic Reasoning, Social Studies and Science," *Journal of Educational Research*, 56 (Feb. 1963), 322-26.

Spencer, P.L. and D.H. Russell, "Reading in Arithmetic," *National Council of Teachers of Math Yearbook*, 25, 1960, 202-23.

Troxel, V., "Effects of Purpose on the Reading of Expository Mathematical Materials in Grade Eight," *Journal of Educational Research*, 55 (Feb. 1962), 221-27.

5. COMPREHENSION

Allshan, Leonard M., "A Factor Analytic Study of Items in the Measurement of

Some Fundamental Factors of Reading Comprehension," Unpublished dissertation, Columbia University, 1964.

Ballard, Grady Lee, "The Effect of Guiding and Motivating Questions Upon the Reading Comprehension of Fourth and Fifth Grade Pupils." Unpublished dissertation, University of Maryland, 1964.

Davis, Frederick B., "Research in Comprehension in Reading," *Reading Research Quarterly*, 3 (Summer 1968), 499-545.

Glock, Marvin and Jason Milman, "Evaluation of a Study Skills Program for Above Average High School Pupils," *Journal of Developmental Reading,* 7 (Summer 1964), 283-89.

Schiller, Sister M.P., "The Effect of the Functional Use of Certain Skills in Seventh Grade Social Studies," *Journal of Educational Research*, 57 (Dec. 1963), 622-24.

6. GROUPING

Allport, Floyd H., "The Influence of the Group Upon Association and Thought," *Journal of Experimental Psychology*, 3 (1920), 159-82.

Anderson, R.C., "Learning in Discussion: A Resume of the Authoritarian-Democratic Studies," *Harvard Educational Review*, 29 (1959), 201-15.

Anderson, R.P. and B.L. Kell, "Students' Attitudes about Participation in Classroom Groups," *Journal of Educational Research*, 48 (1954), 255-67.

Banghart, F.W., "Grouping Structure, Anxiety, and Problem-Solving Efficiency," *Journal of Experimental Education*, 28 (Dec. 1959), 172-74.

Carpenter, C.R., "The Penn State Pyramid Plan: Independent Student Work-Study Groupings for Increasing Motivation for Academic Development." Paper read at the 14th National Conference on Higher Education, Chicago, March 1959.

Carpenter, F., "Toward a Systematic Construction of a Classroom Taxonomy," *Science Education*, 49 (April 1965), 230-34.

Cattell, R.B., "On the Theory of Group Learning," *Journal of Social Psychology,* 37 (1953), 27-52.

Cirelli, J., "What Good Are Committees?" *Instructor,* 71 (May 1962), 93-94.

Durrell, D.D., "Pupil-Team Learning," *Instructor*, 74 (Feb. 1965), 5+.

Engel, H., "Working with Small Groups in the Classroom," *High Points*, 44 (May 1962), 54-57.

Flanders, M.A., "Diagnosing and Utilizing Social Structures in Classroom Learning," *National Social Study Education Yearbook*, 59, pt. 2, 187-217.

Gibb, J.R., "The Effects of Group Size and of Threat Reduction Upon Creativity in a Problem Solving Situation," *American Psychologist*, 6 (1951), 324.

Hedges, William D., "Is Talking Teaching?" *Clearing House,* 41 (Feb. 1967), 334-37).

Horwitz, M., "Feedback Process in Classroom Groups," *National Social Study Education Yearbook,* 59, pt. 2, 218-24.

Laing, J.M. and P.F. Munger, "Group Process Concept," *Education*, 80 (Dec. 1959), 231-34.

Lott, A.J., "Grouping Cohesiveness and Individual Learning," *Journal of Educational Psychology,* 57 (1966), 61-73.

McIntosh, W.R., "Problems Involved in Grouping in Content Areas and Proposed Solutions," *Conference on Reading*, University of Chicago, 1959, 171-74.

Maloney, R.M., "Group Learning Through Group Discussion: A Group Discussion Implementation Analysis," *Journal of Social Psychology*, 43 (1956), 3-9.

Mann, I., "The Teacher's Responsibility: Understanding Group Behavior," *Education*, 81 (Nov. 1960), 171-73.

Olson, W.C., "Implications of the Dynamics of Instructional Groups," *National Social Study Education Yearbook,* 59, pt. 2, 268-80.

Savage, J.F., "Elaborative Thinking, Done Better in Groups?" *Elementary School Journal*, 64 (May 1964), 434-37.

Scheidel, T.M. and L. Crowell, "Idea Development in Small Discussion Groups," *Quarterly Journal of Speech*, 50 (April 1964), 140-45.

Strang, R., "Effective Use of Classroom Organization in Meeting Individual Differences," *Conference on Reading,* University of Chicago, 26, 1964, 164-70.

Trandis, H.C., et al, "Team Creativity as a Function of the Creativity of the Members," *Journal of Applied Psychology*, 47 (1963), 104-10.

Whitehall, John and W.W. Lewis, "Social Interaction in the Classroom" in N.L. Gage (ed.), *Handbook of Research on Teaching*, Chicago: Rand-McNally & Co., 1963.

Ziller, R.C., et al, "Group Creativity Under Conditions of Success or Failure and Variations in Group Stability," *Journal of Applied Psychology*, 46 (Feb. 1962), 43-49.

7. VOCABULARY

Hafner, L.E., "A One-Month Experiment in Teaching Context Aids in Fifth Grade," *Journal of Educational Research*, 58 (1965), 472-74.

Olsen, Arthur V., "Communication Skills—Teaching Word Recognition for Better Vocabulary Development," *Clearing House*, 40 (April 1966), 559-63.

Petty, Walter, et al, *"The Current State of Knowledge About the Teaching of Vocabulary."* National Council of Teachers of English, Champaign, Ill., 1968.

Romano, L.G. and N.P. Georgiady, "Vocabulary Learning as Influenced by the Multi-Media Approach," *Illinois School Research*, 2 (1966), 24-32.

Stauffer, Russell G., "A Vocabulary Study Comparing Reading, Arithmetic, Health and Science Texts," *Reading Teacher*, 20 (Nov. 1966), 141.

West, N.E., "Vocabulary: Basic Factor for Understanding Science," *Science Teacher*, 27 (Dec. 1960), 15.

8. CRITICAL-CREATIVE READING

Betts, Emmet A., "Research on Reading as a Thinking Process," *Journal of Educational Research*, 50 (Sept. 1956).

Birch, H.G. and H.S. Rabinowitz, "The Negative Effort of Previous Experience on Productive Thinking," *Journal of Experimental Psychology*, 4 (June 1951), 121-25.

Buss, Arnold, "A Study of Concept Formation as a Function of Reinforcement and Stimulus Generalization," *Journal of Experimental Psychology*, 40 (1950), 494-540.

Callantine, Mary and J.M. Warren, "Learning Sets in Human Concept Formation," *Psychological Reports*, 1 (1955), 363-67.

Davis, John Edwin, "The Ability of Fourth, Fifth, and Sixth Grade Pupils to Distinguish Between Fact and Opinion in an Experimentally Designed Reading Situation." Unpublished dissertation, University of Oregon, 1964.

Della-Piana, G.M., "Searching Orientation and Concept Learning," *Journal of Educational Psychology*, 48 (1957), 245-53.

Hull, Clark, "The Evolution of Concepts," in *Selected Readings on the Learning Process*, T.L. Harris, ed. (New York) Oxford University Press, 1961, p. 119-33. Abridged from "Quantitative Aspects of the Evolution of Concepts, An Experimental Study," *Psychological Monographs*, 28 (1920), 1-85.

Maney, Ethel Swain, "Literal and Critical Reading in Science." Unpublished dissertation, Temple University, 1952.

Ohnmacht, F.W., "Achievement, Anxiety, and Creative Thinking," *American Educational Research Journal*, 3 (1966), 131-38.

Olson, LeRoy, "Concept Attainment of High School Sophomores," *Journal of Educational Psychology*, 54 (1963), 213-16.

Reed, H.B., "Factors Influencing the Learning and Retention of Concepts: The Influence of Length of Series," *Journal of Experimental Psychology*, 36 (1946), 166-79.

Sochor, E. Elona, "Literal and Critical Reading in Social Studies." Unpublished dissertation, Temple University, 1952.

Stauffer, R.G., "Critical Reading at Upper Levels," *Instructor*, 74 (March 1965), 75+.

————, "The Role of Language in Thinking," in "Diagnostic Teaching Methods and Materials," paper delivered at the 6th Annual Reading Conference of Syracuse University, 1964 edited by Jane H. Root, 87-97.

Taba, Hilda, "The Teaching of Thinking," *Elementary English*, (May 1965), 535-52.

————, "Thinking in Elementary School Children." U.S. Dept. of Health, Education and Welfare, Office of Education, Cooperative Research Project No. 1574. San Francisco State College, 1964.

Vinacke, W.E., "The Investigation of Concept Formation," *Psychological Bulletin*, 48 (1951), 5.

Wenzel, B.M. and C. Flurry, "The Sequential Order of Concept Attainment," *Journal of Experimental Psychology*, 38 (1948), 547-57.

Wittrock, M.C., "Verbal Stimuli in Concept Formation: Learning by Discovery," *Journal of Educational Psychology*, 54 (1963), 183-90.

Wolf, Willavene, Martha L. King, and Charlotte Huck, "Teaching Critical Reading to Elementary School Children," *Reading Research Quarterly*, 3 (Summer 1968), 435-98.

9. GENERAL

Ausubel, David P., "The Use of Advance Organizers in the Learning and Retention of Meaningful Verbal Materials," *Journal of Educational Psychology*, 51 (1960), 267-72.

Courtney, L., "Recent Developments in Reading in the Content Areas," *Conference on Reading*, University of Chicago, 27 (1965), 134-44.

Dalton, Patrick, David Gliesman, Harriet Guthrie, and Gilbert Rees, "The Effect of Reading Improvement on Academic Achievement," *Journal of Reading*, 9 (March 1966), 242-52.

Drew, L.J., "Developmental Reading in Industrial Arts at the Junior-High School Level," *School Shop*, 24 (Oct. 1964), 40-41.

Finger, A., "Use of Content Subjects for Remedial Reading," *High Points*, 43 (Nov. 1961), 67-69.

Fitzgerald, Donald and David Ausubel, "Cognitive versus Affective Factors in the Learning and Retention of Controversial Materials," *Journal of Educational Psychology*, 54 (1963), 73-84.

Foss, F.G., "Do Reading Scores Predict Typing Success?" *Journal of Business Education*, 41 (April 1966), 281-82.

Funk, G., "Reading and Industrial Arts: Interview," *Industrial Arts and Vocational Education*, 50 (Oct. 1961), 24-25+.

Green, F., "Art Helps Us Read," *Arts and Activities*, 57 (Feb. 1965), 17.

Greenberg, Judith W., Joan M. Gerver, Jeanne Chall, and Helen Davidson, "Attitudes of Children from a Deprived Environment Toward Achievement-Related Concepts, *Journal of Educational Research*, 59 (1965), 57-62.

Groff, P.J., "Children's Attitudes Toward Reading and their Critical Reading Abilities in Four Content-type Materials," *Journal of Educational Research*, 55 (April 1962), 313-17.

Harrison, L.J., "Teaching Accounting Students How To Read," *Journal of Business Education*, 35 (Jan. 1960), 169-70.

Heyman, J. and R. Holland, "Reading Improvement in the Industrial Arts Class," *Journal of Industrial Arts Education*, 25 (Jan. 1966), 48-49+.

Johnson, V.R., "Teaching for Better Understanding in Typewriting: Reading, Writing, and Research-Orientation," *Journal of Business Education*, 41 (Jan. 1966), 149-50.

Joly, R.W., "Reading Improvement in Subjects Other Than English," *High Points*, 47 (Jan. 1965), 22-30.

Ramsey, Robert Diehle, "An Analysis of the Appropriateness of the Readability and Difficulty of Instructional Materials in a Junior High School." Unpublished dissertation, University of Kansas, 1961.

Robinson, H. Alan, "Teaching Reading in the Content Areas," *Improvement of Reading Through Classroom Practice*, 9 (1964), 35.

Sigel, I., "The Dominance of Meaning," *J. Genet. Psychology*, 85 (1954), 207.

Smith, N.B., "Reading in Subject Matter Fields," *Educational Leadership*, 22 (March 1965), 382-85.

Strang, R., "Developing Reading Skills in the Content Areas," *High School Journal*, 49 (April 1966), 301-6.

Vawter, G.P., "Music Attuned to Reading," *School and Community*, 51 (Nov. 1964), 21.

Wagner, G., "What Schools Are Doing; Developing Reading Power in the Content Areas," *Education*, 85 (Oct. 1964), 122-24.

Wood, J.L., "Reading and Typewriting," *Journal of Business Education,* 40 (Dec. 1964), 109-11.

II. TEXTS

Abraham, Willard, *The Slow Learner*. New York: Center for Applied Research in Education, 1964.

Amidon, Edmund J. and Ned A. Flanders, *Role of the Teacher in the Classroom*. Minneapolis: Paul S. Amidon, 1963.

Artley, A. Sterl, *Trends and Practices in Secondary Reading*. Newark: International Reading Association, 1966.

Ausubel, David P., *The Psychology of Meaningful Verbal Learning*. New York: Grune & Stratton, Inc., 1963.

Ausubel, David and Richard Anderson, *Readings in the Psychology of Cognition*. New York: Holt, Rinehard & Winston, Inc., 1965.

Bamman, Henry A., Ursula Hogan, and Charels E. Greene, *Reading Instruction in the Secondary Schools*. New York: David McKay Co., Inc., 1961.

Bellack, Arno A. (ed.), *Theory and Research in Teaching*. New York: Columbia University Press, 1963.

Bennis, Warren, et al, *Interpersonal Dynamics*. Homewood, Ill: Richard D. Irwin, Inc., 1968.

Bilodeau, Edward A., *Acquisition of Skill*. New York: Academic Press, Inc., 1966.

Bois, J. Samuel, *Explorations in Awareness*. New York: Harper and Row, Publishers, 1957.

Bruner, Jerome S., et al, *A Study of Thinking*. New York: John Wiley & Sons, Inc., 1956.

Bruner, Jerome S. *On Knowing*. Cambridge, Mass.: Harvard University, 1966.

Bruner, Jerome S., *The Process of Education*. Cambridge, Mass.: Harvard University, 1960.

Bruner, Jerome S., et al, *Studies in Cognitive Growth*. New York: John Wiley & Sons, Inc., 1967.

Bruner, Jerome S., *Toward A Theory of Instruction*. Cambridge, Mass.: Harvard University Press, 1967.

Bugelski, B.R., *The Psychology of Learning Applied to Teaching*, Indianapolis: The Bobbs-Merrill Co., Inc. 1964.

Burton, Dwight, L., *Literature Study in the High Schools*. New York: Holt, Rinehart & Winston, Inc., 1960.

Burton, Dwight L. and John S. Simmons, *Teaching English in Today's High Schools*. New York: Holt, Rinehart & Winston, Inc., 1965.

Clayton, Thomas E., *Teaching and Learning*. Englewood Cliffs: Prentice-Hall, Inc., 1965.

Dawson, Mildred and Henry A. Bamman, *Fundamentals of Basic Reading Instruction*. New York: David McKay Co., Inc., 1959, 1963.

Dechant, Emerald V., *Improving the Teaching of Reading*. Englewood Cliffs: Prentice-Hall, Inc., 1964.

Deese, James, *The Structure of Associations in Language and Thought*. Baltimore: The John Hopkins Press, 1965.

Deighton, Lee C., *Vocabulary Development*. New York: The MacMillan Company, 1964.

Durrell D.D., *Improving Reading Instruction*. New York: Harcourt, Brace & World, Inc., 1956.

Fabun, Don, *The Dynamics of Change*. Englewood Cliffs: Prentice-Hall, Inc., 1967.

Fay, Leo, et al, *Improving Reading in the Elementary Social Studies*. Washington: National Council for the Social Studies, 1961.

Gage, N.L. (ed.), *Handbook of Research on Teaching*. Chicago: Rand McNally & Co., 1963.

Gagne, Robert M., *Learning and Individual Differences*. Columbus: Charles E. Merrill Books, Inc., 1967.

Heilman, Arthur, *Teaching Reading*. Columbus: Charles E. Merrill Books, Inc., 1961, 1967.

Herber, Harold L., *Developing Study Skills in Secondary Schools*. Newark: International Reading Association, 1965.

————, *Success With Words*. New York: Scholastic Book Services, 1966.

Hook, J.N., *The Teaching of High School English*. New York: The Ronald Press Co., 1965.

Hullfish, H. Gordon and Philip G. Smith, *Reflective Thinking: The Method of Education*. New York: Dodd, Mead & Co., 1961.

Joyce, Bruce R. and Berj Harootunian, *The Structure of Teaching*. Chicago: Science Research Associates, Inc., 1967.

Kephart, Newell C., *The Slow Learner in the Classroom*. Columbus: Charles E. Merrill Books, Inc., 1960.

Keppel, Francis, *The Necessary Revolution in American Education*. New York: Harper Row, Publishers, 1966.

Keyes, Kenneth S. Jr. *How to Develop Your Thinking Ability*. New York: McGraw-Hill, 1950.

King, Martha L., et al (eds.). *Critical Reading*. New York: J.B. Lippincott Co., 1967.

Klausmeier, Herbert J. and Chester W. Harris, *Analysis of Concept Learning*. New York: Academic Press Inc., 1966.

Krumboltz, J.D. (ed.), *Learning and the Educational Process*. Chicago: Rand-McNally & Co., 1965.

McGrath, Joseph E. and Irwin Altman, *Small Group Research*. New York: Holt, Rinehart & Winston, Inc., 1966.

Mager, Robert F., *Preparing Instructional Objectives*. Palo Alto: Fearon Publishers, 1962.

Mallery, Daivd, *High School Students Speak Out*. New York: Harper and Row Publishers, 1962.

Marksheffel, Ned D., *Better Reading in the Secondary School*. New York: The Ronald Press Company, 1966.

Massey, Will J. and Virginia D. Moore, *Helping High School Students to Read Better*. New York: Holt, Rinehart & Winston, Inc., 1966.

Miel, Alice (ed.), *Reading Improvement in the Junior High School*. New York: Teachers College Press, 1963.

_____, *Teaching the Slow Learner*. New York: Teachers College Press, 1951.

Miles, Matthew B., *Learning to Work in Groups*. New York: Teachers College Press, 1967.

National Society for the Study of Education, *The Innovation and Change in Reading Instruction – '67 Yearbook*. Chicago: University of Chicago Press, 1968.

_____, *Development in and Through Reading*. (60th part I). Chicago: University of Chicago Press, 1961.

_____, *The Dynamics of Instructional Groups. (59th part II)*. Chicago: University of Chicago Press, 1960.

_____, *Individualizing Instruction,* (61st part I). Chicago: University of Chicago Press, 1962.

_____, *Reading in the Elementary School (48th)*. Chicago: University of Chicago Press, 1962.

_____, *Reading in the High School and College* (47th part II). Chicago: University of Chicago, 1948.

Osgood, Charles E., et al, *The Measurement of Meaning*. Chicago: University of Illinois Press, 1967.

Petty, Walter Y., et al, *The State of Knowledge about the Teaching of Vocabulary*. Champaign, Ill: National Council of Teachers of English, 1968.

————, *Issues and Problems in the Elementary Language Arts*. Boston: Allyn & Bacon, Inc. 1968.

Ramsey, Wallace Z. (ed.), *Organizing for Individual Differences*. Newark: International Reading Association, 1967.

Reeves, Ruth, *The Teaching of Reading in our Schools*. New York: The Mac-Millan Company, 1966.

Riessman, Frank. *The Culturally Deprived Child*. New York: Harper & Row, Publishers, 1962.

Robinson, H. Alan (ed.), *Reading: Seventy-five Years of Progress*. Chicago: University of Chicago Press, 1966.

————, *Recent Developments in Reading*. Chicago: University of Chicago Press, 1965.

————, *The Underachiever in Reading*. Chicago: University of Chicago Press, 1962.

Robinson, H. Alan and Sidney J. Rauch, *Corrective Reading in the High School Classroom*. Newark: International Reading Association, 1966.

————, *Guiding the Reading Program*. Chicago: Science Research Associates, Inc., 1965.

Robinson, Helen M. (ed.), *Controversial Issues in Reading and Promising Solutions*. Chicago: University of Chicago, Press, 1961.

————, (ed.), *Precedents and Promise in the Curriculum Field*. New York: Teachers College Press, 1966.

Rosenthal, Robert and Lenore Jacobson, *Pygmalion in the Classroom*. New York: Holt, Rinehart & Winston, Inc. 1968.

Russell, David H., *Children's Thinking*. Waltham, Mass.: Blaisdell Publishing, 1956.

Sauer, Edwin H., *English in the Secondary School*. New York: Holt & Rinehart & Winston, Inc., 1961.

Sherk, John K. (ed.), *Speaking of Reading*. Syracuse: Syracuse University Press, 1964.

Smith, Henry P., *Psychology in Teaching*. Englewood Cliffs: Prentice-Hall, Inc., 1962.

Smith, Henry P. and Emerald V. Dechant, *Psychology in Teaching Reading*. Englewood Cliffs: Prentice-Hall, Inc., 1961.

Smith, Nila B., *Reading Instruction for Today's Children*. Englewood Cliffs: Prentice-Hall, Inc., 1963.

Socher, Elona, et al, *Critical Reading*. Champaign, Ill: National Council of Teachers of English, 1959.

Strang, Ruth M., Constance M. McCullough, and Arthur Traxler, *Problems in the Improvement of Reading*. New York: McGraw-Hill Book Company, 1946 and 1961.

Taba, Hilda and Deborah Elkins, *Teaching Strategies for the Culturally Disadvantaged*. Chicago: Rand McNally & Co., 1966.

Trabasso, Tom and Gordon H. Bower, *Attention in Learning: Theory and Research*. New York: John Wiley & Sons, Inc., 1968.

Waetjen, Walter B., *Human Variability and Learning*. Washington: Association for Supervision and Curriculum Development, 1961.

————, *New Dimensions in Learning*. Washington: Association for Supervision and Curriculum Development, 1961.

Wellington, C. Burleigh and Jane Wellington, *Teaching for Critical Thinking*. New York: McGraw-Hill Book Company, 1960.

Whitehead, Frank, *The Disappearing Dais*. London: Chatto and Windus, 1966.

INDEX